Life on the Breadline

Life on the Breadline

This book is dedicated to everyone whose life
has been damaged by a decade of austerity
and to all who are struggling to transform
the structural injustice of poverty.

'The moral arc of the universe is long,
but it bends towards justice.'
(Martin Luther King Jr, 1968)

Mary, Jonathan and Bethany – You are my inspiration.
Thank you.

Life on the Breadline

*Theology, Poverty and Politics
in an Age of Austerity*

Chris Shannahan

scm press

© Chris Shannahan 2025

Published in 2025 by SCM Press

Editorial office
3rd Floor, Invicta House,
110 Golden Lane,
London EC1Y 0TG, UK
www.scmpress.co.uk

SCM Press is an imprint of Hymns Ancient & Modern Ltd
(a registered charity)

Hymns Ancient & Modern® is a registered trademark of
Hymns Ancient & Modern Ltd
13A Hellesdon Park Road, Norwich,
Norfolk NR6 5DR, UK

British Library Cataloguing in Publication data

A catalogue record for this book is available
from the British Library

ISBN: 978-0-334-06369-8

EU GPSR Authorized Representative
LOGOS EUROPE, 9 rue Nicolas Poussin, 17000, LA ROCHELLE, France
E-mail: Contact@logoseurope.eu

Typeset by Regent Typesetting

Contents

Acknowledgements

This book has been a long time coming and there have been many people who have supported, strengthened, challenged and encouraged me along the way. Without you this book would still be little more than an idea. First, and foremost, I want to say a massive 'Thank you' to my wife Mary and our children Jonathan and Bethany, and to my son-in-law Danny for your love, encouragement and unswerving support every step of the way since I set out on the Life on the Breadline project back in 2018. Secondly, I'd like to thank the Economic and Social Research Council for funding 'Life on the Breadline: Christianity, Poverty and Politics in the 21st century' between 2018 and 2021 and to my colleagues at the Centre for Peace and Security at Coventry University for your colleagueship, interest and support. Third, it was a privilege to work alongside such an amazing Life on the Breadline project team – thank you for everything: Dr Stephanie Denning, Professor Robert Beckford and Professor Peter Scott for your friendship, guidance, support and wisdom. Fourth, I want to say an enormous 'Thank you' to our Life on the Breadline case study partners for being so open hearted, so generous with your time and for sharing your journey with us. Without you, *Breadline* would have never made it out of the library – Church Action on Poverty, B30 Trussell Trust food bank, Hodge Hill United Church, Power the Fight, Notting Hill Methodist Church and the Inspire Centre. I hope this book helps to bring about the change we all long for. And finally, thank you to SCM Press for seeing the potential in my ideas and for agreeing to publish this book. To my editors at SCM, David Shervington and Rachel Edge, thank you for your patience, your advice and your guidance. It's been great working alongside you making this book the best it can be.

List of Figures

Photographs were taken by Chris Shannahan between 2019 and 2020, and illustrations were painted by the artist Beth Waters for Life on the Breadline and she gave kind permission for their use.

Introduction

Austerity represents a clear and present danger to the social fabric of breadline Britain. The poverty it has unleashed violates individuals, families and whole communities. Like an octopus, the tentacles of such traumatizing poverty have slithered into every corner of our lives. Drawing on the Life on the Breadline project, which I led between 2018 and 2021, this book will explore Christian responses to contemporary poverty in the UK during the Age of Austerity that followed the 2010 General Election. The chapters that follow represent an interdisciplinary, fieldwork-led expression of political theology, but more than that, this book emerges from my own conviction that theology can be a force for liberative social change, enabling the Church to live up to its calling to 'transform structural injustice'.

Austerity – impact and ideology

The last 15 years have resembled a perfect storm as different facets of poverty have compounded one another during what I refer to in this book as an Age of Austerity. Former Conservative Prime Minister David Cameron and Chancellor of the Exchequer George Osborne insisted that there was no alternative, that the justification for the austerity they introduced was exclusively economic and that everybody needed to shoulder the shared burdens it would bring as the government sought to respond to the impact of the 2008 global financial crash and the recession that followed in its wake. However, in this book I will demonstrate that this was not true. Austerity was not an unavoidable economic necessity, but a conscious political choice shaped by a neoliberal vision of economy, culture, State and civil society. The decision to impose long-lasting austerity policies hit people already left out or left behind far harder than others and the repeated assurances that we were 'all in this together' were never true. Women (Hall 2018), children (Edmiston et al., 2017), Black and Brown Britons (Runnymede Trust 2018) and people with disabilities have been harder hit than other social groups.

As I will show in this book, who we are, what we look like and where we live has a direct impact on how hard austerity has hit us.

In 2008, the year of the global financial crash, the faith-inspired charity Trussell Trust distributed 26,000 three-day food parcels at its food banks. By 2024 this number had shot up to 3.1 million and more than 10% of households in the UK regularly skipped meals because of increasing levels of food insecurity. Just before the 2010 UK General Election, 2.9 million children were living in poverty. This figure had increased to 4.5 million by 2024. In 2011, Child Benefit was frozen, followed by the freezing of all other working-age benefits in 2016, and the introduction of the so-called 'bedroom tax' in the 2012 Welfare Reform Act, which reduced people's benefits by a further 25% if they had a spare room in their house. At the time of writing, wages are still lower in real terms than they were when the financial crash paralysed the global economy. Unemployment may be less of a scourge than in previous years, but employment became increasingly fragile and insecure during the Age of Austerity. Whereas just 168,000 people were employed on zero-hours contracts in 2010, this figure had risen to more than one million by 2024. Over the same period destitution has doubled and more than 345,000 people are officially homeless. Austerity-age poverty has ruptured the social fabric of British society. In this book I will argue that theologians are facing a *Kairos* moment of judgement and opportunity. How will we respond?

Rooted in research

This book emerges from the exhaustive three-year fieldwork-led political theology Life on the Breadline project, which was funded by the Economic and Social Research Council, which I led from 2018 to 2021.[1] The project, which I discuss in detail in Chapter 2, represented the first major fieldwork-led project by academic theologians in the UK to explore the nature, scope and impact of Christian responses to poverty in the UK since the global financial crash. Whereas social scientists have extensively studied faith-based responses to austerity measures and their impact, there have only been a tiny number of relatively small qualitative research projects and just a handful of publications on austerity-age poverty within theology. *Life on the Breadline* represents a theological first.

Leaving our disciplinary bunkers and getting out of the library

It has become very fashionable to proclaim how interdisciplinary our research is. However, based on our experience during the Life on the Breadline project, I would suggest that the claim to be interdisciplinary can, quite often, owe more to style than substance. This is not to say that all contemporary theologians have stubbornly chosen to remain safe within the comfort zone of our own disciplinary bunker. Such a claim would be disingenuous, unfair and would ignore the ways in which critical engagement with disciplines as varied as political philosophy, postcolonial criticism, gender studies, the sociology of religion and cultural studies have deepened, challenged and enriched political theology, Black theology and feminist/womanist theology, for example. However, such interdisciplinarity is still too rare and too sporadic. In the chapters that follow I will demonstrate how a sustained, in-depth critical engagement with aspects of peace studies, human geography, the sociology of religion, trauma studies, the theorizing of intersectionality and studies of postsecularism is essential and can critique, challenge and contextualize an austerity-age theology of liberation. I will argue that such thorough interdisciplinarity needs to become the norm within political and contextual theology, rather than the exception.

Furthermore, this book will model an approach to contextualized political theology that is rooted in and shaped by extensive qualitative primary research, as I show in Chapter 2. The Life on the Breadline project revolved around six varied extended ethnographic case studies, in-person and online focus groups, semi-structured interviews, walking interviews and an online survey of Church leaders, modelling an approach that can ensure theoretical and theological analysis is informed by and arises from rich primary data. Political theologians need to spend as much time out in the community as they do in the library.

Rigorous but not neutral

In this book I demonstrate that the credibility of an emergent austerity-age theology of liberation rests on three interrelated criteria. First, it is essential for such a theology to be rooted in the everyday life, energy and cultural authenticity provided by fieldwork. Second, it is vital for theologians to ensure that our work is nuanced, interdisciplinary, theoretically solid and rigorous and intellectually multidimensional. These commitments provide this book with is contextual credibility and its academic currency. However, its theological energy and drive emerges from my conviction that theology needs to be a force for liberative social change; a discourse that arises from and is shaped by a personal and academic commitment to God's preferential option for the poor to challenge structural injustice. My commitment is to research that is rigorous but not to neutrality, which, I argue, amounts to collusion in the face of ideologically motivated austerity.

Towards a new Theology of Liberation

In light of my standpoint and understanding of the nature and purpose of theology in a structurally unjust society, this book represents an attempt to begin to sow the seeds of an interdisciplinary fieldwork-led austerity-age theology of liberation. This commitment was central to our research during the Life on the Breadline project and reflects my own understanding of the calling of the theologian and the challenge facing academic theology and the Church after more than a decade of austerity. In the chapters that follow I will show how differing Christian responses to contemporary poverty can play a part in the fashioning of a culturally resonant theology of liberation that has the capacity to stimulate the liberative praxis needed to 'transform structural injustice' and support all who struggle to embody God's preferential option for the poor in the face of systemic poverty and deepening inequality.

Summary of chapters

This book moves from social analysis to a critical discussion of our Life on the Breadline research and the varying Christian approaches to poverty that we identified and analysed during our fieldwork before concluding in the closing chapters by beginning to sow the seeds of a new interdisciplinary theology of liberation that will need nurturing and developing further in future research and publications.

In Chapter 1, I lay the theoretical foundations for the arguments I make throughout the book as I discuss the nature, causes and impact of contemporary poverty. I explore the importance of language and the power of public and political discourse to fashion a narrative about the nature and causes of poverty that becomes embedded in our hearts and minds and can foster very different responses to social exclusion. I discuss and critique the historic and contemporary individualizing of poverty in policy and theology and the ways in which it has become increasingly moralised and weaponized to distinguish between so-called 'deserving' and 'undeserving' poor. I argue that we need to understand theoretical discussions about poverty as an example of systemic injustice, as a form of debilitating violence and as a multidimensional phenomenon that we experience in an intersectional manner if we are to forge the holistic theoretical understanding needed upon which to build a nuanced theology of liberation.

In Chapter 2, I turn to a description of the emergence of the Life on the Breadline project in 2018, at the mid-point of the 'Age of Austerity'. I discuss the project's methodology and key insights and introduce the original approach to hermeneutics taken during the research. I introduce and explore the 'nitty-gritty' grounded approach to hermeneutics we adopted to reflect the plurality of contrasting experiences and views we encountered, and the transformative approach to meaning-making we forged through the dub hermeneutics that I developed as a means of engaging in an emancipatory form of hermeneutical analysis. I site the book within the broad family of theologies of liberation, arguing that the theologian's task is to share in the struggle to 'transform structural injustice' as an engaged organic intellectual. I summarize the key findings of our Life on the Breadline research and introduce the four broad approaches to the Christian engagement with poverty that we uncovered – 'Caring', 'Campaigning and Advocacy', 'Self-help and Enterprise' and 'Community Building'.

In Chapters 3 to 6 I introduce, analyse and assess the four broad approaches to the Christian engagement with austerity-age poverty that we uncovered during our Life on the Breadline fieldwork. I draw on the ethnographic case studies, interviews, online survey and focus groups we used during the project to frame these distinct but intersecting approaches as an ecosystem of Christian responses to contemporary poverty. In Chapter 3, I introduce the most widespread Christian response to poverty that we encountered during our research, the 'Caring' approach. I discuss the roots of the 'Caring' responses to poverty in a vision of the Church as a servant community that is motivated by a theological vision of the common good and human flourishing to meet the physical and pastoral needs of people who are damaged by debilitating poverty. I explore the theological foundations of this approach and, by drawing on primary research from the Life on the Breadline project consider the strengths and weaknesses of this form of response to austerity and the implications it has for the role the Church plays in the public sphere.

I move in Chapter 4 to describe, analyse and assess the more politicized 'Campaigning and Advocacy' approach to systemic poverty and structural injustice and discuss the theological roots of this, often marginalized, tradition of more radical Christian social action, in a vision of God's preferential option for the poor and the framing of the Church as a liberative movement called to speak truth to power and 'transform structural injustice'. Drawing extensively on primary data from Life on the Breadline research, I explore the impact that this approach has on the role the Church plays in the public sphere and the part it can play in fashioning an austerity-age theology of liberation. In Chapter 5, I consider a third, quite different approach to the Christian engagement with poverty that we encountered during our research. The 'Self-help and Enterprise' approach, which envisions the Church as an empowerer and enabler, draws a great deal of its support from evangelical and Pentecostal Christian traditions and foregrounds self-reliance, aspiration and business and social enterprise as responses capable of empowering individuals who are limited or damaged by poverty to realize their potential and flourish. I draw on examples from the Life on the Breadline project to illustrate the features and breadth of the 'Self-help and Enterprise' approach and critiques of the tradition's attitude towards the causes and systemic nature of poverty. Chapter 6 concludes my analysis of the ecosystem of the Christian approaches to austerity-age poverty that we uncovered during the Life on the Breadline research with an examination of the 'Community Building' approach that we encountered in several of our case studies. In this chapter I discuss the 'Community Building' vision of the Church as a companion community and its emphasis on contextualized, grassroots solidarity and relational Incarnational spirituality as the building blocks for a holistic engagement with multidimensional poverty and the search for inclusive, egalitarian community.

In Chapters 7 and 8 I draw on the arguments I have developed in previous chapters and on further Life on the Breadline data to begin to lay the methodological and thematic foundations for an austerity-age theology of liberation. I argue that theologians face a moment of truth and that the Church stands at a *Kairos* moment and suggest how they can respond to this time of judgement and opportunity to fashion a multifaceted holistic theology of liberation that has the potential to forge the liberative praxis needed to 'transform structural injustice' in this seemingly unending Age of Austerity.

Notes

1 The Life on the Breadline project team consisted of Dr Chris Shannahan (Project Lead), Dr Stephanie Denning, Professor Robert Beckford and Professor Peter Scott. More information and free resources can be found on the project website at https://breadlineresearch.coventry.ac.uk/. Locations or individuals' names are only used where consent has been given.

1

Wrestling an Octopus: Theorizing Contemporary Poverty

Introduction

In his 1964 Nobel Peace Prize lecture, Martin Luther King Jr compared poverty to 'a monstrous octopus [that] … projects its nagging, prehensile, tentacles into lands and villages all over the world'. King embraced complexity and plurality but far too often theological engagements with poverty focus on experience and biblical reflection, while ignoring the theoretical insights of our social science colleagues, or cherry picking the easy-to-swallow bits and kicking the more awkward insights into the long grass. It is time for theology to overcome its intellectual myopia. In this book I argue that theologians need to move beyond a super-ficial engagement with social and political theory to develop a deeper and more receptive critical dialogue with vital insights that can enhance and enrich theological analyses of austerity-age poverty. I suggest that theologians need to engage with key theoretical debates, if we want to fashion an intellectually and culturally credible liberative theology of austerity-age poverty. In this chapter I show that debates about the language we use to discuss poverty, the individualizing and moralising of poverty, the systemic nature of injustice, the interrelation between poverty and capitalism, the need to develop an intersectional theological framework and poverty as a form of multidimensional violence need to be embedded in the work of theologians more deeply than ever before. If we fail to open ourselves to such insights, theologies of austerity-age poverty will find themselves talking only to each other and will be unable to stimulate the liberative praxis needed to forge transformative social change.

The way we talk about poverty

Even though we often take it for granted, language is never neutral. The words we use speak volumes about our social location and our standpoint. Consequently, a clearer understanding of the symbolic nature of language can help us to develop a more holistic understanding of the socio-cultural, political and existential significance of the words we use when talking about poverty. This exploration of the symbolic nature of language is rooted deep in the human attempt to make sense of the world and our place in it. The analysis of its use as a system of symbolic meaning-making is closely aligned with the emergence of semiotics in the late nineteenth century and, in particular, the lectures of Ferdinand de Saussure (2006) in Geneva between 1907 and 1911. For Saussure, language was a structured system of signification within which words or phrases (signifiers) communicated encoded meanings about specific phenomena, objects or experiences (the signified). Writing half a century ago the anthropologist Clifford Geertz (1973) wrote about the symbolic significance of culture. The structuralist semiotics of linguists like Saussure and anthropologists like Claude Lévi-Strauss (1955) tended to frame language as an apolitical system of signification that revolved around universal linguistic forms and patterns. Like Lévi-Strauss, Geertz (1973, p. 5) saw culture as a 'web of significance'. However, unlike his structuralist counterparts, Geertz insisted that we can only fully understand such meaning-making in relation to the context to which it speaks.

Consequently, it is important for theologians to recognize that the decontextualized use of tools like semiotics or discourse analysis to excavate the meaning of the words we use cannot compete with the nuanced understanding made possible through an experiential exploration of the contextual resonance of language. Theological analyses of the language of poverty have been too slow to recognize the ways in which extended empirical research can give life, energy, depth and nuance to our analyses. The language we use arises from and helps us to make sense of the world around us (Geertz, 1973, p. 93). In his development of social semiotics, Michael Halliday (1978) made a similar point, arguing that the process of signification emerged from and could only be understood in relation to real-world social relationships. The language we use is shaped not only by our own experience, but by wider public and political discourses. Consequently, as we think about the way we talk about poverty, we need to consider the narratives of meaning such discourse communicates. With this in mind, it is important to supplement social semiotic practice with an engagement with the critical discourse analysis first developed by Norman Fairclough (1992,

p. 73ff). Critical discourse analysis draws on social semiotics to locate language in relation to broader social processes. This brings 'text' (the words used), 'discursive practice' (the nature or context of the specific discourse) and 'social practice' (wider social processes) into a critical dialogue, enabling us to develop a greater understanding of systems of inequality and oppression, in order to facilitate progressive social change. Jørgensen and Phillips (2002, p. 62) suggest that discourse is a 'socially and historically situated' 'form of action through which people can change the world'. In the context of my own search for a liberative theology of austerity-age poverty it is the capacity of language to justify injustice or paint a picture of an alternative egalitarian future that is at the forefront of my mind.

As we consider the ways in which we talk about poverty in breadline Britain social semiotics and critical discourse analysis can help to illuminate the relationship between 'text', 'discursive practice' and 'social practice'. Poverty discourses reflect broader policy and ideological narratives. By interrogating this symbolic relationship, we can form a fuller understanding of the theological and political significance of the ways in which we talk about poverty and the extent to which it reinforces or subverts the structural injustice that characterizes social relations in austerity-age Britain. By framing the ways in which we talk about poverty in this way, it becomes possible to apply what Pierre Bourdieu (1979) calls the 'symbolic power' of such discourse to broader understandings of social relations. For Bourdieu (1979, p. 79) 'symbolic systems are instruments of knowledge which exert a structuring power' to 'construct reality'. Such symbols can help the ruling class to construct a hegemonic discourse that reinforces the status quo. Drawing on the social semiotics of Halliday and Fairclough's critical discourse analysis can help us to identify the use of such 'symbolic power' in discussions about contemporary poverty in the UK. Fairclough (1992, p. 137) identifies three elements in the formation and interpretation of human discourse: the words we use ('text'); relevant political or public discourse ('discursive practice') and wider social processes ('social practice'). He suggests that the purpose of critical discourse analysis is to, 'systematically explore often opaque relationships of causality and determination between ... discursive practices, events and texts and ... wider social and cultural structures, relations and processes'. In the table I show how this approach can be used to interrogate the ways in which we talk about contemporary poverty. This perspective, when allied with a use of the hermeneutics of suspicion (Segundo, 1976) can enable a focused liberative theological analysis that recognizes the power of language to suppress and justify systemic poverty or to subvert the structural injustice upon which it rests.

The political significance of language

Table: The language of poverty

Text	Discursive Practice	Social Practice
skiver, striver, hard-working, chav, NEET, scrounger, thrifty, spendthrift, work-shy	individualized moralizing deserving/undeserving	austerity, neoliberalism, welfare cuts
low income, underprivileged, affluent, destitute, getting by, comfortable, privileged, hardship, needy, disadvantaged, 'cost of living crisis'	individualized not structural	later New Labour/Keir Starmer and, to a degree, Boris Johnson and Rishi Sunak
marginalized, oppressed, socially excluded, deprived, shame/stigma	systemic, collective, conscious exclusion	redistributive/capitalism/ structural injustice

The language we use to talk about contemporary poverty exemplifies broader public discourse, which, in turn, reflects wider social processes and ideological perspectives. Clarke and Newman (2012, p. 299ff) liken the austerity narrative to alchemy – the weaving of a public discourse that re-framed deepening poverty and the retreat of the welfare state as the first hopeful stirrings of empowered individuals in a dynamic neo-liberal 'Big Society' – from tired communalism to energetic localized citizenship. Clarke and Newman (2021, p. 301) argue that the use of such alchemy by David Cameron and George Osborne was intended to elicit a form of false consciousness that accepted their hegemonic rationale for austerity.

Whilst we often think of the word 'myth' as a way of saying something is not true, the Greek term 'mythos', from which it is derived, simply refers to a story that seeks to express fundamental existential or cultural truths and values in a persuasive narrative form. Mark Gardiner and Steven Engler (2010) liken myths to maps which help communities to navigate their place in society. The Structuralist anthropologist Claude Lévi-Strauss (1955, p. 430) argues that myths are linguistic devices that seek to explain 'the present and the past, as well as the future', whereas the mythologist Joseph Campbell (1988) views them as narrative searches for meaning – attempts to make sense of life. Chiara Bottici (2011, p. 41) speaks of the ways in which myth is used within political discourse almost unnoticed – 'slipping into our unconsciousness, political myths can deeply influence our most fundamental perceptions ... and thus escape ... critical scrutiny'.

Commentaries on contemporary poverty in the UK are woven into broader, often subconscious, political myths related to its causes and the nature and purpose of the austerity policies introduced following the 2010 General Election. Christopher Flood (2002, p. 8) describes a political myth as a 'narrative which serves ideological functions'. It is, therefore, possible to speak of the austerity agenda that Conservative Prime Minister David Cameron and his Chancellor, George Osborne, introduced following the General Election as a political myth. The political myth of austerity presented welfare spending cuts as unavoidable economic necessities in the face of a growing deficit and the global recession that followed the 2008 financial crash. Austerity was the only way to 'save' the nation. The austerity myth pinned the blame for UK poverty on the policies of the 2007–10 Labour Government led by Gordon Brown and implicated us all for our recklessness and financial irresponsibility (Cooper and Whyte, 2017, p. 4ff). Speaking in 2009, a year before coming to power, Cameron told the Conservative Party Conference, 'We will confront Britain's culture of irresponsibility and that will be hard to take for many people. And we will tear down Labour's big government bureaucracy, ripping up its time-wasting, money-draining, responsibility-sapping nonsense.'[1]

Cameron and Osborne insisted that poverty was not systemically rooted in global capitalism but was the fault of Labour's poor management of the economy and our financial irresponsibility as individuals. They therefore side-stepped any need to address questions of structural injustice. Their austerity myth turned the economic meltdown that resulted from flaws in the privatized banking system into a crippling public sector debt (Clarke and Newman, 2012, p. 299ff). We were told that we all need to make sacrifices because, according to Cameron's 2009 speech at the Conservative Party Conference, 'We are all in this together'. Like all myths, the austerity myth pointed us to the future as well as the past, echoing the neoliberalism from which it sprang. The solution to the deepening poverty and growing inequality that followed the 2008 financial crash lay, not in a bureaucratic collectivist State that sapped innovation but energizing entrepreneurial spirit and individualized localism: a 'Big Society'.

The power of the austerity myth revolved around the capacity of specific words to echo and amplify a broader social discourse. The 2012 Welfare Reform Act embedded the emergent Age of Austerity in legislation. This Act of Parliament provided the vocabulary and set the policy course for a decade of deepening poverty and increasing inequality. Reaching back to centuries-old binary moral motifs about the 'able-bodied' and 'idle' or the 'deserving' and 'undeserving' poor, the political myth of austerity found its voice in the words of Chancellor George Osborne at the 2012 Conservative Party Conference. Adopting an individualized and moralistic tone, Osborne implicitly echoed the broader neoliberal social discourse that ran like a thread through the policy agenda of the Cameron-led 2010–15 Conservative/Liberal Democrat coalition government.

The language that Osborne used evoked an austerity myth that valorized fairness, aspiration, hard work and a commitment to shared sacrifice. Austerity, he claimed, was an economic necessity needed to 'repair a badly broken economy'.[2] Osborne framed the austerity myth within a social discourse of fairness, claiming this to be a characteristic of Britishness – 'We know what the British mean by fair. That those who put something in should get something out.' Fairness, aspiration, effort and shared sacrifice were presented as intimately interconnected – the moral foundation of Osborne's austerity myth: 'We support those who aspire so we can help those most in need … The cost of paying our debts cannot possibly be borne by one section of society alone.' On this basis Osborne sought to frame the deep welfare and public spending cuts that characterized austerity policies, and their deeply unequal impact, as a fair means of spreading the burden of the sacrifice needed to build an aspirational economy that rewarded hard work. Osborne claimed that during the Blair and Brown Labour governments the 'state had become too expensive' and public sector pensions unaffordable. Implicitly evoking the individualistic localism that characterized Cameron's 'Big Society' as the basis for an aspirational new 'One Nation' social contract, Osborne sought to make a moral, as well as an economic, argument for austerity, claiming to speak for hardworking teachers who refused to strike, corner-shop owners open until midnight, commuters leaving home before their children get up, entrepreneurs working hard on the next start-up and pensioners saving hard for their grandchildren.

Osborne claimed that 'We modern Conservatives represent all those who aspire, all who work, save and hope, all who feel a responsibility to put in, not just take out.' It was on this basis that he sought to justify his binary moral references to 'workers' and 'shirkers' – 'It is wrong that it's possible for someone to be better off on benefits than they would be in work.' Where, he asked, 'is the fairness for the shift-worker, leaving home in the dark hours of the early morning who looks up at the closed blinds of their next-door neighbour sleeping off a life on benefits?' Built on this foundation, the austerity myth resisted extra taxation for the super-wealthy because 'wealth creation is not something to be penalised' or a so-called 'mansion tax' but advocated public spending cuts because 'the government spends too much' of people's money and the introduction of Universal Credit (to replace six existing benefits) 'so work always pays'. In closing his 2012 Conservative Party speech, Osborne hammered home the ethical basis for austerity, returning to his binary worldview which pitted 'workers' against 'shirkers', enterprise against dependency and a cumbersome over-reaching state against a nimble and empowered civil society. How, he asked, 'can we justify the incomes of those out of work rising faster than the incomes of those in work?'. 'Our entire economic strategy', he insisted, 'is an enterprise strategy. We will be the government for the people who aspire.'

The political myth that Cameron and Osborne fashioned and the language they deployed provided austerity with its utilitarian rationale and its deeper neoliberal ideological justification. Whilst it was inflected with echoes of a One Nation ethic and references to aspiration, fairness and shared sacrifice, the primary focus of the austerity was a binary narrative which defined people in unreflective either-or terms as 'workers' or 'shirkers'. The reference to 'strivers' and the 'skivers' within austerity mythology carried echoes of the Victorian discourse of the 'deserving' and the 'undeserving' poor. Contemporary debates about poverty in the UK are interwoven with discussions about the austerity agenda of successive Conservative governments since 2010. However, aspects of the dichotomous moral narrative fashioned by Cameron and Osborne were also present in the language used by Labour Prime Ministers Tony Blair and Gordon Brown to valorize so-called 'hard-working families' and distinguish them from benefit claimants at the 2005 General Election.

This 'skiver' versus 'striver' discourse is the inheritor of a debate that finds its roots in the medieval Church's emphasis on the importance of almsgiving as a means of helping people who were destitute and living on the margins of society. Whilst the giving of alms was seen as an essential marker of faith, a more punitive accompanying narrative distinguished between those who were genuinely destitute and those who were seen as 'vagrants'. In the Early Modern era distinctions were made between the 'able-bodied', the 'impotent' and the 'idle' poor, and in 1601 the Elizabethan Poor Law formalized this objectification of people living in poverty. Two hundred years later in the Poor Law of 1834, these distinctions were moralized still further in the Act's categorization of people in poverty as 'deserving' or 'undeserving'. Although the Poor Law originates in Victorian England, the reified characteristics that the Act attributed to the 'deserving' and the 'undeserving' live on in the public discourse about 'skivers', 'shirkers' and 'hard-working families' that continues to frame UK poverty in the twenty-first century (on the Left as well as the Right). Rachel Muers (2021, p. 42) notes the rhetorical and political force that 'the moral categorization of people in poverty' has on the public imaginary and on attitudes towards the imposition of austerity policies on people and communities who are already left out or left behind. Muers argues that such moral categorization serves as a reminder of the ways in the binary and reductionist objectification of people as 'deserving' or 'undeserving' enables those with power to avoid asking themselves awkward ethical questions about the morality of austerity and the systemic inequalities it reflects. The objectification of people through the adoption of such a discourse by successive UK governments since the 2008 financial crash has served to diminish people's agency. Our Life on the Breadline research suggests that this is also a trap that many Christian responses to austerity-age poverty have tended to fall into. All who seek a truly emancipatory austerity-age theology of liberation need to ensure that a commitment to the voice, dignity and agency of people with direct experience of poverty lies at the heart of theological analyses of structural injustice.

During his imprisonment in Benito Mussolini's Italy, Antonio Gramsci began to write about the political importance of culture in his *Prison Notebooks*. Gramsci's ideas about the nature and impact of hegemony on social relations can help us to develop a fuller understanding of the political significance of the language we use when talking about systemic poverty. Unlike many other Marxist theorists of his generation, Gramsci (2007, p. 168ff) argued that culture bore within it the potential to oppress or to liberate and represented a key arena for class struggle. For Gramsci, culture provided the ruling class with a means of depicting unjust social relations as normative and inequality as an expression of the natural order. Gramsci referred to this use of culture as a means of social control and domination, intended to elicit false consciousness, as cultural hegemony. The hymn 'All Things Bright and Beautiful' exemplifies Gramsci's understanding of hegemony. Written in 1848 by Cecil Frances Alexander, 'All Things Bright and Beautiful' is now largely seen as a children's hymn. However, the Victorian original was not so child-friendly: 'The rich man in his castle, the poor man at his gate, God made them high and lowly and ordered their estate.' Alexander's bouncy tune masked the hegemonic use of worship to paint poverty and inequality as ordained and blessed by God. Whilst the explicit hegemony of the Victorian 'All Things Bright and Beautiful' may be a thing of the past, worship remains an important arena of the existential struggle against systemic poverty and a context within which the cultural violence of structural injustice can be challenged and liberative consciousness raised.

The pioneer of peace studies, Johan Galtung (1990, p. 291), sees hegemony as a form of cultural violence. Culture, he argues, is used to weave an ideological narrative that justifies the structural violence of systemic inequality. For Galtung (1990, p. 292), cultural violence 'works by changing the moral color of an act ... making reality opaque'. Because of its ubiquitous power, culture, he suggests, can 'preach, teach, admonish ... and dull us into seeing exploitation and/or repression as normal and natural, or into not seeing them ... at all' (1990, p. 295). The political myth of austerity as shared sacrifice and the moralistic discourse of successive UK governments that frames endemic poverty and deepening inequality as natural, rather than the debilitating consequence of structural injustice exemplifies cultural violence. The Joint Public Issues Team (JPIT) is an ecumenical think-tank that supports the social action of the British Methodist Church, the United Reformed Church and the Baptist Union of Great Britain in association with the Church of Scotland. As George Osborne's 'skivers' versus 'strivers' rhetoric began to circulate, JPIT (2013, pp. 4–5) interrogated the flawed but widely adopted narrative it popularized. In particular they challenged six widely disseminated myths that reflected Osborne's depiction of poverty as individual failure. JPIT demonstrated that the assertions that people are poor because 'they are lazy and don't want to work', 'are addicted to drink and drugs', they can't 'manage their money properly', 'are on the fiddle' and that they 'have an easy life on benefits' and were responsible for the global financial crash were all unsubstantiated value judgements.

Austerity will not be overcome until the ballooning of food banks, child poverty, food insecurity, homelessness, low pay and poor housing become morally unacceptable. As Gramsci and Galtung demonstrate, ideas and language matter. They can maintain or subvert the status quo. Manuel Castells (2010, p. 360) observes, 'Whoever wins the battle for people's minds will rule, because mighty rigid apparatuses will not be a match in any reasonable timespan for minds mobilized.' Gramsci refers to this existential battle as a 'cultural war of position' (2007, p. 168ff). If the hegemonic normalization of poverty is to be subverted and the 'war of position' won, the false consciousness it engenders must first be recognized. In the early 1960s Paulo Freire (1970) drew on the work of Gramsci in his liberative educational programmes teaching illiterate peasants in rural Brazil. In his seminal book *Pedagogy of the Oppressed* that arose from this work, Freire (1970), argues that oppressed communities can only attain true liberation when they become 'conscientized' – critically aware of the nature and causes of the structural injustice that oppresses them. In his later *Pedagogy of Indignation*, Freire defines conscientization as 'the building of a critical awareness' of the systemic causes of poverty and inequality (2004, p. 66). In this book I argue that the damage of a decade of austerity in breadline Britain can only be truly overcome when such a critical awareness breaks the hegemonic hold of dominant moralizing poverty narratives. Our research within Life on the Breadline suggests that the Church stands at a *Kairos* moment. Commitment to a vision of the common good within which all people can flourish and to reflecting God's preferential option for the poor characterize the Church's engagement with poverty but, in our experience, are hampered by being distant and, largely, cushioned from the brutal rawness of austerity and a nervousness about moving beyond a 'caring' love of neighbour into the fraught world of political activism. The journey towards a conscientized Church, it seems, is far from over. This tension ran through our research and weaves through every chapter of this book.

'Get on your bike' – Individualizing and moralizing poverty

In 1981, Norman Tebbit told the Conservative Party Conference about the experience of his unemployed father: 'He didn't moan or blame the government. He got on his bike and looked for work 'til he found it.'[3] In the intervening 45 years, successive UK governments on the Left, as well as the Right, have, with occasional exceptions, continued to individualize poverty. People living in poverty have found themselves blamed for being poor – they don't try hard enough or are morally inadequate, we are told. In her examination of New Labour, Ruth Levitas (2005, p. 7) observed a shift from a bold early redistributive energy towards a centre-right moral conservatism, which framed poverty as 'pathological ... rather than endemic'. A decade later, against the backdrop of the recession that followed the 2008 global financial crash and violent unrest in many English towns and cities during 2011, Conservative Prime Minister David Cameron suggested that Britain was morally 'broken'. Alluding to a long-running TV comedy show, *Shameless*, which focused on a seemingly dysfunctional family enjoying an easy life on benefits, Cameron suggested that the experience of poverty and the moral failings of individuals were intimately interconnected. Echoing the Blairite focus on individual responsibility and Cameron's 'broken Britain' mantra, Chancellor George Osborne assured the 2012 Conservative Party Conference that the government would support 'strivers' and 'hard-working families' and make life harder for 'shirkers' and 'skivers'. This dichotomous moral narrative and the valorizing of 'hard working families' has wound its way down the years, and the term continued to feature prominently in the publicity of both Labour and Conservative Parties ahead of the 2024 General Election. Writing as this moral discourse was becoming embedded in austerity-age Britain, the political journalist Owen Jones (2012) spoke of the ways in which political and public narratives about 'welfare dependency' were used to stigmatize people living in poverty. Kayleigh Garthwaite (2016, p. 277ff) drew on her research in the north-east of England to make a similar point, illustrating the ways in which people who were referred to food banks felt ashamed because of this stigmatizing narrative. Our 2018–21 Life on the Breadline research into Christian responses to austerity-age poverty in the UK uncovered this sense of shame among food bank users in one of our Birmingham case studies of the Trussell Trust B30 food bank. Stigma can damage communities, as well as individuals. Our Life on the Breadline case study of the work of Hodge Hill Church on a large Birmingham housing estate, for example, illustrates the ways in which the internalization of negative narratives about the neighbourhood can foster a debilitating sense of collective shame. Liz Beddoe and Emily Keddell (2016, p. 155) summarize: 'Blame and shame, heightened by discourses of social abjection, are powerful weapons with which to empower political disengagement … Stigma intensifies the othering of people who are poor, side-stepping structural explanations of violence and neglect.' In Hodge Hill, the use of Asset-Based Community Development counters such debilitating narratives, empowering each other and fostering a shared commitment to the common good, as I explain in Chapter 6.

Most of the Church leaders whom we interviewed or surveyed during Life on the Breadline argued that the causes of poverty were systemic. However, one Church leader from the North of England reminded us that the moralizing individualization of poverty and echoes of old 'deserving'/'undeserving' binaries continue to resonate within some local congregations: 'There is a sense that it is still the individual's fault if they are poor' (Life on the Breadline survey, 2020). The Joint Public Issues Team (2013, p. 4) challenged this perception, as well as the myths noted above: 'The myths exposed in this report, reinforced by politicians and the media, are convenient because they allow the poor to be blamed for their poverty, and the rest of society to avoid taking any of the responsibility.' I have argued elsewhere (Shannahan, 2019a) that exposing the fallacy of the 'skivers' and 'shirkers' motif is an indispensable part of the battle to delegitimize the hegemonic depiction of austerity-age poverty and inequality as unfortunate or part of life's natural order. I discuss this existential struggle further below in my analysis of the violence of poverty.

Such a depiction of poverty echoes the tradition of liberal individualism that originated in the work of the seventeenth-century philosopher John Locke and the eighteenth-century economic liberalism of Adam Smith. This perspective valorizes individual agency and ethical responsibility, meritocratic entrepreneurship and economic liberalism, and has dominated most political discourse in the UK since the early 1980s. Poverty is presented as a moral, rather than a structural problem. It is argued that its roots lie in growing social atomism and a 'broken' social contract and not the systemic flaws of capitalism because there is no such thing as society, just individuals and their families (to paraphrase Margaret Thatcher's 1987 claim). During the Age of Austerity that followed the 2010 UK General Election, the coalition government's response to poverty encouraged individuals to become more active citizens building a good-neighbour focused 'Big Society' rather than adopting the collectivist redistributive ethic that characterized the early years of the New Labour decade (Espiet-Kilty, 2016). Cameron's vision of empowered individuals acting in a voluntary capacity to enhance community well-being at a local neighbourhood level accompanied, and echoed, a neoliberal political and economic agenda that valorized the volunteering of individuals and dismissed the value of collective action (Kisby, 2010). Ray Gaston and Steven Shakespeare (2010, p. 797) cautioned local churches against supporting the 'Big Society' agenda as a means of sustaining their own social action, arguing such engagement represents a form of 'collusion'. The Big Society, they said, is 'a Big Lie … a smokescreen, another ideological veil. Its pretence of radical change is simply a means of persuading us to live in submission to the great God Capital.'

The systemic nature of poverty

Life is not predetermined, and neither is the deeply ingrained poverty that scars life for so many people in contemporary Britain. As individuals we are accountable for our actions and decisions, but not for the structural injustice that limits our opportunities and the choices we make. I have suggested above that theologians and theorists, practitioners and policymakers need to debunk the persistent but flawed moralizing narrative that blames people in poverty for being poor. Poverty is systemic. Consequently, a credible theology of liberation in an age of ongoing austerity needs to move beyond flawed analyses that divorce poverty from its structural roots and apolitical visions of the common good. Before reflecting on the traumatizing violence of multidimensional poverty it is important, therefore, to emphasize its systemic nature. Three points need to be made.

First, in theological terms it is important to clearly frame poverty as a form of systemic sin, rather than individual moral inadequacy. The traditional understanding of sin as specific words or actions that intentionally wound another person or undermine the will and nature of God highlights the importance of individual agency but runs the risk of neglecting the damage caused to individuals by unjust social systems, systemic inequality and social policy. The tradition of contemporary Catholic Social Teaching that began to emerge during the Papacy of Leo XIII and, in particular, in his 1891 encyclical, *Rerum Novarum*, can help us to think of sin in less individualized terms. Gregory Baum (1994) reminds us that Catholic Social Teaching suggests that what it refers to as 'social sin' results from the activities of individuals that undermine the common good by institutionalizing injustice or embedding it in policy. Pope John Paul II's *Sollicitudo Rei Socialis* suggests that poverty is caused by 'structures of sin', rather than individual moral sinfulness (1987, paragraph 36). Albert Nolan strikes a balance between individual responsibility and structural injustice, arguing that whilst, 'social structures are produced and reproduced by human agency', they 'constrain or enable people' (2007, p. 627). Social structures can, he continues, be seen as 'materially sinful because of the pain and suffering they inflict upon people' (p. 632). The Pope's Synod of Bishops drew on the commitment of the 1968 Latin American Bishops' Conference in Medellín to the core values expounded within liberation theology, regarding the recognition of the traumatizing damage caused by the 'social manifestations of sin' evidenced in 'unjust systems and structures' (World Synod of Catholic Bishops, 1971, paragraphs 51 and 5). Going further, the United States Council of Roman Catholic Bishops spoke of structural injustice as an expression of 'social sin' (1986, paragraph 77). Such shifts in Catholic Social Teaching were informed by the writings of the first generation of Latin American liberation theologians and, in particular, the movement's pioneer Gustavo Gutiérrez who suggested that, 'Sin is a social, historical fact, the absence of brotherhood' that is 'evident in oppressive structures ... as fundamental alienation, the root of a situation of injustice and exploitation' (1974, p. 175). Gutiérrez goes on, 'Sin is present in the denial that a human being is sister or brother to me. It is present in structures of oppression, created for the benefit of the few' (1983, p. 62). This recognition that poverty is rooted in the 'structures of sin' that result from 'social sin' can help us to subvert and overcome dominant models of political discourse in the UK that continue to frame it in individualized terms. Furthermore, such reflections can provide contemporary Church leaders with the theological resources our Life on the Breadline research suggests they need to shift Christian engagement with austerity-age poverty from welfare to sustained action intended to 'transform structural injustice'.

Second, therefore, poverty results from social processes, rather than poor individual choices. As I argued above, the moralizing individualization of poverty that we have witnessed under successive Labour and Conservative governments in the UK for more than 40 years has been supported by a public discourse that demonizes people living in poverty and blames them for being poor. Such an approach enables policymakers and practitioners to quietly ignore the awkward fact that deep-seated and persistent poverty is caused by policy decisions that benefit the few and not the many and which are embedded in systems of governance and social and economic policy.

Writing about the rise of globalized capitalism, Manuel Castells summarizes: 'Social exclusion is a process, not a condition' (1998, p. 73). Whilst Castells and Saskia Sassen wrote about global processes their words ring true a generation later in breadline Britain. Writing about the emergence of a network of global cities, Sassen argued that the processes of globalization have created and deepened global and local inequalities: 'Alongside these new global and regional hierarchies of cities is a vast territory that has become increasingly peripheral, increasingly excluded from the major economic processes that fuel growth in the new global economy' (1994, p. 4). In a similar vein Castells suggested that the new networked global economy created 'black holes' within informational capitalism (1998, p. 162). Such 'black holes' of exclusion, powerlessness and poverty represent, argues Castells, a 'fourth world' that may be physically next-door to wealth and power, but to all intents and purposes, might as well be on another planet (1996). Our Life on the Breadline case study of Christian responses to the Grenfell Tower fire and the dramatic inequality that characterizes life in the Royal Borough of Kensington and Chelsea illustrates Castells' argument with graphic clarity, as I demonstrate in Chapter 4.

Third, poverty and inequality are inextricably linked with the neoliberal economic philosophy that drove the Age of Austerity introduced by David Cameron and George Osborne following the 2010 UK General Election. Discussion, therefore, of a so-called 'cost of living crisis' should not depict it as an unforeseen accident, nor the unavoidable tragic consequence of the Covid-19 pandemic that began in 2020 or the Russian invasion of Ukraine in 2022. Rather, the 'crisis' needs to be understood as the price of a decade of stringent austerity, the withdrawal of the State and an increasing reliance on the voluntary sector to provide the safety net for people living in poverty. Whilst the term 'neoliberalism' can be used in vague, often pejorative, terms to dismiss Conservative government policies as uncaring, its careful use can help us to place the systemic nature of austerity-age poverty in a broader ideological context. Neoliberalism is an economic perspective rooted in a libertarian philosophical tradition stretching back to the classical liberalism of the early nineteenth century, as I noted above. Sometimes simply referred to as free-market economics, neoliberalism supplanted a largely settled social consensus in the UK that developed in the decades following the Second World War, which emphasized the importance of a strong Welfare State as a means of social support and the fostering of a common good that did not undermine capitalist economic policies. This consensus began to fray in the US and the UK towards the end of the 1970s with neoliberal advocates like Margaret Thatcher in Downing Street and Ronald Reagan in the White House. Placing a strong emphasis on deregulating the economy and removing welfare programmes that were perceived to inhibit entrepreneurialism, neoliberalism sought to create the economic conditions within which individuals could flourish. Within the Cameron/Osborne neoliberal framework the foundations of the caring 'Big Society' they spoke of were individual charity, good-neighbourliness, localism and the voluntary sector. The Welfare State was not to be dispensed with completely but shrunk. It was recognized that the State had a limited role to play in fostering the common good but only so long as it did not stifle entrepreneurship and competition, which were depicted as the drivers of social mobility (Farnsworth and Irving, 2018). Such a perspective has generated wealth for some, but as we have seen during the Age of Austerity, it has done nothing to address the structural injustice that limits broader social mobility. Neoliberalism may make it easier to develop profitable businesses and might provide the conditions within which some people can flourish but there is a social price to be paid as individual opportunity is prioritized over the common good (Piketty, 2014). In the UK, inequality has deepened as the Welfare State has withdrawn and economic and employment regulations have been loosened. We have never 'all been in this together' as former UK Chancellor George Osborne claimed. We need to understand that deepening inequality and poverty are not accidental consequences of the austerity pursued by successive Conservative governments in the UK; they are built into neoliberal capitalism (Feldman, 2019). It is my argument in this book that such policies rupture the social fabric of British society and a shared commitment to the common good.

The violence of poverty

Poverty is an insidious form of violence that can suffocate the life out of us. Poverty scars us physically, emotionally and spiritually and its overwhelming impact can disempower us and numb us to the systemic injustice that gives it life and robs us of our future. Gutiérrez alludes to such violence in *A Theology of Liberation*: 'Poverty means death: lack of food and housing, the inability to attend properly to health and education needs, the exploitation of workers, permanent unemployment, the lack of respect for one's human dignity' (1988, p. xxi). Furthermore, he argues that 'In the Bible, poverty is a scandalous condition inimical to human dignity and, therefore, contrary to the will of God' (1974, p. 291).

I have argued elsewhere (Shannahan, 2019a) that liberation theologians need to engage in a deeper dialogue with the pioneering peace studies of Johan Galtung if they are to explain the complex violence of poverty in a persuasive manner. I have suggested that a use of Galtung's (1969) triad of direct, structural and cultural violence can transform theological analyses of structural injustice. Galtung suggests that the 'vicious cycle' of direct, structural and cultural violence feed into and compound each other (1990, p. 295). Galtung adopted a deliberately broad definition of violence as deliberate actions, forces or factors that inhibit people from realizing their potential (1969, p. 168ff). Vittorio Bufacchi (2005) suggests, with some justification, that this notion that anything that prevents a person from fulfilling her or his potential is a form of violence is too broad. However, it remains the case that Galtung's conceptualization of violence, depicted in Figure 1, provides us with the impetus needed to reconsider the multifaceted nature of poverty and the damage it causes.

Galtung suggests that direct violence refers to specific actions taken by individuals that are intended to cause harm (1969, pp. 170–71). Direct violence can be psychological as well as physical and lead to verbal or spiritual damage just as much as physical harm. Direct violence revolves around a specific event – shame and silencing, as well as knives and guns (Galtung, 1990, p. 294). Galtung implies that structural violence is, to a degree, a synonym for injustice (1969, p. 171). Embedded in policies, systems and practices, structural violence, argues Galtung, is depersonalized and 'silent' and provides an institutional framework within which person-to-person violence takes place (1969, p. 173). Cultural violence provides the moral or ideological camouflage that normalizes structural and direct violence. Galtung puts it eloquently, suggesting that cultural violence refers to 'the symbolic sphere of our existence – exemplified by religion and ideology, language and art ... that can be used to justify or

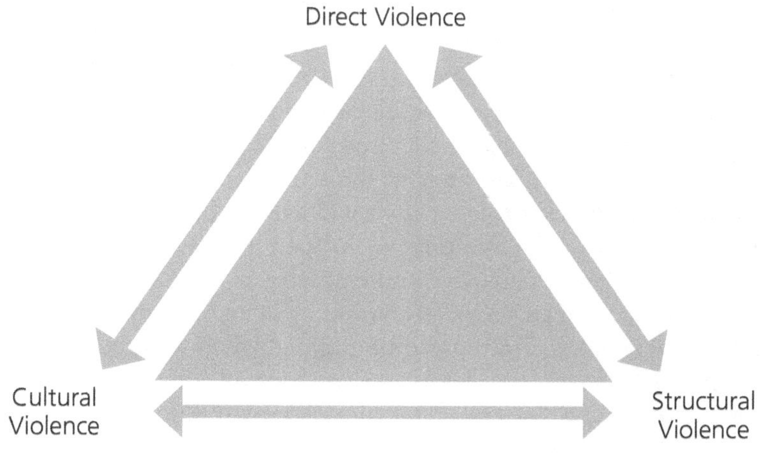

Figure 1. Johan Galtung's Triad of Violence

legitimize direct or structural violence ... Stars, crosses and crescents ... come to mind' (1990, p. 291).

In Gramscian terms, cultural violence refers to the use of culture to fashion a hegemonic public discourse that justifies injustice. Galtung speaks of 'violence that works on the body and violence that works on the soul' (1969, p. 169). Poverty represents an insidious form of direct violence that scars our spirit, as well as our physical and mental health. Gutiérrez puts it like this: 'Material poverty is a sub-human condition ... to be poor means ... to be exploited by others ... not to know you are a person' (1974, p. 289). In her analysis of the exploration of oppression within the Bible, Elsa Tamez notes how poverty is described as leading to the 'degradation of the human being ... [and] ... a seizure of the divine image in the person' (1982, p. 12).

As we discovered during our Life on the Breadline project, the Age of Austerity hasn't just ruptured the social fabric of British society, it has sucked the life out of local communities and damaged the physical and mental well-being of millions of women, men and children across the UK. Our case study of the London-based Power the Fight organization that works with churches to support, mentor and act as an advocate for young people who have been touched by knife crime, highlights the link between a £1 billion cut in spending on youth and children's services and the upsurge in serious youth violence. Our Life on the Breadline fieldwork also shone a light on the ways in which the seemingly unending challenge of food insecurity impacts on our mental health. The number of three-day food parcels provided by the faith-inspired Trussell Trust (the UK's largest food bank provider) grew from under 26,000 in

2008–09 (the year of the global financial crash) to more than 3.1 million in 2023–24.[4] One of our Life on the Breadline case studies focused on one of the largest food banks in the West Midlands, an area where the number of three-day food parcels distributed by Trussell Trust food banks has grown from 121,000 in 2017 to 269,000 in 2024. Here we witnessed the psychological damage wrought by the need to continually rely on food parcels to manage between Universal Credit payments. One woman embodied this emotional pain: 'people are killing themselves you know, bab, and dying. I've contemplated it, why struggle like this for another ten, fifteen years' (Denning et al., 2021, p. 14). Another person at B30 highlighted the debilitating nature of such pain: 'Poverty affects people's moods, everybody seems miserable, depressed, anxious, worried, a lot of debt, struggling for food and you know just the basics really of life, struggling to pay bills.'

Our Life on the Breadline case study of the work of Hodge Hill Church on the Bromford estate in East Birmingham further illustrates poverty's soul-sapping violence. Built in the 1960s, the Bromford estate has been depicted as a 'problem estate' – a forgotten place characterized by welfare dependency and worklessness (Shannahan, 2012). On the basis of the Indices of Deprivation, Bromford can be characterized as a multiply deprived community. Statistically the estate is one of the 5% most multiply deprived neighbourhoods in England. Such social exclusion preceded the 2008 financial crash but the austerity agenda of successive Conservative governments since 2010 robbed the community of many of its remaining public services, deepening and embedding pre-existing poverty and structural injustice.

Above I discussed how public discourse – the words we use and hear, the images we create and the TV programmes we watch – can resemble a form of cultural violence, deployed to bolster a political myth. An expression of such cultural violence as it relates to contemporary poverty was found in former Prime Minister David Cameron's 2011 speech about his government's nascent 'troubled families' initiative, which he framed as a response to that summer's violence in English town centres and shopping areas. Cameron pointed to what he suggested was a '*Shameless* culture' whereby people in poverty enjoyed an easy life on benefits, rather than working hard. Cameron insisted that such families 'cause so much misery for others' – 'parents choosing to live life on the dole' and 'teenagers rampaging around the neighbourhood before turning to crime', even though his assessment of moral failure owed more to ideologically driven stereotypes than real life.[5]

The rap musician Plan B pointed acerbically to the fallacy at the heart of Cameron's analysis. In his iconic track, 'Ill Manors', Plan B spoke of

2011's street violence, suggesting that 'There's no such thing as broken Britain, we're just bloody broke in Britain' (Plan B UK, 2012). In a very different way the Joint Public Issues Team also critiqued Cameron's claims and wider Conservative rhetoric about poverty: 'By his own measures, David Cameron's "troubled families" are not the "neighbours from hell" that he describes, but, instead "neighbours in need"' (2013, p. 10). In spite of this corrective, the narrative blaming and shaming people living in poverty has gained widespread cultural traction. Kayleigh Garthwaite points to the stigmatizing of people who are forced to rely on food banks to feed their families. Garthwaite (2016, p. 278) suggests that the moral discourse that framed poverty as a shameful example of individual failure was 'fuelled by Conservative government rhetoric and "poverty porn" representations of people seeking emergency food'. Such physical, psychological and spiritual scarring can be mitigated but will never be overcome until the cultural violence that rationalizes, individualizes and moralizes contemporary poverty is seen for what it is – a hegemonic form of social control intended to elicit, maintain and reinforce a collective form of false consciousness that swallows the ideologically driven political myth of austerity. Gramsci argued that the struggle against this cultural violence resembles a 'war of position' (2007, p. 168ff) between the ideological forces that underpin and defend structural injustice and those that articulate a vision of an inclusive and egalitarian society that is characterized by a shared commitment to the common good. This struggle to subvert the narrative that provides moral justification for systemic poverty and inequality will not be an easy one to win. To re-frame what John Paul Lederach calls the 'moral imagination' of society we need to reimagine our common life (2005, p. 23). As Gutiérrez observes, such reorientation demands 'a conversion ... to the oppressed person, the exploited social class, the despised race' (1974, p. 205). For Freire, this liberative rebirth can only occur once we become conscious of the fact that oppression is not part of the natural order of things but results from systemic injustice (1970; 2004). Only through the development of such critical awareness can the hegemonic hold of the political myth that justifies austerity be broken.

Poverty is a form of direct and structural violence that is provided with moral camouflage by the deployment of cultural violence. Galtung argues that structural violence is, 'built into the structure and shows up as unequal power and unequal life chances' (1969, pp. 171, 173). It is often indirect and silent. However, its impact was evident in the years that followed the 2012 Welfare Reform Act, the introduction of Universal Credit beginning in 2013, the freezing of benefits from 2016 onwards, housing deregulation and extensive ongoing public spending cuts. Such austerity policies resulted in dramatic increases in homelessness and destitution, food bank use, endemic low pay and insecure zero-hours contracts, perfectly exemplifying the features of structural violence. Cooper and Whyte refer to the Age of Austerity as 'a bureaucratised form of violence that is implemented in routine and mundane ways' (2017, p. 4). The grind of austerity resembles the slow violence that Rob Nixon wrote of in relation to environmental damage. Nixon suggested that 'slow violence ... occurs gradually and out of sight, a violence of delayed destruction that is dispersed across time and space, an attritional violence that is typically not viewed as violence at all' (2011, p. 2). While Nixon's focus was on climate change, like Powers and Rakopoulos (2019) and Cooper and Whyte (2017), I suggest that the term 'slow violence' perfectly captures the incremental, slowly soul-sapping damage of austerity-age poverty.

Our Life on the Breadline case study of Christian responses to the Grenfell Tower fire in June 2017 illustrated the ways in which analyses of structural, cultural and direct violence and collective trauma can strengthen theological analyses of austerity-age poverty. I have argued elsewhere that the Grenfell tragedy was not ultimately caused by a faulty fridge or broken sprinklers and fire doors but by decades of deregulation and underinvestment in social housing (Shannahan, 2022, p. 274ff). Cooper and Whyte (2017) suggested that the Grenfell Tower fire was a form of slow institutional violence; a disaster waiting to happen due to the dramatic spending cuts imposed by Kensington and Chelsea Borough Council following the 2010 General Election. Tracy Shildrick, however, reminds us that the contemporary crisis in social housing did not begin after the 2008 financial crash, but almost 30 years earlier at the beginning of the 1980s (2018, p. 784ff). For Shildrick, the roots of the housing injustice that culminated in the Grenfell fire lie in the neoliberalism of the Thatcher decade, which laid the ground for the withdrawal of the State, the culture of deregulation, the valorization of the private sector and the weakening of government commitments to fostering the common good we have witnessed during the Age of Austerity. The Grenfell tragedy reminds us that austerity is a form of structural violence that is justified through the deployment of forms of cultural violence that demonize people living in poverty.

Of all that has been written about the Grenfell Tower fire it is perhaps the poetry of Ben Okri that has best evoked the visceral and devastating violence of the tragedy: 'In this Age of Austerity the poor die for others' prosperity ... If you want to see how the poor die, come see Grenfell Tower' (Okri, 2018). Okri's poetry invites us to engage more fully with the ways in which trauma theory can inform our understanding of contemporary poverty. In the months following the Grenfell Tower fire the number of local residents exhibiting symptoms of post-traumatic stress disorder grew dramatically. The damage of the tragedy continued to reverberate through North Kensington and three years later, in 2020, it was revealed that more than 10,000 people had been treated for post-traumatic stress disorder.[6] The collective trauma that resulted from the Grenfell fire illustrates the tragic human cost of austerity economics. Such trauma, suggests Caroline Garland (2019), resembles an unhealed wound that damages communities, as well as individuals, and Gilad Hirschberger argues that the collective trauma of events like the Grenfell fire 'shatters the basic fabric of society' (2018, p. 1). In recent years the study of trauma has begun to emerge as a new field of discussion within political theology, as seen, for example, in the work of Karen O'Donnell and Katie Cross (2020; 2022). Engagement with this new expression of political theology can enrich theological analyses of the deep-rooted violence of contemporary poverty and the long-lasting damage it causes. The building of such a nuanced analysis will enable theologians to understand and respond with credibility to the multi-dimensional damage of contemporary poverty. I discuss this in greater depth in Chapters 4 and 8.

The jigsaw of poverty – developing an intersectional gaze

Too often, theological analyses and faith-based responses have implied that poverty is one-dimensional and our experience of it is uniform. Such a perspective hinders theoretical understanding and weakens anti-poverty activism because it neglects the multidimensional character of poverty and the intersectional nature of our experience. Writing about the multifaceted experiences of oppression amongst African American women, Kimberlé Crenshaw (1989) was the first to coin the term 'intersectionality'. Crenshaw wrote about the interrelation of attitudes towards gender, ethnicity and social class. She suggested that such attitudes coalesce in a complex pattern of oppression within which sexism, racism and classism interweave and compound one another. Crenshaw stresses that intersectionality does not represent a 'new totalizing theory of identity' (1991, p. 1244) but a tool that can help us to better understand the interwoven nature of our experience and the need to avoid reductionist or one-dimensional policy, practice or analysis.

Whilst Crenshaw wrote from a legal standpoint, her reflections on intersectionality have provided researchers from many different disciplines with a new and far more nuanced means of examining identity and social relations. Although theologians are often comfortable with intellectual complexity, the nuance and multidimensional analysis of social relations made possible through a use of the concept of intersectionality has not yet made much of an impact within theology. Grace Ji-Sun Kim and Susan Shaw have begun to explore how an engagement with the concept can enable contemporary theologians to fashion more holistic analyses of the interconnection between power, identity and difference (2018, p. 2). In a UK context, Karen O'Donnell and Katie Cross (2022) have drawn together a range of academics and activists to explore the political and theological significance of trauma through an intersectional lens. It was within this collection of essays that I argued that theologians need to approach contemporary poverty, as evidenced by the 2017 Grenfell Tower fire, through an intersectional lens if they are to grasp its complexity. Within our Life on the Breadline project, we worked with the artist Beth Waters to illustrate the intersecting and interlocking nature of the differing faces of poverty. Poverty doesn't just reach its suffocating tentacles into every corner of our lives, it comes in different guises, each feeding into and off each other. Poverty is like a jigsaw, as Figure 2 indicates. Only by grasping its multidimensional and interlocking nature can we begin to fashion a genuinely holistic austerity-age theology of liberation.

Figure 2. The Jigsaw of Poverty (Beth Waters for Life on the Breadline)

I spoke earlier of the psychological and existential violence wrought by poverty, alluding to its multidimensional nature. The Church Urban Fund (CUF), which was established by the Church of England in 1987 in response to growing levels of social exclusion during the Thatcher decade, offers a valuable understanding of poverty that highlights the importance of an intersectional mindset. The CUF depicts poverty as 'complex and multidimensional' – a 'web of interlinked factors that together have a significant impact on an individual's ability to flourish' (2014, p. 1). Soon after the election of New Labour in the 1997 General Election, Tony Blair established the Social Exclusion Unit to respond to the complexity of marginalization in the UK after 17 years of Conservative government. New Labour adopted an intentionally intersectional approach, suggesting that, 'Social exclusion is a shorthand label for what can happen when individuals or areas suffer from a combination of linked problems such as unemployment, poor skills, low incomes, poor housing, high crime environments, bad health and family breakdown' (Social Exclusion Unit, 2001, p. 10).

Although I have argued elsewhere (Shannahan, 2019a) that New Labour's approach to poverty increasingly stigmatized individual people in poverty as the Blair decade progressed, the importance of their recognition of the multidimensional nature of social exclusion should not be forgotten. In a similar manner, Levitas et al. (2007) note the multifaceted nature of social exclusion, referring to its three interrelated spheres (resources, participation and quality of life). The breadth of such policy formation is important to recognize. In spite of its lack of a sustained focus on structural injustice, the social exclusion narrative of the early twenty-first century reminds us of the need to rid ourselves of the temptation to frame poverty in one-dimensional terms. It is with this in mind that the Church Urban Fund's description of poverty as a web of interconnected threads can help theologians to grasp the need to adopt an intersectional frame of reference and a matrix mindset in theological analyses of contemporary poverty. The CUF suggests that we need to think about a 'poverty of resources', a 'poverty of relationships' and a 'poverty of identity', which interweave, feeding into and off each other. A focus on such interwoven complexity and the ways in which the intersectional nature of our experience influences how we experience contemporary poverty needs to become a central theme in an emergent theological analysis of austerity.

Conclusion

In this chapter I have laid the theoretical foundations for my exploration of the Christian approaches to austerity-age poverty that we identified and analysed during Life on the Breadline. I have discussed the nature and the causes of austerity-age poverty and its relationship with wider and deeper structural injustice. I have argued that the development of a theoretically rigorous theological engagement with the complexity of contemporary poverty rests on the willingness of theologians to step out of their comfort zone and engage in the kind of critical depth with social science analyses of austerity that continues to be all too rare. I have demonstrated the power of the language we use to discuss the nature and causes of poverty and the ways in which public discourse can be utilized as a form of hegemonic cultural violence that justifies, individualizes and moralizes poverty. As a basis for arguments in later chapters I have suggested that only an understanding of our intersectional experience of the systemic, violent and multidimensional nature of austerity-age poverty can form the basis for the theology of liberation I am searching for in this book. In the next chapter, I turn to a detailed discussion of the Life on the Breadline research project, from which this book arises.

Notes

1 The full text of Prime Minister David Cameron's 2009 Conservative Party Conference speech is available here: https://www.theguardian.com/politics/2009/oct/08/david-cameron-speech-in-full.

2 George Osborne's speech to the 2012 Conservative Party Conference is at https://www.newstatesman.com/business/economics/2012/10/george-osbornes-speech-conservative-conference-full-text, accessed 31.03.2023.

3 Norman Tebbit's On Your Bike Speech, September 1981, https://www.youtube.com/watch?v=sU_pDM1N7io, accessed 29.09.2022.

4 See https://www.trussell.org.uk/news-and-research/latest-stats/end-of-year-stats, accessed 15.04.2025.

5 The full text of Prime Minister David Cameron's speech can be found at https://www.gov.uk/government/speeches/troubled-families-speech, accessed 24.05.2023.

6 ITV News, 'Grenfell Uncovered: Hundreds of children treated for trauma after the Grenfell fire', *ITV News*, 24 January 2020, https://www.itv.com/news/london/2020-01-24/grenfell-uncovered-hundreds-of-children-treated-for-trauma-after-the-grenfell-fire, accessed 19.07.2021.

2

Researching Christian Responses to Austerity-Age Poverty

Introduction

Theological analyses of contemporary poverty that avoid primary research cannot capture the visceral damage it causes. As theologians we need to get serious about fieldwork if we want our research to inform policy and help the Church to 'transform structural injustice'. We need to recognize that if we turn a deaf ear to the lessons our social science colleagues have to teach us then our analyses of contemporary social problems will lack depth, cultural resonance, nuance and credibility. All too often, though, increasingly common theological claims to inter-disciplinarity are not borne out in practice, possibly reflecting a kind of academic virtue-signalling rather than a serious commitment to interdisciplinary research. In the previous chapter I sought to develop a holistic understanding of contemporary poverty by engaging in depth with key insights from social and political theory. This chapter draws on our Life on the Breadline qualitative theological research to illustrate the importance of rooting interdisciplinary contextual political theology in extensive fieldwork. I discuss the development of the project, the methodology we adopted during fieldwork and the key theological themes and insights that arose from our work, before highlighting the challenges that our research poses for theologians, activists, policymakers and the Church. This will provide the empirical foundation for my sowing of the seeds of a new liberative theology of austerity-age poverty in later chapters.

Life on the Breadline – a theological first

Christian theologians have written about poverty and structural injustice for centuries (Shannahan, 2019a). In the aftermath of the 1832 Reform Act, the Tolpuddle Martyrs, led by Methodist lay-preacher

Figure 3. A Food Bank Nativity Scene (Beth Waters, Life on the Breadline 2018)

James Loveless, challenged unjust labour laws to form the world's first agricultural workers' union in 1834. Radical Christian preachers such as Joseph Rayner Stephens gave voice to the emergent egalitarianism of the Chartist movement's call to challenge the impact of the 1834 Poor Law on people already living in poverty (Yeo, 1981). Against the backdrop of the industrial revolution, Christian Socialists such as F. D. Maurice critiqued the growth of urban poverty in the ballooning cities of Victorian England (Norman, 1987).

A century later in Latin America, in the face of deepening inequality during the 1960s, the work of radical educationalist Paulo Freire (1970) resourced the emerging Liberation Theology of figures such as Gustavo Gutiérrez (1974), who argued that in a structurally unjust society the God of Creation who shaped all people in the divine image necessarily has a preferential option for the poor. Since 1947, the William Temple Foundation think-tank has developed theological research on faith and social and economic justice and the role of the Church in the public sphere, in the tradition established by former Archbishop of Canterbury, William Temple. Much more recently the pioneers of Black liberation theology in the UK, Robert Beckford (2000; 2004) and Anthony Reddie (2019) have written about the intersection between racialized oppression, racism and structural injustice, not least since the rise of economic neoliberalism under Margaret Thatcher in the 1980s, and in relation to the impact of the 2016 Brexit vote to leave the European Union.

These selected examples are not intended to provide an exhaustive overview of theological analyses of poverty. Rather, they illustrate two things of importance in the context of this book. First, most theological engagement with poverty, inequality and structural injustice has occurred in the past, in other parts of the world or as an intersectional factor in theological analyses of 'race', racism and struggles for racial justice. Second, unlike our social science colleagues, academic theologians, to date, have barely referenced the Age of Austerity that followed the 2010 General Election in any critical depth. That is not, however, to suggest that there have been no theological analyses of aspects of contemporary poverty in the UK as I indicate below in relation to three forms of response.

First, as faith groups' engagement in the public sphere has become increasingly common during the Age of Austerity, a small number of papers have asked how this influences our understanding of the purpose of theological discourse in the face of structural injustice. In the aftermath of the global recession that followed the 2008 financial crash, for example, Andrew Bradstock (2010, p. 135ff) argued that the Church had an ethical responsibility to challenge the valorizing of the financial market and the assumptions that underwrote austerity economics. Bradstock (2010, pp. 139–40) argued that theology can enable such a challenge in relation to economic marginalization, pointing, like Chris Baker and Elaine Graham (2018), to the important insights that the public theologian John Atherton can offer to those engaged in this debate. Ray Gaston and Steven Shakespeare (2010) wrote more forthrightly about the need to see Prime Minister David Cameron's Big Society initiative, not as a progressive example of active citizenship, but as ideological camouflage for austerity economics. At the outset of the 'Age of Austerity', Gaston and Shakespeare reminded us that because 'Jesus stands in solidarity with those who have nothing' the Church has a fundamental responsibility to 'resist the lure of the Big Society and to work instead with those who resist the cuts to jobs and services' (2010, pp. 800, 801).

Second, a small selection of papers have discussed food banks as faith-based responses to food poverty, although, with the exception of Charles Pemberton (2020), this tentative discussion has been largely literature-based, rather than engaging directly with the experience of food bank users. Helen Cameron (2014) commended the pastoral value of faith-based food banks to people experiencing poverty. However, she also warned of the dangers of the Church unintentionally colluding with the austerity economics that forced people to turn to food banks to feed their families. Building on this foundation, Chris Allen (2016) and Charles Pemberton (2018, 2020) used the food bank model as the basis for a discussion about theology and Christian social action in an Age of Austerity. For Allen, the food bank illustrates the weaknesses of dominant Christian traditions of social action – charity and campaigning for social justice. Such perspectives, he argues, can foster dependency and disengagement and need to be supplanted by a modelling of new inclusive forms of community building that emphasize fellowship, reciprocity and hospitality. In response, Pemberton challenges Allen's reading of the food bank, suggesting his call for a new hospitality to be 'insufficiently radical' (2018, p. 2). Pemberton (2020) argues that the food bank need not be a disengaged, apolitical and objectifying place but can, instead, become a transformative political space that enables new forms of anti-austerity activism to arise. Such papers hint at some of the broader theoretical, economic and theological themes I discuss in this book but the intersectional connections with other aspects of austerity that theologians need to explore are not considered.

Third, Patricia Jones (2019) and Shannahan (2022) have analysed the challenges that the confluence of what Jones calls 'welfare state retrenchment', housing injustice and homelessness during the Age of Austerity, pose for political theologians (2019, p. 154). In my reflection on Christian responses to the 2017 Grenfell Tower fire, I argue that the tragedy symptomizes the trauma-inducing cruelty of austerity and needs to be seen as an almost inevitable by-product of neoliberal capitalist housing policies (Shannahan, 2022, p. 275). In a similar vein, Jones invites theologians to reflect on the existential damage caused by austerity poverty and the ways in which such individual and communal wounding can undermine our common life (2019, p. 154). She writes, 'There is a profound ethical and theological challenge to the common good in the uncomfortable reality that some members of society have such low expectations and aspirations.' The value of such theological engagements with aspects of austerity-age poverty should be acknowledged and need to stimulate deeper, more intersectional, interdisciplinary analyses of austerity by contemporary theologians. However, with the exception of the emerging interdisciplinary arts-based theology of Wren Radford (2022a; 2022b), there is little sign, at the time of writing, of many theologians within the academy rising to this challenge.

The Life on the Breadline research project provides a huge bank of original primary data, rooting theological analysis in the everyday experience of austerity-age poverty, extensive ethnographic fieldwork and engagement with local, regional and national Church leaders from across the UK. Emerging in 2018, at the mid-point of a decade of biting austerity and growing inequality, Life on the Breadline was the first major empirically based project led by academic theologians to uncover and analyse the impact of austerity policies on a breadth of Christian responses to UK poverty since the 2008 global financial crash. Life on the Breadline modelled the thorough interdisciplinarity and in-depth fieldwork that needs to guide the future development of political theology if it is to gain traction beyond a theological audience and influence policymakers and practitioners. Consequently, in this chapter I explore our development of Life on the Breadline, the methodology we adopted and the insights we gained during the project. This will form the basis of the theology of austerity-age poverty that I argue for in this book.

Theologians – participants, not bystanders

Researchers have a duty to be rigorous, but we can never claim with any credibility to be neutral because absolute objectivity is a fantasy promoted by social insiders. It is inevitable that our work either subverts or colludes with structural injustice. I do not claim to be neutral and am consciously committed to the vision summarized by Cornel West. Writing of the role of the Black intellectual in the USA, West argues the need to become an insurgent, subverting hegemonic structures of injustice (1985, p. 122). For West, the intellectual's job is to 'speak a truth that allows suffering to speak [to]… create a vision of the world that puts into the limelight the social misery that is usually hidden or concealed by the dominant viewpoints of a society' (1999, p. 551). In a similar vein, Antonio Gramsci argues that the intellectual needs to become 'an organiser and not just … a simple orator' (1971, p. 10) and Gustavo Gutiérrez suggests that the theologian is called to be 'an organic intellectual with links to the popular liberation undertaking' (1974, p. 32). It is my hope that the resources we developed within Life on the Breadline and the arguments I fashion in this book can provide the foundations for an emergent austerity-age theology of liberation. Indeed, I suggest that, if theology does not act as a resource for the building of an inclusive, egalitarian society, then it is of little use in the struggle to transform structural injustice (Shannahan, 2014, p. 4). This stance has implications for the way in which we make-meaning, 'do' theology, envisage our task as theologians and evaluate the impact of our work.

Meaning-making in an age of austerity

The austerity-age theology of liberation that I argue for in this book can be seen as a form of liberative theological action research (Cameron et al., 2010; Graham, 2013) in three respects. First, it arises from my personal commitment to a model of theological research that resources all who work for justice in the face of ideologically inspired austerity. Second, it emerges from my own extended engagement with people whose lives and communities have been scarred by austerity and structural injustice. Third, it is my hope that this book will play some part in providing people with the analytical and theological tools needed to help the Church to fulfil its calling to 'transform structures of injustice'. In order to meet this goal, I need to find a credible way of organizing and categorizing insights drawn from our Life on the Breadline fieldwork and a hermeneutical perspective that can help me to make theoretical and theological sense of these discourses.

Typologies are a tried and trusted analytical tool within social research where they are widely used to capture and categorize data and within strands of biblical theology as a means of gathering and analysing scriptural passages on similar themes. They can organize and rationalize different data sources in a manner that enables comparison and systematic analysis (Collier, LaPorte and Seawright, 2012). However, the use of typologies in social research has three potential drawbacks. First, typologies can falsely imply that dynamic social phenomena are fixed or static. Second, typological analyses can become universalizing and decontextualized (Stapley et al., 2022, p. 1). Third, typologies can be hindered by selective sampling, albeit unconsciously, by the researcher. This cautionary word should be borne in mind by all who seek to understand Christian engagement with austerity-age poverty but does not completely negate their value when seen as useful, if limited, tools.

Literature-based explorations of Christian approaches to poverty are vital. The theoretical and theological insights that such discussions generate should not be dismissed as second-hand by social scientists who prioritize empirical research. However, it is also important for book-bound political theologians to move beyond the written page to embrace in-depth engagement with the communities we seek to understand in our work. Fieldwork disrupts intellectual security as we encounter the complexity, mess, contradiction, inspiration and challenge of everyday life in breadline Britain. Theology needs to be disrupted.

Homi Bhabha's (1994) exploration of the dialogical nature of culture can resource theological analyses of overlapping traditions of Christian engagement with austerity poverty. What we identified during Life on the Breadline was a discernible but shifting framework of different traditions of Christian social ethics, missiology and ecclesiology. Listening to Bhabha's reflections on the possibilities of liminal living can enhance our understanding of faith-based engagement with austerity. For Bjørn Thomassen, 'Liminality refers to … a moment of freedom between two structured worldviews' (2014, p. 7). Negotiating meaning in the liminal third space of breadline Britain is not straightforward given the evolving nature of the relationship between seemingly distinct traditions of Christian social ethics and missiology. Chris Baker notes that the third space is 'politically enigmatic', warning that 'Attempts to build coherent political and community-development programmes on the basis of ... multi-discourse politics are notoriously difficult' (2009, p. 24). Bhabha, however, points to the liberative potential of this fluid third space – 'The borderline work of culture ... creates a sense of the new as an insurgent act of cultural translation' (1994, p. 10). We glimpsed such liberative liminality during our research, but can the Church foster an insurgent transformation of multifaceted structural injustice in the third spaces we encounter in an increasingly postsecular public sphere?

Although we identified an ecosystem of four discernible Christian responses to contemporary poverty during Life on the Breadline and drew these together in a loose typological framework, our fieldwork points to their evolving and dialogical interconnection. These are not fixed ideal types. As I show below approaches converge, diverge and evolve over time. Indeed, the same networks or organizations can shift between modes of engagement or embrace elements of more than one tradition of Christian social action. Consequently, we did not impose rigid dividing lines between different responses. Such evolving engagement bears within it the seeds of a new theology of liberation that can begin to force the structural injustice of austerity-age poverty into retreat in an increasingly fluid postsecular cultural context.

The fieldwork-led analysis of the ecosystem of Christian approaches to contemporary poverty is an important first step. However, unless we find a way of making theological sense of this ecosystem of Christian social action, an austerity-age theology of liberation will fail to move beyond the cul-de-sac of sociological description. In his reflection on the African American experience of historic and contemporary oppression, Anthony Pinn (1999) speaks of the contrasting ways in which music has been used to make sense of collective suffering. Pinn advocates a 'nitty-gritty hermeneutics' that wrestles honestly with the contradiction and mess of structural injustice and our responses to it, rather than squeezing social realities into an *a priori* commitment to liberation (1999, p. 116ff). If an austerity-age theology of liberation is to be culturally credible it needs to recognize the untidiness and fluidity of life in breadline Britain and acknowledge those moments where the Church is co-opted into or colludes with structural injustice (Beckford, 2004). Political theology needs to be honest if it is to faithfully reflect the complexity of contemporary culture, even when this is uncomfortable and contradicts what we hold dear. In fashioning a new austerity-age theology of liberation it is tempting to smooth away the contradictions between different Christian perspectives or to gently nudge approaches to one side if they echo the contours of neoliberal economics, individualize the causes of poverty or promote the prosperity gospel. However, honestly reflecting the spectrum of Christian approaches to austerity, poverty, structural injustice and the role of the Church in the public sphere is more likely to lay the foundations for a lasting theology of liberation than a picture that is falsely neat and tidy.

Pinn offers wise advice that we need to heed, but it is also important to remember that nobody who writes about austerity-age poverty is a neutral observer. As I have made plain, I am not a disinterested bystander but an activist-researcher whose work revolves around the conviction that in a structurally unjust society the God of love who creates all people in the divine image necessarily has a preferential option for the poor. How then can I make sense of the traditions of Christian engagement with poverty that we encountered during Life on the Breadline in such a way that I honestly reflect untidiness and contradiction, whilst building an austerity-age theology of liberation? In responding to this question, bringing the work of Paul Ricoeur and Juan-Luis Segundo into dialogue with Pinn's nitty-gritty hermeneutics and the dub DJs of Dancehall Reggae can help us to fashion a liberative hermeneutical perspective for an Age of Austerity. Our interpretation of a text or, in my case, differing Christian responses to poverty, is shaped by our positionality and our standpoint. Ricoeur points to the importance of context when he implies that the hermeneutical task revolves around an interrogation of the texts that shape our lives (1971). Such texts, for Ricoeur, can include cultural activities and the existential narratives embedded in public discourse. Given that such discourses are dynamic, rather than fixed, they should be seen as contextual expressions of Christian social ethics that reflect varied interpretations of biblical and theological teaching about poverty. The question to bear in mind, therefore, is not whether Christian engagement with austerity-age poverty is political (consciously or unconsciously) but whether it affirms the status quo or seeks to 'transform structural injustice'.

Juan Luis Segundo pioneered the use of the hermeneutical circle within Latin American liberation theology. Theology is not, he argues, 'applied to human realities inside some antiseptic laboratory that is immune to the ideological tendencies and struggles of the present day' (1976, p. 7). Segundo suggests that the liberation theologian must always express a 'suspicion that anything involving ideas, including theology, is intimately bound up with the existing social situation, at least in an unconscious way' (1976, p. 8). Segundo speaks of the need to interrogate experience and dominant theological traditions with 'ideological suspicion' in the articulation of a new liberative theology (1976, p. 9). This hermeneutics of suspicion was first conceptualized by Ricoeur in *Freud and Philosophy* (1965/1970 English translation). Ricoeur points to Sigmund Freud, Karl Marx and Friedrich Nietzsche as exemplars of the need to approach texts and dominant discourses of meaning with a hermeneutics suspicion, in order to combat the false consciousness they can elicit, as a necessary step towards the articulation of a new liberative narrative (Ricoeur, 1970, p. 32ff). Denis Stewart suggests that 'Suspicion opens up the text to a new reading' (1989, p. 306).

This dialogue between Ricoeur, Segundo and Pinn provides the foundation for my 'suspicious' re-reading of the traditions of Christian engagement with poverty that we identified during Life on the Breadline. However, we need to turn to the dub practice of Dancehall DJs if we are to translate such radical suspicion into a liberative model of Christian anti-poverty activism. Dub is a technique used by DJs and record producers to fashion a new piece of music on the rhythmic foundations of an existing track. One of the few theologians to explore the hermeneutical potential of dub practice is the pioneer of British Black liberation theology, Robert Beckford (2006). Drawing on the tradition of epistemological deconstruction and reconstruction within Black British cultural studies, exemplified by Stuart Hall (2021) and Paul Gilroy (2000), Beckford argues that dub represents a conscious act of reconstructive emancipation: 'Dub is more than a musical technique: it is ... a quest for meaning' (2006, p. 67). For Beckford, dub practice, 'is guided by an emancipation ethic which seeks out redemptive themes in history, culture and society' (2006, pp. 91–2). I have argued elsewhere that dub practice can provide political theology with a creative methodological tool capable of resourcing the development of a counter hegemonic liberative hermeneutical framework (Shannahan, 2010, p. 237ff). The interconnection between the theological sharpness of Segundo, Pinn's call for a nitty-gritty honesty, Ricoeur's hermeneutics of suspicion and the liberative potential of dub practice provides us with the kind of hermeneutical framework we need to forge an austerity-age theology of liberation. Consequently, it is this dub hermeneutics, as depicted in Figure 4, that I draw upon to guide my analysis of 'Caring', 'Campaigning and Advocacy', 'Self-help and Enterprise' and 'Community Building' Christian responses to contemporary poverty in later chapters.

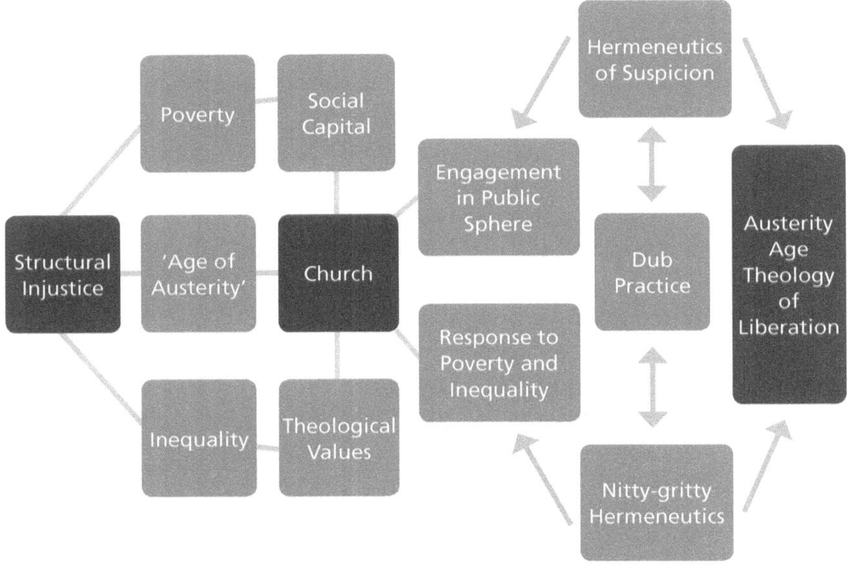

Figure 4. Dub Hermeneutics

An austerity-age dub

'Caring', 'Campaigning and Advocacy', 'Self-help and Enterprise' and 'Community building' Christian approaches to poverty reflect a spectrum of theological, ecclesiological and missiological perspectives and attitudes towards the Church's role in the public sphere. Whilst each approach has been analysed individually by theologians and social scientists, the spectrum of models of Christian engagement with austerity-age poverty have not been brought into a critical, fieldwork-led, dialogue within political theology – until now. As I show in this book these four approaches reflect differing historic traditions of social ethics, theology and ecclesiology. However, as we discovered during Life on the Breadline, it would be a mistake to see these responses as contradictory or unconnected. Each approach reflects a distinct theological engagement with poverty and vision of the role of the Church in the public sphere. However the 'Caring', 'Campaigning and Advocacy', 'Self-Help and Enterprise' and 'Community Building' responses we identified during our research interweave, converge, diverge and evolve over time. It is, therefore, more appropriate to speak of a Christian ecosystem of responses to austerity-age poverty than a formalized or tightly framed typology.

Culture and context

By the beginning of the twenty-first century, it was clear that religion had not, as many previously ardent secularists had predicted (Weber, 1930/2011; Wilson, 1966; Berger, 1967), faded from public view (Berger, 1997; Habermas, 2006; Casanova, 2012). Faith remained culturally, sociologically and politically important. Towards the end of the New Labour decade, Michael Hoelzl and Graham Ward (2008) pointed to what they called the new visibility of religion within civil society politics. This new visibility highlights three distinct but overlapping phenomena that impacted on our research during Life on the Breadline.

First, the renewed political significance of faith groups and their increasing visibility in the public sphere reflect a cultural shift away from a secularized modernity towards a postsecular social landscape. Elaine Graham summarizes: 'the world appears to be ... entering an unprecedented political and cultural era' (2013, p. xiii) within which the seemingly solid secular certainties of modernity are becoming increasingly fluid and uncertain. This is not a return to a pre-secular age but a movement beyond the reductionist mindset that depicted religion and politics as irreconcilable – the public and the private as binary opposites. This cultural shift is exemplified by the work of the political philosopher Jürgen Habermas (2006; 2008) who re-affirms the role faith-based organizations play in the public sphere.

Second, the increasing visibility of the Church in civil society politics should be read against the backdrop of a shrinking Welfare State. A year before the 2010 UK General Election, the Conservative Party leader David Cameron argued the need for an age of financial prudence, contrasting this with what he suggested was Labour's irresponsible spending (Evans and Walker, 2020) and preparing the ground for the 'Age of Austerity' that the coalition government he led introduced. The austerity agenda that was introduced by Cameron and his Chancellor of the Exchequer, George Osborne, exemplified the valorization of the market, the private sector and localized voluntary action that characterizes neoliberalism (Harvey, 2005, p. 2). The collective was depicted as a barrier to social mobility and displaced by the philanthropy of individual entrepreneurs as government ceded its place to the market. Guy Feldman summarizes, 'By dismantling social safety nets that protect the poor and replacing them with market-based antipoverty interventions, neoliberalism has transformed social welfare programs and what they do' (2019, p. 344).

Third, the Church's increasingly visible role within the public sphere during the Age of Austerity raises important questions about the nature and the use of its social capital in local communities. Whilst it was Robert Putnam (2000) who brought its discussion into the political mainstream, we need to turn to the work of Pierre Bourdieu to understand the theoretical roots of the concept of social capital. Bourdieu began to systematize his thinking about social capital in his 1979 book *Distinction* in which he explored the use and interrelation of economic, social, cultural and symbolic capital. Although the economic capital of many local churches is limited, they possess significant levels of cultural, symbolic and social capital because of their status as interpretive communities and their rootedness in local neighbourhoods, what Bourdieu calls 'the aggregate of the actual or potential resources which are linked to a durable network of institutionalized relationships of mutual acquaintance and recognition' (1986, p. 249). Whilst he wrote about associational life in the USA, Putnam's work can help us to understand the potential of local churches to respond to austerity-age poverty in the UK. Putnam is primarily concerned with the extent to which bonding capital and bridging capital underpin and enable civic life (2000, pp. 22–3). He writes, 'Bonding social capital constitutes a kind of sociological superglue, whereas bridging social capital provides ... WD-40.' High levels of bonding capital can strengthen belonging and support within groups but, without the dialogue and outward-facing networking made possible by bridging capital, can become excluding and introverted. Bridging capital can foster dialogue and greater collaboration between different social groups but is, arguably, insufficient to animate effective activism in the face of asymmetric power relations in structurally unequal contexts. A more politicized approach, which was explored by Simon Szreter (2002), is referred to as linking capital. Sretzer suggests that linking capital refers to 'relationships of exchange' between unequal communities that 'take on a democratic and empowering character where those involved are endeavouring to achieve a mutually beneficial goal on the basis of mutual respect, trust and equality of status, despite the manifest inequalities in their respective positions' (2002, p. 579).

The renewed visibility of faith groups in the public sphere, particularly in the face of a retreating Welfare State during the Age of Austerity, and their enduring social capital have been increasingly widely recognized and explored (Baker, 2009; Bretherton, 2010, 2015; Dinham et al., 2009; Beaumont and Cloke, 2012; Cloke et al., 2019; Shannahan, 2014). Adam Dinham summarizes, 'Academics, policymakers and practitioners are grappling with the emphatic return of faith to the public table' (2009, p. 1). The key question, it seems, is not, whether the Church retains social capital, but how it uses it in a structurally unjust society. It is this question that ran through our Church leader interviews and online survey, our practitioner interviews and ethnographic case studies during Life on the Breadline. The different Christian approaches to poverty that we identified during our research represent varied responses to this question. As I consider each of these four approaches I reflect on three questions. First, what does this approach suggest about the calling of the Church? Second, what does this approach reveal about theological understandings of austerity-age poverty? Third, what does this approach tell us about the ways in which the Church should use its social capital and the role it should play in the public sphere and the extent to which it is capable of fulfilling its calling to 'transform structural injustice'?

Methodology

Life on the Breadline was not the first project led by academic theologians to use interviews or case studies as a key source for theological analysis as three examples illustrate. First, over the last 20 years there has been a tentative but growing interest in qualitative research methods within practical theology as John Swinton and Harriet Mowat (2016) demonstrate. Swinton and Mowat suggest that qualitative research methods provide practical theologians with a nuanced means of examining and interpreting the messy fluidity of human practice and the social world (2016, p. 28ff). They point to the ways in which the use of constructivist insights about the social construction and location of knowledge (Berger and Luckmann, 1966; Pass, 2004; Hay, 2016) and our understanding of our experience within qualitative research methodologies can enrich the work of practical theologians. A second example of the use of fieldwork within practical theology is found in the development of the Network for Ecclesiology and Ethnography by Pete Ward and Christian Scharen, which was established in 2007.[1] Scharen (2012), Ward (2012) and Ward and Tveitereid (2022) argue that the extended fieldwork and naturalistic approach to data gathering that characterize participant observation, semi-structured interviews and focus groups, makes ethnography the perfect approach to qualitative research into the Church and Christian community.

Third, the work of Luke Bretherton (2010; 2015) shows how ethnographic methods can enable the development of more holistic models of political theology, as his in-depth analyses of the broad-based community organizing network Citizens UK demonstrates. Life on the Breadline sits within this tradition of political theology. It would be disingenuous, therefore, to claim that ours was the first project led by

UK-based academic theologians to use qualitative research methods. However, none of the examples cited above have explored Christian engagement with poverty since the 2008 global financial crash. In fact, at the time of writing, Life on the Breadline remains the only extended empirically based theological project to analyse the multidimensional impact of the Age of Austerity on Christian responses to poverty and inequality in the UK. The project modelled the contextual interdisciplinary form that needs to become normative within political theology.

Grounded in experience through our use of the pastoral cycle (Green, 1990) and drawing on methodological insights from contextual theology (Schreiter, 1985; Bevans, 1992) and our ethnographic fieldwork, Life on the Breadline established an iterative dialogue between primary data, the social sciences and political theology. Approximately 800 people participated in our research. Adopting a triangulated approach to data collection, which combined six ethnographic case studies; focus groups; extended semi-structured interviews; informal walking interviews; two overnight residential consultations and an online survey enabled us to fashion the most extensive evidence-based yet assembled in the UK of Christian action on austerity-age poverty.

Mindful of the complex, contextual and contested nature of knowledge, Life on the Breadline adopted a constructivist (Berger and Luckmann, 1966) approach to fieldwork that engaged with 'top-down' and 'bottom-up' perspectives on contemporary poverty and Christian social action. By bringing the perceptions of strategic regional and national Church leaders into dialogue with the insights of grassroots activists and practitioners we were able to develop a holistic picture of contemporary Christian engagement with poverty in the UK. We interviewed 17 national Church leaders from 13 UK-wide Christian denominations; conducted an online survey of 104 regional Church leaders from England, Northern Ireland, Scotland and Wales; facilitated six photo-elicitation focus groups; interviewed more than 60 grassroots practitioners; developed six in-depth ethnographic case studies (in Birmingham, London and Manchester) and led three National Poverty Consultations, involving a total of approximately 90 participants. It should be noted that research participants and locations have only been named in this book where explicit consent was given. Where this was not the case I have indicated the region within the UK within which a Church leader serves.

National Church leader interviews

The purpose of our Church leader interviews during 2019 and 2020 was to gain the perspective of people who held senior national leadership roles within Christian denominations about the Church's engagement with austerity-age poverty. Those whom we interviewed did not necessarily engage themselves in grassroots Christian responses to poverty on a day-to-day basis. They were, however, in a position to provide a strategic 'top-down' overview and assessment of their denomination's approach and attitude towards social justice and engagement in civil society politics. Key national leaders from the following denominations (or ecumenical networks) each spent about one hour in conversation with us – the Cherubim and Seraphim Church, the Church of England, the Church of Scotland, the Anglican Church in Wales, the Evangelical Alliance, the Independent Methodist Church, the Irish Council of Churches, the Methodist Church of Britain and Ireland, New Frontiers/Jubilee+, the Orthodox Church, the United Free Church of Scotland, the United Reformed Church and the Wesleyan Holiness Church. National leaders from other denominations, notably the Roman Catholic Church, the New Testament Church of God, the Redeemed Christian Church of God and the Baptist Union of Great Britain were all invited but were either unresponsive or did not feel able to accept our invitation. It is important to note, therefore, that we were not able to interview the national leaders of all Christian denominations in the UK. However, our regional Church leader survey reflected views from a wider range of Christian denominations, including those which decided not to participate in our national Church leader interviews. It remains the case therefore, at the time of writing, that our Life on the Breadline interviews still reflect the widest and most ecclesiologically diverse sample of national Church leaders to have been interviewed on the Church's response to austerity policies and contemporary poverty.

Regional Church leader survey

Our national Church leader interviews provided Life on the Breadline with a strategic overview of differing Christian attitudes to contemporary poverty. However, almost inevitably, the reflections of national leaders were generalized and removed from local contexts. For a more fine-grained perspective we turned to regional Church leaders who held senior leadership positions in different geographical regions within the UK. A total of 104 Church leaders from 17 different denominations across England, Scotland, Northern Ireland and Wales participated in our survey: Baptist Union of Great Britain, Church of England, Church of God of Prophecy, Church of Ireland, Church of Scotland, Church in Wales, Coptic Orthodox Church, Elim, Independent Methodist Church, Methodist Church of Britain and Ireland, Quakers, Roman Catholic Church, Salt and Light, Seventh Day Adventist, the Synod of German Speaking Congregations, the Salvation Army and United Reformed Church.

Our survey provided us with a more nuanced picture of the nature of contemporary poverty, its connection with national government austerity policies, impact in local communities and on grassroots Christian activism than the strategic overview presented by national Church leaders. Furthermore, the denominational and geographical spread of regional Church leaders provided a greater breadth and reach than previous theological analyses that were more limited by geography or ecclesiological tradition. Most regional Church leaders suggested that since the 2010 General Election they had seen a significant rise in the number of people using food banks, the numbers of people who are homeless, are sleeping rough, who have insecure or low-paid jobs, are suffering with mental health problems, living in poor quality housing or are facing destitution.

Ethnographic case studies

As well as our Church leader interviews and survey, Life on the Breadline revolved around six varied, ethnographic case studies of Christian engagement with contemporary poverty in Birmingham, London and Manchester. During each case study a member of the project team engaged in participant observation, led focus groups and conducted informal walking interviews alongside more formal semi-structured interviews. The case studies were selected to highlight different aspects of poverty and exemplify differing Christian responses and theological and ecclesiological traditions. Whilst our national Church leader interviews and regional Church leaders' survey spanned the UK, our case studies focused specifically on the three largest British cities. Further work is ongoing in rural contexts.

In Birmingham we developed two case studies. Our case study of the Trussell Trust B30 food bank highlighted the dramatic ongoing growth of food poverty during the Age of Austerity, in particular, as a result of sweeping cuts to welfare spending following the 2012 Welfare Reform Act. B30, which was based in the ecumenical Cotteridge Church

(Church of England, Methodist, United Reformed Church), exemplified networked Christian social action, combining the 'Caring' and 'Campaigning/Advocacy' approaches to poverty that I discuss in detail in later chapters. The second of our Birmingham case studies profiled the use of Asset-Based Community Development (ABCD) by Hodge Hill Church (Church of England/United Reformed Church) on the Firs and Bromford housing estate in east Birmingham. In statistical terms, the estate is amongst the 5% most multiply deprived in Britain and is part of the most multiply deprived Parliamentary constituency in Birmingham. Hodge Hill Church's engagement with poverty is shaped by the ABCD principles first articulated in a US context by Kretzmann and McKnight (1993), which invert dominant deficit-based approaches to community development by focusing primarily on assets present within a community. This case study exemplified the 'community building' approach to poverty that I discuss in Chapter 6.

We developed two case studies in London. First, we worked alongside Notting Hill Methodist Church to explore faith-based responses to the 2017 Grenfell Tower fire in which 72 people died (Shannahan, 2022) and the wider issues of homelessness, destitution, poor housing and housing justice. The Grenfell Tower tragedy exemplified the slow structural violence of poverty that I discussed in Chapter 1. Just a few hundred yards from Grenfell Tower, Notting Hill Methodist Church provided immediate pastoral care and unconditional welcome in the immediate aftermath of the fire, was a focal point for 'Campaigning' vigils for housing justice, and engaged in 'Advocacy' through its involvement in Shelter's 2019 *Building for our Future: A Vision for Social Housing* report. Our second London case study focused on the faith-inspired charity Power the Fight, which was established in 2019 in response to growing levels of serious youth violence during the Age of Austerity.[2] The organization draws much of its support from Black Pentecostal and evangelical churches and bases its 'Advocacy' alongside policymakers in London and 'Caring' approach to supporting young people caught up in or impacted by serious youth violence, and their families, on its community empowerment cycle, which I discuss further in Chapter 5. Power the Fight's work illustrates the multidimensional nature of austerity-age poverty and the advantages of using an intersectional analysis to assess the uneven nature of its impact. Whilst Power the Fight's primary focus is on supporting young people who have been affected by serious youth violence and on advocacy, advice and training alongside policymakers, this work cannot be fully understood unless we recognize the impact of austerity policies on youth provision, community facilities and social inclusion projects in London. Between 2011 and 2021 youth services budgets in London alone were cut by 44% (£36 million p.a.).[3] During the same period, 600 statutory youth worker positions were cut, and 130 youth clubs were closed. In 2020, youth work charity the YMCA reported that youth service budgets across England and Wales had been cut by 70% (approximately £1 billion) since 2010.[4] Power the Fight's work needs to be read against this context of spending cuts and growing poverty.

Our final two case studies were in Manchester and considered the work of the anti-poverty NGO Church Action on Poverty and the Inspire Centre. Emerging from the vision of members of Inspire United Reformed Church, the Inspire Centre was established in 2010 to provide a community hub that would welcome all people unconditionally, with a particular focus on serving marginalized communities. Whilst not focusing specifically on challenging austerity-age poverty, Inspire's mission of welcome, inclusion, community building and empowerment should be read against the backdrop of its commitment to transforming structural injustice. Inspire provided us with an opportunity to reflect on how 'Community Building' focused social enterprise models a different approach to social action and social justice than more traditional 'Caring' or 'Campaigning' approaches.[5] Established in 1982, Church Action on Poverty is a faith-inspired social justice charity. For more than 40 years, Church Action has been at the forefront of ecumenical Christian anti-poverty 'Campaigning' and 'Advocacy'. This case study enabled us to analyse and reflect upon their geographically dispersed nationwide approach to networked anti-poverty activism. Church Action is not a large organization but its influence on the anti-poverty activism of Christians from a wide range of denominations has been very significant. In part this reflects its status as a partner of the Churches Together in Britain and Ireland ecumenical network, which represents almost all national Christian denominations in the UK. Church Action exemplifies the effectiveness of creative network-based engagement with poverty. Christian denominations are far more widely dispersed, rooted in historic traditions of social action and embedded in local communities than NGOs like Church Action. However, whilst Church Action is not rooted in every community, does not have the resources of many Christian denominations and has limited capacity, its focus on awareness raising, its flat management structures, determined focus on poverty, rather than a wide range of other priorities and its use of broad-based community organizing principles, has enabled it to become one of the most influential faith-inspired anti-poverty NGOs in the UK. Its online presence and use of social media; its active engagement with approximately 10,000 grassroots supporters; educational work; connections with other ecumenical networks like the Joint Public Issues Team and the support of approximately 100 local churches that use its annual Church Action on Poverty Sunday worship resources has enabled it to mount a wide range of targeted issue-based campaigns since its founding more than 40 years ago. During Life on the Breadline we focused on Church Action's Food Power Network, Local Pantries project, End Hunger UK, Self-Reliant groups and Church on the Margins initiative. I discuss Church Action's 'Campaigning' and 'Advocacy' in Chapter 4.

National Poverty Consultation

During Life on the Breadline we hosted a National Poverty Consultation in collaboration with Church Action on Poverty. The consultation, run in 2018, 2019 and 2021 (online), drew together approximately 90 Church leaders and Christian anti-poverty activists for a 48-hour period of mutual support, sharing good practice, strategizing and planning new initiatives. This dispersed network model of Christian anti-poverty activism echoes the shift from institution-based activism towards the more fluid social movement-oriented approach exemplified by Niall Cooper's 2021 *Building Dignity, Agency and Power Together* report.

The views of Church leaders

Core values

A commitment to two foundational Christian doctrines ran through the responses of the national and regional Church leaders who participated in Life on the Breadline. First, Church leaders stressed the social implication of the *imago Dei* – the conviction arising from Genesis 1.27 that humanity is made in the image of God. Since all are made in the divine image every person bears something of the Creator within them. We are equally precious because God has created us all. Alluding to Jesus' Parable of the Sheep and the Goats (Matthew 25.31–45), one Church of Scotland leader from the North of Scotland summarized – 'We are all made in God's image. Whatever we do for the least of people we do for Christ Jesus.' Second, the doctrine of the Incarnation was believed to underpin the Church's commitment to solidarity and social justice. John 1.14 tells us that 'the Word became flesh and lived among us'. This belief that, in the person of Jesus, God becomes our brother, shares our life and stands in solidarity with oppressed humanity, is not just a foundational Christian doctrine but the bedrock of the Church's anti-poverty activism. A United Reformed Church leader from Yorkshire summarized: 'The incarnate Christ is at the heart of the world, its people's lives, relationships, societies and cultures, communities and nations. Therefore, all that damages the well-being, peace and justice of these is at the heart of God' (Life on the Breadline online survey, 2020).

For most of the Church leaders who participated in the project, these two doctrines formed the basis of their commitment to an ethic of servanthood and social responsibility. In many cases this was informed by Common Good teaching that was shaped by Catholic Social Teaching, Anglican Social Theology, or contemporary re-workings of the social gospel, first developed by the US Baptist pastor Walter Rauschenbusch (1917) in the early twentieth century. Most Church leaders aligned their denomination's engagement with poverty with what might be called a 'Matthew 25 model' of Christian discipleship. This approach was characterized by an egalitarian understanding of Jesus' commandment to 'Love your neighbour' (Mark 12.30–31) and stand in solidarity with the hungry, the homeless, the captive and the marginalized: in feeding the hungry, clothing the naked and giving shelter to the homeless, Christians are feeding and welcoming Jesus himself. A Salvation Army leader from the North of Scotland spoke of the call to 'reflect Jesus' attitude to the least and the lost' and a London-based leader within the Lutheran German Speaking Congregation of Great Britain talked of 'finding Christ in our poor brother or sister'. For a Methodist District Chair from Northern England who spoke with us there is a 'Gospel imperative to be a good neighbour' (Life on the Breadline online survey, 2020). In the face of government policies that worsen poverty and deepen inequality, such unconditional neighbour love can be seen as a political intervention in a society where structural injustice undermines the common good, as I suggest in Chapter 3. However, most of the Church leaders did not speak in such terms. Instead, such activism was framed in the language of loving service.

A significant minority of Church leaders spoke articulately of the need to move beyond a welfare-based apolitical 'caring' to much more explicitly political 'campaigning' that addresses the systemic causes of contemporary poverty. Many Church leaders alluded to the Marks of Mission as a template for contemporary Christian social action. First adopted by the Anglican Consultative Council in 1984, the Marks of Mission sought to distil the central pillars of Christian mission into five short statements of faith (Zink, 2017). Later adopted by the UK-wide ecumenical network Churches Together in Britain and Ireland, the Marks of Mission have had a big influence on the development of Christian missiology and social ethics in recent decades. The fourth Mark of Mission has influenced the Church's approach to activism, suggesting that the Church is called to 'transform unjust structures in society'.[6] One Church leader from West Yorkshire summarized this perspective, arguing that poverty needs to be seen as 'a consequence of injustice rather than the result of personal choices' (Life on the Breadline online survey, 2020). Dr Nicola Brady, the General Secretary of the Irish Council of Churches at the time of our research (Interview, 2020), suggested that Christians are called to tackle the root causes of poverty because of the biblical commandment to work for justice, as well as providing pastoral care and emergency support for people living in poverty. Liam Purcell of Church Action on Poverty (Interview, 2020) made a similar point, arguing that 'we need to talk about the root causes of poverty. It's not enough to do local social action.'

The assertion that in an unjust society God necessarily has a preferential option for the poor, which has formed the bedrock of liberation theology since its emergence in Latin America, was seen as an inspiration by leaders from the Baptist Church, the Church of England, the Church of Scotland, the Methodist Church, the Roman Catholic Church, Salt and Light and the United Reformed Church. The Church is called, suggested a United Reformed Church leader from Southern England, to stand in solidarity with the oppressed with 'the God of the outsider'. Another United Reformed Church leader from the South-West of England spoke of the importance of a commitment to 'God's preferential option for the poor and a concern that justice and mercy go hand in hand' and a Church of Scotland leader from the West of Scotland argued that the Church is called to recognize and prioritize 'the theological imperative of the Priority of the Poor'. Such a commitment was common amongst Church leaders but was usually expressed in largely generalized and apolitical terms. The Revd Dr Richard Frazer, the Convenor of the Church and Society of the Church of Scotland, was more forthright. Frazer challenged the Church to move beyond what he called 'a sticking plaster approach to handouts' to address the 'underlying causes of poverty' (Life on the Breadline interview, 2019).

The nature and causes of austerity-age poverty

As I have shown above, the views of the national and regional Church leaders who participated in Life on the Breadline reflected differing theological perspectives. However, the relative size, strength and self-confidence of different Christian denominations appeared to be an equally important factor in their responses. Church of England bishops and senior leaders from the Church of Scotland appeared to be relatively secure and self-confident. Given their status as Established Churches this self-confidence and readiness to speak of the need for the Church to challenge policymakers by speaking truth to power was, perhaps, not surprising. The leaders of smaller, more fragile, denominations such as the Church of the Cherubim and Seraphim, the Independent Methodist Church and the United Free Church of Scotland, expressed greater hesitation, suggesting that they did not have the capacity, the strength or the profile to influence political leaders or to mount extensive campaigns to challenge systemic poverty.

Of the regional church leaders who participated in our Life on the Breadline survey, 86% suggested that poverty had deepened, and inequality increased in their region since the 2010 General Election. Fifty-six Church leaders referred to a dramatic rise in the numbers of people needing to use food banks, 43 told us that homelessness had risen over the last decade and 19 said that many more children were living in poverty in their area. Church leaders pointed to many indicators of growing levels of poverty – more people in work using food banks; the closure of rural shops and post offices; poorer public transport; the fact that the provision of free hot meals has become a normal, rather than an exceptional feature of church life; the growth of food banks in seemingly affluent areas; the rise in personal debt; increasingly unaffordable rents; the significant increase in the number of people surviving on zero-hours contracts; increasing pressures on mental health; an increasing inability to afford healthy food at the supermarket and the growing number of baby-banks and second-hand shops specializing in baby clothes.

Such reflections remind us of our intersectional experience of austerity-age poverty and of the need to resist one-dimensional responses. The church leaders whom we spoke with appeared to grasp both the complex jigsaw of poverty and our intersectional experience of it. Furthermore, many displayed an awareness of the systemic causes of contemporary poverty, pointing in particular to the negative impact of the following in their regions – ongoing low average incomes, the so-called 'cost of living crisis', welfare reforms, and especially, the roll-out of the Universal Credit scheme and a decade of government spending cuts. Of the regional church leaders who completed our online survey, 59% believed that Conservative government welfare reforms were the biggest single cause of increasing levels of poverty since the 2010 General Election. Some 38% felt the biggest single cause was low wages, 35% suggested it was personal debt and 31% pointed to high rents; 26% identified the 'cost of living' crisis as the primary cause of poverty, 12% highlighted unemployment and just 3% pointed to poor individual decision-making as the key factor.

Social action on poverty – faith in action

A Salvation Army officer from the North of Scotland told us that 'most congregations are engaging regularly with those affected by poverty' (Life on the Breadline online survey, 2020). In a similar fashion a Church of Scotland Church leader from Edinburgh suggested that their denomination 'is very vocal on tackling poverty at a national level and that has flowed down to the local level' (Life on the Breadline online survey, 2020). An Anglican Church leader from the South of England summarized the theological basis for Christian engagement with austerity-age poverty: 'Jesus had a heart for the poor. Caring for those in poverty and fighting injustice is core to our faith. When we do this, others come to join us' (Life on the Breadline online survey, 2020). In spite of this, many Church leaders from different denominations across the UK suggested that most local churches have often been largely cushioned from the brutal violence of austerity. A Church of Scotland leader put it this way: 'Christians care but owing to demographics are largely isolated from the worst effects of poverty' (Life on the Breadline online survey, 2020) and a Welsh Baptist leader observed that, 'congregations tend to be middle class' (Life on the Breadline online survey, 2020).

A United Reformed Church leader from Southern England added to this perception of disengagement, suggesting that 'on average congregational members are relatively comfortable and tend to see the issues as more personal than structural' (Life on the Breadline online survey, 2020). Revd Micky Youngson, former President of the British Methodist Conference, told us, 'I think the Church has continued to respond to the needs of the communities that we're in. The problem is we're less in the communities of abject need than we are in more comfortable communities' (Interview, 2020). Youngson went on to point to a dilemma. The Church, she suggested, is increasingly committed to a welfare-based model of Christian social action and is motivated by love and grace but remains largely disengaged from the visceral realities of austerity. She put it like this: 'Austerity has prompted a lot of Methodist churches to … run a food bank or be involved in a night shelter. If you wanted to … you could say it's slightly arms-length … the comfortable rescuing the uncomfortable but I think there's more love and grace in it than that.' Several church leaders implied that this distance from the impact of austerity was often combined with a moralizing and individualizing of poverty. A Methodist leader from the North-West of England spoke of a persistent 'sense that it's still the individual's fault if they are poor' (Life on the Breadline online survey, 2020) and a Divisional Commander in the Salvation Army from Southern England suggested that, 'there is still a feeling of deserving and undeserving. Generally, it is thought by congregations that if you try you will thrive' (Life on the Breadline online survey, 2020). In spite of this, almost all of the Church leaders with whom we spoke expressed the view that the struggle to defeat poverty and inequality should be seen as a fundamental aspect of the gospel and be placed at the centre of contemporary understandings of mission and discipleship.

Regional Church leaders referred to a wide variety of activities that local churches engaged in as they responded to poverty. The top ten anti-poverty activities that regional Church leaders told us were run or supported by local churches in their regions were food banks (mentioned by 99% of Church leaders), clothes and toy banks (87%), holiday clubs (81%), community meals (76%), homelessness shelters (66%), money advice services (64%), advice centres (61%), breakfast clubs (54%), cooking classes (46%) and community supermarkets (14%).

Some 38% of regional Church leaders told us that anti-poverty social action within their denomination was largely developed by individual churches in response to need in their local neighbourhood. However, Church leaders also suggested that most Christian engagement with austerity-age poverty is undertaken in collaboration with partners or as part of broad-based networks; 93% suggested that such activities were undertaken ecumenically with other Christian partners and 28% suggested that these activities were interfaith collaborations; 73% told us that such social action was undertaken in partnership with faith-based charities and NGOs and 56% referred to Church–secular NGO partnerships.

Most Church leaders placed a focus on welfare based 'Caring' responses to poverty and generalized 'advocacy' rather than more prophetic 'Campaigning' for structural economic and political change. An Anglican Mission Enabler from the West of England told us that 'it's easier to respond practically but to stay out of campaigning and advocacy', going on to suggest that 'getting political is always controversial. It is so intertwined with party politics and people are really anxious about mixing party politics and faith.' A Pentecostal leader from the South-East of England suggested that the Church could 'only deal with the symptoms of poverty' because 'the real cause of poverty falls outside of our realm of influence and needs governmental involvement'. A Salvation Army leader from the West of Scotland made a similar point – 'I think we are better placed to tackle the consequences of poverty than the root causes.' Whilst acknowledging this, an Anglican bishop from the South of England spoke of the limited value of addressing only the impact of poverty, rather than its systemic causes: 'We aren't bad at pulling bodies out of the river, just not very good at stopping them being thrown in further upstream.' A Baptist Church leader from the North-West of England also critiqued the limitation of Christian social action to apolitical 'Caring', pointing to the Church's calling to embody God's preferential option for the poor: 'God is a God of justice. We are in a place to tackle the causes of poverty … It is important for us to be that prophetic voice' (Life on the Breadline online survey, 2020).

Can the Church make a difference?

The responses of Church leaders reflected a spectrum of views about the capacity of the Church to translate its commitment to 'transform structures of injustice' into effective action. Some Church leaders felt that their denomination was too small to have any impact on government policy. An Anglican bishop from the South of England pointed to an inward-looking ethos: 'Too much congregational energy is devoted to institutional survival' (Life on the Breadline online survey, 2020). Such a perspective can reflect an institutional mindset or point towards a conservative ecclesiology that does not prioritize social action, or which perpetuates individualized understandings of wealth, poverty, faith and the gospel. However, it is important to recognize that this is not necessarily the case. There is a security that Anglican churches enjoy, given the Church of England's status as an established Church and the presence of 26 of its bishops in the House of Lords, that other Christian traditions do not. As one Salvation Army leader told us, 'We are running out of money and are dependent on local charities' (Life on the Breadline online survey, 2020). Not all denominations in the UK have the same status, wealth, strength or security. This needs to be understood when we comment upon the ways in which different churches engage with poverty.

Some Church leaders, like a Methodist Chair of District in the North-West of England, argued that 'The current government take a doctrinaire approach and seem unwilling to hear criticism or challenge' and a leader within the Church of Scotland suggested that 'government is not interested in the views of ordinary people, still less the Church'. The Church, he argued, 'has no credible national voice' (Life on the Breadline online survey, 2020). Others, however, suggested that 'the established Church still has a voice at the power table' (Anglican bishop, Life on the Breadline online survey, 2020). Such contrasting perspectives remind us of the political importance of the social location of different Christian traditions and their relationship with power élites. This diversity of experiences leads us to ask whether the Church has the capacity or the will to translate its social capital into effective united action to defeat austerity-age poverty. A Church of Scotland leader from the Scottish borders lays down the challenge to which the whole Church needs to respond: 'The UK churches together have a membership large enough to exert pressure on the government' (Life on the Breadline online survey, 2020). The question we need to ask, therefore, is whether the Church is willing to be bold enough to translate its bridging social capital and collective influence into a more politicized form of linking capital in order to speak truth to power and 'transform [the] structural injustice' of austerity-age poverty.

Conclusion

Our national Church leader interviews, regional Church leader survey, practitioner interviews and six ethnographic case studies within Life on the Breadline painted the most detailed picture of Christian responses to austerity-age poverty yet developed by academic theologians in the UK. We did not provide an absolutely exhaustive summary of all forms of Christian engagement with contemporary poverty. Given the breadth and dynamism of the Christian community, claims to encapsulate the entirety of the Church's engagement with poverty in a single project or analysis should be treated with scepticism. However, in this chapter I have demonstrated the critical importance of extended fieldwork within multidisciplinary political theology. By engaging in depth with local Christian communities and NGOs, regional Church leaders and national Church leaders I have illustrated the breadth of Church responses to austerity in the UK and begun to sketch out some of the perspectives that inform the theoretical and theological interpretive framework of Christian engagement with contemporary poverty, which I introduce in the next chapter. This hermeneutical framework will provide the foundation for the liberative theology of austerity-age poverty I seek to develop in this book, and outline key challenges that the Church must face if it is to use its enduring social capital to fulfil its calling to transform structural injustice.

Notes

1 See more about the Network for Ecclesiology and Ethnography at https://www.ecclesiologyandethnography.net/.

2 See https://www.powerthefight.org.uk/, accessed 25.10.2023.

3 Sian Berry, 2021, 'London's Youth Service Cuts 2011–2021: A Blighted Generation', London: City Hall, https://www.london.gov.uk/sites/default/files/sian_berry_youth_services_2021_blighted_generation_final.pdf.

4 See YMCA, 2020, *Out of Service: A Report Examining Local Authority Expenditure on Youth Services in England and Wales*, London: YMCA, https://ymca.org.uk/wp-content/uploads/2024/08/YMCA-Out-of-Service-report.pdf.

5 See https://www.lev-inspire.org.uk/ for more information (accessed 26.10.2023).

6 The 'Marks of Mission' were first adopted in 1984. See https://www.anglicancommunion.org/mission/marks-of-mission.aspx.

3

'Caring'

Introduction

'Caring' Christian approaches to poverty are motivated by a vision of the Church as a servant community and a theological commitment to the common good. This perspective is characterized by a missiological commitment to building a society within which all people can flourish and a strong focus on ongoing pastoral care for all who are left out or left behind. Given its focus on neighbour-love and servanthood, it is perhaps not surprising that this represents the dominant Christian response to austerity-age poverty and the approach most widely courted by government. Its pastoral focus tends to present fewer challenges to government and for local churches for whom engagement in civil society politics is problematic, as I will show in this chapter. However, the differing Christian approaches to poverty that we identified during Life on the Breadline are not fixed, but fluid. Consequently, 'Caring' responses to austerity, for example, can merge with or encompass aspects of 'Campaigning', 'Community Building' and 'Self-Help and Enterprise' models of social action. The pastoral impact of 'Caring' Christian responses to austerity-age poverty has been immense. Our Life on the Breadline research has illustrated the breadth, extent and value of such an approach to people with direct experience of poverty in greater empirical depth than any previous theological studies. The question to be faced, therefore, is not whether 'Caring' responses to austerity offer support to countless people who are weighed down by the burden of poverty, but whether this welfare-based common good model of social action has the capacity to challenge and 'transform structural injustice'. I will suggest in this chapter that whilst 'Caring' can be seen as a political intervention in a structurally unjust society, this approach to the Christian engagement with austerity-age poverty is hindered by the Church's nervousness about moving beyond charity into the muddy waters of civil society politics.

The common good

The roots of the common good theological ethic that underpins the 'Caring' approach to poverty are found in the virtue ethics of Aristotle. In *Politics*, a compendium of his thinking about civic life, Aristotle argues that the goal of political debate and the mark of good governance is a commitment to the foundational importance of the common good of the citizens of a city. In his *Nicomachean Ethics*, Aristotle (1962 edition) suggests that, 'The attainment of the good for one person alone is a source of satisfaction; yet to secure it for a nation ... is nobler and more divine.' More than a thousand years later in the *Summa Contra Gentiles*, the medieval theologian Thomas Aquinas argued that for followers of Jesus the pursuit of the common good is a fundamental expression of Christian faith because it reflects our calling in Mark 12.30–31 to love God with all our heart, our mind, our soul and our strength, and our neighbour as ourselves. In the sixteenth century CE, Ignatius of Loyola expressed a similar sentiment in his suggestion to the first Jesuits that all of their actions should be focused on strengthening the common good of the whole of humanity (Hollenbach, 2002, pp. 5–6).

The roots of such common-good thinking predate Christianity but the concept, if not always the term itself, is a foundational feature of 'Caring' Christian approaches to contemporary poverty. Its theological framing is evident in the Bible as three examples illustrate. First, the prophet Jeremiah identifies a commitment to the common good in his summary of the calling of the people of Israel during their Exile in Babylon – 'Seek the welfare of the city where I have sent you into exile and pray to the Lord on its behalf for in its welfare you will find your welfare' (Jeremiah 29.7). In the face of brutal social dislocation, the community of faith is called to dedicate itself to playing an active role in the public sphere to foster the well-being of wider society. Second, in the parable of the Sheep and the Goats in Matthew 25.31–46, Jesus equates God's solidarity with the oppressed with a radical enacting of the common good: when you feed the hungry, clothe the naked, welcome the stranger, you feed and clothe and welcome me. The measure of discipleship is not tied to church growth but to an embodiment of Jesus' preferential option for the poor. Third, in Acts 2.43–47 we read about the earliest Christian community in Jerusalem, where all things were held in common and people sold 'their possessions and goods' and distributed 'the proceeds to all as any had need' (Acts 2.45).

Catholic Social Teaching

Whilst the tradition is ultimately rooted in the writing of the thirteenth-century theologian Aquinas about the common good, contemporary Catholic Social Teaching finds its origins in Pope Leo XIII's 1891 encyclical *Rerum Novarum.* Leo declared that commitment to the common good must lead people of faith to challenge the emergent urban poverty of the late Victorian era (Leo XIII, 1891, paragraph 42). Writing in 1996, the Catholic Bishops' Conference of England and Wales summarized the heart of common good thinking within Catholic Social Teaching: 'We believe each person possesses a basic dignity that comes from God ... The test therefore of every institution or policy is whether it enhances or threatens human dignity and indeed human life itself' (1996, paragraph 13). Ahead of the 2010 UK General Election, the Council of Bishops suggested that the policies proposed by candidates standing for election should be judged in relation to the extent to which they foster or undermine the common good (2010, p. 8ff). In her 2015 Newman Lecture, Anna Rowlands suggests that common-good thinking within Catholic Social Teaching revolves around an exploration of what it means to '... live well together in peace, rendering mutual assistance and in so doing learning to participate in the life of God' (2015, p. 4).

Speaking of political discourse in the UK, Rowlands suggests that 'our public conversations about austerity [have] been highly divisive ... it has seemed at times as if the notion of virtue itself required a willingness to speak in such divisive terms: the deserving versus the undeserving poor, strivers versus skivers' (2015, p. 4). She argues that common-good thinking can articulate 'suffering, failure, pain and tragedy', whilst also enabling 'a response to difficulty and human suffering that is more than silence, suppression, distraction or consumption' (2015, p. 5). Rowlands points to three interrelated strands of Catholic Social Teaching that arise from God's communion with humanity in Jesus: the inherent dignity of all people, the human need for belonging and fraternity and the gospel call to stand in solidarity with all who are left out or left behind (2021, p. 239ff).

These themes resonate with the 'Caring' responses to the austerity-age poverty we encountered in Life on the Breadline. Rowlands argues that common-good thinking should not be viewed as a consensual smoothing-away of difference, inequality or injustice. Rather an appeal to egalitarian solidarity in a context within which human connectedness and dignity are undermined represents a call to counter-hegemonic social action. Whether such social action has the capacity to translate a common good into political action that has the potential to transform structural injustice is, however, less certain. Hollenbach argues that there is a need to interrogate the extent to which such appeals to the common good collude with or challenge structural injustice (2002, p. 19ff). As I demonstrate in later chapters, whilst the 'Caring' response to austerity-age poverty is invaluable and can be seen as a political intervention in a society where the value of the common good is actively undermined, it is essential to draw on a hermeneutics of suspicion when judging its capacity to resource the transformation of structural injustice when the institutional Church itself is part of the establishment. We need, as I will show towards the end of this chapter, to dub 'Caring' approaches to systemic poverty on the basis of a clear liberative ethic.

The social gospel

The second expression of common-good thinking that we encountered during Life on the Breadline was rooted in the social gospel tradition that has shaped most liberal Protestant social action for more than a century. Particularly active during the late 1870s and 1880s, the Ohio Congregational pastor Washington Gladden was arguably the earliest advocate of the implicationist social gospel. His 1877 book *The Christian Way: Whither it leads and how to go on* exemplified the social gospel's challenge to the US Church in the face of growing urban poverty and inequality. Gladden argued that Jesus' proclamation of the Kingdom of God had implications for economics and politics as well as the life of individual believers. A second key voice in the social gospel movement was the Baptist pastor Walter Rauschenbusch from New York. His experience pastoring in Hell's Kitchen led Rauschenbusch (1917) to insist that the endemic urban poverty and stark inequality that characterized growing US cities contradicted the will of a God who created all people in the divine image and was an expression of systemic sin. Chris Baker argues that the social gospel movement 'challenged both laissez faire capitalism and Protestant individualism with a reformulation of the Christian faith that stressed the doctrine of God's immanence, via the Incarnation of Christ, in the human suffering of the world' (2009, p. 71). Baker suggests that social gospel advocates emphasized the 'political and social dimensions of [Jesus'] proclamation of the Kingdom of God with regard to the commitment to practice justice but especially ... to the poor and marginalized' (2009, p. 71).

The energy of the social gospel movement began to dissipate in the aftermath of World War One, as liberal Protestantism's reforming social ethic was displaced by the crisis-oriented neo-orthodoxy exemplified by

Karl Barth's 1919 text *The Epistle to the Romans*, which critiqued the narrative of inevitable human progress. In spite of this decline in the face of the political and spiritual crises embodied by the horrors of World War One, the socio-cultural rupturing of revolution, economic depression and the rise of fascism across Europe, the influence of the social gospel movement remained an important, if implicit, influence on the Church's engagement with poverty. It was reflected in the pragmatic Christian Realism of Reinhold Niebuhr in the US and Archbishop William Temple in the UK from the 1930s onwards as seen, for example, in Temple's 1942 text *Christianity and Social Order*, which helped to pave the way for the creation of the Welfare State. In more recent decades theologians such as Ronald H. Preston and John Atherton have exemplified Christian Realist social gospel thinking. Furthermore, social gospel thought helped to shape the work of the Christian Socialist movement, and more recently Christians on the Left, as well as informing key Church reports such as the 1985 Anglican *Faith in the City* report and its 2006 ecumenical successor, *Faithful Cities*. The tradition remains an important, if often subconscious, influence on ongoing Christian social action.

Servanthood and neighbour love

The core theological values that underpin 'Caring' responses to poverty are rooted in four widely cited biblical passages. First, John 13.34–35 sketches out the broad philosophical basis for 'Caring' responses to poverty, rooting them in an ethic of love – 'A new commandment I give you: Love one another. As I have loved you, so you must love one another.' Second, Mark 12.30–31 emphasizes the outwards-facing nature of such love and its focus on our neighbour – the person who is in need: 'Love the Lord your God with all your heart and with all your soul and with all your mind and with all your strength … [and] love your neighbour as yourself.' Third, John 13.1–17 tells the story of Jesus washing his disciples' feet. At the heart of his ministry is a commitment to loving service – those who follow him are called to be servants too. It is this mindset that characterized most of the 'Caring' responses to poverty that we encountered during Life on the Breadline. Fourth, Matthew 25.31–46 makes it clear that challenging social exclusion is not a peripheral aspect of Christian discipleship but the foundation upon which it is built. This parable of the Last Judgement in Matthew 25.31–46 represents a radical call to stand in active solidarity with all who are oppressed – the hungry, the homeless and the refugee. By standing with the oppressed, Christians stand with Jesus himself.

The influence of such common-good thinking, Catholic Social teaching and the values of the social gospel movement were apparent in the 'Caring' responses to austerity-age poverty that we encountered in many of our national Church leader interviews, the regional Church leaders survey and several of our Life on the Breadline case studies. Such 'Caring' approaches reflect the implicationist tradition of Christian social action, as seen, for example, in *Faith in the City*, which suggests that Jesus' 'proclamation of the Kingdom of God had ... profound social and political implications' (Archbishop of Canterbury's Commission on Urban Priority Areas, 1985, p. 48), even though the heart of the gospel message was essentially focused on the individual and their relationship with other people and with God. The Anglican political theologian Kenneth Leech was deeply critical of the implicationist tone of *Faith in the City*, suggesting that it neglected the fact that the 'proclamation that God was in Christ reconciling the world to himself [and] the vision of a transformed society' is inherently political (1997, p. 139). Whilst Leech's critique of the depoliticizing of Christian engagement with structural injustice is persuasive, it remains the case that implicationist welfare-based approaches to servanthood and neighbour love still represent the dominant model of the Church's engagement with poverty. It is important to ask, however, whether such implicationism and the side-stepping to the political nature of Jesus' teaching on the Kingdom of God and solidarity with marginalized communities inhibit the Church's ability to engage in patterns of servanthood and neighbour love that can transform structural injustice.

Church as servant community – fostering the common good

'Caring' Christian responses to contemporary poverty are motivated by a vision of the Church as a servant community that is called to embody God's love, enable human flourishing and foster the common good. This ecclesiological perspective reflects the implicationist reading of the teaching ministry of Jesus that I spoke of above, embodying his command to love neighbour and stranger and to welcome and serve people who are socially excluded. During Life on the Breadline, the District Superintendent of the Wesleyan Holiness Church summarized this perspective succinctly: 'Love God and love people. That's the whole of Christianity' (Interview, 2020). George, a volunteer at the B30 food bank in South Birmingham, told us that this 'Caring' response to poverty was 'Christianity in action' (Life on the Breadline focus group, 2019). Such a 'Caring' ecclesiology frames generosity, welcome, servanthood and neighbour love as foundational values, what one Methodist District Chair called 'the Gospel imperative to be a good neighbour' (Life on the Breadline online survey, 2020) or what a Salvation Army officer from the West of Scotland referred to as the call to 'serve suffering humanity' (Life on the Breadline online survey, 2020).

The implications of Jesus' ministry for the self-understanding of the Church and its engagement with contemporary poverty are framed in largely individualized welfare-based terms. First and foremost, Christian faith is understood in relation to an individual's personal experience of God's love and their spiritual relationship with Jesus. Servanthood, neighbour love, standing alongside those with direct experience of poverty and 'Caring' for all who are left out or left behind are seen as ways of responding to the implications of Jesus' teaching for the ways in which we live and order society. An Anglican leader from the South of England suggested that 'Social responsibility is at the heart of the Gospel ... Jesus had a heart for the poor and marginalized; he taught us to love our neighbour, to act justly, love mercy, walk humbly and set the captives free' (Life on the Breadline online survey, 2020). The language of 'social responsibility' is commonplace in many UK churches and reflects the sincere but apolitical and individualized commitment of a 'Caring' Church that is, to a large degree, cushioned from the systemic brutality of austerity. Arguably, proclaiming the importance of social responsibility is a commitment only those who are socially included can make. A Salvation Army officer from the North of Scotland typified this ecclesiological perspective, whilst hinting at the dilemmas it raises in the face of structural injustice: 'Responding to poverty is prioritised as an act of serving others or offering hospitality. Campaigning and advocacy are more political and, therefore, may be seen as too partisan' (Life on the Breadline online survey, 2020). I argue below that pastorally oriented 'Caring' engagements with poverty in a society that consciously undermines the common good can be interpreted as relational political interventions in the public sphere. The perspective shared by this Salvation Army officer (and many others with whom we spoke during Life on the Breadline) raises important questions about the Church's self-understanding, its interpretation of its engagement in the public sphere, its interpretation of God's preferential option for the poor and its capacity to fulfil its calling to 'transform structural injustice'. This is a theme I discuss in further detail towards the end of this chapter.

The value of the implicationist 'Caring' social action that arises from this vision of the Church should not be dismissed or devalued. The breadth of responses from regional Church leaders emphasizing the role of such Christian engagements with contemporary poverty in their region and denomination highlights the positive impact of the 'Caring' tradition of social action across the UK. The pastoral value of the Church's role in 'bandaging the wounds' of people broken by austerity needs to be recognized, even if it leaves the structural injustice and cultural violence that feeds the normalizing of poverty intact. However, when he spoke to us during Life on the Breadline, the Archbishop of the Anglican Church in Wales hinted at the need to develop an ecclesiological and missiological perspective that builds a more critical and politically engaged approach on the foundation of this pastorally centred ethic of servant neighbour love: 'poverty prevents flourishing ... and where we see people's aspirations being crushed, opportunities removed ... it's just terribly unjust' (Interview, 2020). The archbishop's reflection illustrated the fluid, interconnected and evolving character of the ecosystem of Christian approaches to contemporary poverty that we uncovered during the project. Reflecting a fusion of 'Caring', 'Campaigning' and 'Advocacy', the archbishop's comments echoed much earlier interventions by senior Church leaders in Lent 2014, just as austerity measures were beginning to bite in the aftermath of the 2012 Welfare Reform Act. As part of the Church Action on Poverty-inspired End Hunger UK campaign, more than 40 senior Roman Catholic, Church of England, Methodist, Church in Wales and Quaker leaders signed a joint open letter critiquing the David Cameron-led coalition government and arguing that its austerity policies had directly led to a massive rise in the numbers of people relying on food banks to feed their families (Watt, 2014). Also, during Lent 2014, Vincent Nicholls, the Archbishop of Westminster and newly installed leader of the Roman Catholic Church in England and Wales, told journalists that he felt that the government's austerity policies were deepening poverty and fuelling inequality, when he was interviewed in the *Daily Telegraph* newspaper and on BBC Radio 4 (Weaver, 2014). Just a few weeks later, in his 2014 Easter Day sermon, Justin Welby, the Archbishop of Canterbury, described the work of food bank volunteers as a witness to the solidarity and presence of the Risen Christ with people whose lives were being scarred by austerity-age poverty (Kallsen, 2014). Such examples illustrate the way in which 'Caring' responses to systemic poverty can take on the character of pastorally focused political interventions and how 'Caring' and 'Advocacy' can converge, bring local congregations and national Church leaders together and complement one another.

The self-reflection of the British Methodist Church and the Anglican Communion over recent decades highlights the convergences between 'Caring' and 'Campaigning and Advocacy' responses to contemporary poverty, approaches to the Church's engagement in the public sphere and the tensions between movement-based and institutionalized ecclesiologies. The first example of ecclesiological reflections about the calling of the Church arose from the Anglican Consultative Council's (ACC) discussions about the nature of Christian mission. The 1984 ACC meeting in Badagry in Nigeria sought to summarize the calling of the Church in four succinct phrases – what became known as the Marks of Mission (Anglican Consultative Council, 1985). This articulation of a holistic Anglican missiology envisioned evangelism and social justice as complementary, rather than contradictory expressions of mission.

In the years that followed the 1984 ACC meeting in Nigeria, the impact of this articulation of the Marks of Mission rippled across the Anglican Communion and were adopted by the General Synod of the Church of England in 1996.[1] Jesse Zink (2017, p. 144) alludes to the extensive influence of the Marks of Mission on Anglican missiology, suggesting that they 'have attained an omnipresence within Anglican and Episcopal thinking'. Possibly because of its larger national and global footprint, the Anglican Communion's Marks of Mission have been more influential on the wider Church than Methodism's 'Our Calling' process, which I discuss below, and had a broader ecumenical impact. Since 2017, the Marks of Mission have shaped the missiology of the ecumenical network Churches Together in Britain and Ireland, which has more than 50 member national Churches from a wide variety of ecclesiological and theological backgrounds, and were endorsed in 2020 by the General Assembly of the Church of Scotland as the basis for its local, regional and national work.[2] The fourth Mark of Mission suggests that the Church is called 'To seek to transform unjust structures of society', although in 2012 the phrase 'to challenge violence of every kind and to pursue peace and reconciliation' was added. The assertion that the purpose of engaging in the public sphere is to transform structural injustice reinforces the challenge to the 'Caring' Church to become a prophetic 'Campaigning' liberative movement. There is little doubt that the Church became increasingly visible during the Age of Austerity – a key player in response to growing poverty. What is less clear is the extent to which such 'Caring' enabled a more effective and sustained response to the commitment to transform structural injustice.

In 2000, the British Methodist Conference adopted a report entitled 'Our Calling' as a summary of its understanding of the mission and purpose of the Church in a new millennium. One of the four key areas of 'Our Calling' was 'Service' – 'The Church exists to be a good neighbour to people in need and to challenge injustice.'[3] Offering a slightly less assertive echo of the Anglican Communion's fourth Mark of Mission, 'Our Calling' exemplifies a welfare-based common-good 'Caring' response to poverty that revolves around an ethic of servanthood and neighbour love. However, Methodism's support for the Joint Public Issues Team, the 2020 launch of the Church at the Margins scheme, its development of the Walking with Micah initiative (2021–23), the 2023 adoption of the *Justice Seeking Church* report and its participation in the ecumenical Let's End Poverty network ahead of the 2024 UK General Election exemplify the spirit of the social gospel movement and a clearer commitment to supplementing its 'Caring' ethos with a support for a 'Campaigning and Advocacy' approach to challenging poverty.[4] Such national Methodist initiatives have raised the profile of contemporary poverty as a missiological issue within Methodism and helped to stimulate involvement in advocacy oriented anti-poverty actions. The Church at the Margins programme has begun to forge a commitment to a bottom-up ecclesiology fashioned by people experiencing poverty, but at the time of writing the long-term future of this initiative is uncertain. Furthermore, the 2023 *Justice Seeking Church* report provides a valuable Methodist summary of aspects of Christian understandings of justice. Amongst its 'Six Principles for Justice' is an echo of God's preferential option for the poor: 'God consistently shows a bias to people experiencing poverty and those who are excluded – The search for justice must attend to those who live in poverty, and those who are marginalised in other ways, as a priority' (Methodist Church, 2023, p. 27). The report speaks of the need to move beyond an individualized 'Caring' response to poverty – 'The Bible challenges structural injustice ... This takes contemporary readers far beyond a concern for individual acts of charity, as Christians seek directly to act against systemic injustice' (2023, p. 32). Its creative and holistic depiction of what it calls 'systemic change' as a tree whose leaves represent structural change, a stem representing relational change and roots that indicate the need for transformative underpinning values and beliefs, hints at the multidimensional nature of the justice to which the report commits Methodism (2023, p. 51). Given this prophetic alignment of Methodism with the core values of liberation theology it is important to ask whether this commitment has been translated into consistent action in the public sphere. Our Life on the Breadline research suggests that the fulfilment of this sense of calling is sporadic rather than consistent and still hampered by a concern about being perceived as 'political'. From our experience a national embrace of the calling to 'Campaign' against structural injustice has yet to translate into meaningful action at Circuit or local church level in any sustained way.

Like the companion Church at the Margins initiative, the *Justice Seeking Church* report serves as a reminder of the social justice tradition within Methodist heritage. However, our Life on the Breadline research implies that there is a danger that this Methodist heritage has been nudged to one side in favour of a depoliticized emphasis on individualized servanthood and welfare-based neighbour love, resulting from a hesitant nervousness about engagement in the public sphere. It is for this reason, I would suggest, that the *Justice Seeking Church* report needs to be seen as the beginning of a process, rather than its end. In theological terms, the report's authors seemingly align Methodism with an implicationist social gospel tradition that is shaped by a broad commitment to an egalitarian common good and God's preferential option for the poor. The report hints at the need for a transformative engagement with structural injustice, citing, for example a commitment to the call within the Marks of Mission to 'transform unjust structures'. However, even though the word 'injustice' is mentioned 81 times, little is said about the systemic nature and causes of such structural injustice, its links with neoliberal capitalism and the ideologically motivated austerity agenda that has shaped British political life since the 2010 General Election.

'Caring' and the public sphere

What implications does the 'Caring' approach to contemporary poverty have for the Church's engagement in the public sphere and the use of its social capital in the face of systemic injustice? If we want to offer a nuanced response to this question we need to move beyond one dimensional unreflective answers. Adopting a 'nitty-gritty' hermeneutical perspective can help us to recognize and grapple with the complexity of 'Caring' Christian traditions of social action on the ground.

Our Life on the Breadline research identified the following characteristics of 'Caring' Christian engagements in the public sphere and the understandings of the Church that they embody. First, it was widely suggested by Church leaders that the transformative nature of the Christian gospel should be seen in holistic, but essentially implicationist, terms. The Anglican Bishop of Chichester summarized, suggesting that the gospel 'is about transformation and freedom – impacting individuals, communities, nations and the world' (Interview, 2020). A United Reformed Church leader from the South-West of England went further, suggesting that a 'Caring'-focused vision of the Church's role in the public sphere revolves around a commitment to 'God's preferential option for the poor; a concern that justice and mercy go hand-in-hand; a sense that we cannot proclaim the gospel to someone without also meeting need – being Christ' (Life on the Breadline online survey, 2020). This reflection raises an awkward but important question – are proclaiming the gospel and meeting physical need different activities or are they one and the same?

Second, our Life on the Breadline research made it clear that implicationist 'Caring' engagement in the public sphere is inspired by a vision of the common good within which all people are included, all people are valued, and all people can flourish and where the debilitating and excluding trauma of poverty is forced into retreat. As the Archbishop of Wales noted, we all have 'a right to flourish' (Interview, 2020). Third, as implied above, 'Caring' Christian interventions in the public sphere during the Age of Austerity are overwhelmingly premised on the twin ethics of servanthood and neighbour love that inform the implicationism of Catholic Social Teaching and the social gospel. 'Caring' engagement in the public sphere during the Age of Austerity has largely responded to the challenge Dietrich Bonhoeffer laid before the German Church in the face of Nazi dictatorship by 'bandaging up the wounds' of people and communities 'broken beneath the wheels' of austerity, rather than ramming a 'spoke into the wheel' of injustice itself (Bonhoeffer cited in Bethge, 1995, pp. 316–17).

Such welfare-based social action, which has prioritized pastoral care over politics, has immense value and must never be dismissed. However, what became clear during Life on the Breadline was that servanthood, neighbour love and 'bandaging up the wounds' in the face of an ideological commitment to austerity at the heart of government that consistently undermines the common good cannot defeat systemic poverty. In this context, what might it mean in pastoral, pedagogical and political terms for the Church to assert God's preferential option for the poor and the claim its calling is to 'transform the structures of injustice'? Can, as I have hinted above, 'Caring' be re-imagined as a potentially liberative pastorally centred political act? This is a question I turn to towards the end of this chapter.

Robert Beckford writes about the experience of Black Pentecostal churches and argues that what he sees as their lack of sustained engagement in the public sphere relates to three temptations (2004, p. 29ff). Some, he argues, have 'sold out' to a materialistic prosperity-oriented gospel, as I discuss in Chapter 5. Others, he argues, have been 'bought out', exchanging a prophetic critique of structural injustice for the financial security of grants that fund youth and community work. And finally, some churches have been 'scared out' of the inner city, relocating to the perceived safety of the suburbs. Writing about the emergence of interfaith politics, Luke Bretherton comments on the temptations that he suggests faith groups can fall prey to in a postsecular context (2011,

p. 355ff). Bretherton suggests that faith groups can be 'coopted and instrumentalized by the state' (2011, p. 355). Independence is lost in return for perceived influence as faith groups find themselves used to foster greater social cohesion or to step in when welfare spending is cut. Arguably, even if it is only unconscious, 'co-option' blurs the lines between apolitical servanthood and politically blessed 'Caring'. Bretherton further suggests that faith groups can turn inwards (2011, p. 356). Tempted by a form of communalism, faith groups can limit their engagement in the public sphere to a form of identity politics – strong on bonding capital but with little emphasis on bridging or linking capital. Beckford and Bretherton make strong arguments. Based on our Life on the Breadline fieldwork, I would suggest that each of the temptations to which they refer represents a political choice that the Church has chosen to make, even though this is not how such decisions are framed. The pertinent question, therefore, is not whether the Church's 'Caring' presence in the public sphere is political, but whether such social action colludes with or subverts structural injustice.

During Life on the Breadline, most of the Church leaders whom we interviewed or surveyed, whilst arguing that Christians had an important role to play in the public sphere, depicted the Church's 'Caring' engagement with austerity-age poverty as a form of servant neighbour love, rather than politics. Such social action was largely depicted as a person-centred pastoral response to urgent practical need, rather than collective engagement with structural injustice, even where Church leaders recognized the political dimensions of such social action. 'Caring' responses to austerity-age poverty were framed as practical expressions of the fundamental commitments to human flourishing, solidarity and the common good, rather than political interventions in the public sphere. Many Church leaders with whom we spoke remain nervous about moving beyond welfare-based responses to poverty into what they implied was the problematic world of politics, as I noted in the previous chapter. However, as the examples below from Life on the Breadline demonstrate, it would be a mistake to think we can draw a hard and fast line between seemingly apolitical welfare based 'Caring' responses to the symptoms of poverty and politically engaged 'Campaigning' approaches to challenging structural injustice.

There are no neat summaries that encapsulate the essence of 'Caring' Christian engagements with contemporary poverty. In a sense, what our Life on the Breadline research has highlighted is the painful irony that 'Caring' Christian responses to contemporary poverty are, arguably, changing everything and nothing at the same time. They are part of the solution, but they are, arguably, also part of the problem. Some

Church leaders felt that churches are 'generally well engaged in their communities and clergy reasonably alert to social justice' (Methodist leader from Yorkshire, Life on the Breadline online survey, 2020). An Elim Pentecostal Church leader from Northern England hinted at the need for the Church to develop a prophetic and proactive role in the public sphere – 'Being salt and light in our communities and looking after the poor' (Life on the Breadline online survey, 2020). An Anglican leader, also from the North of England, hinted, albeit obliquely, at the political nature of Christian discipleship, pointing to the interwoven nature of individual discipleship and collective action for the common good – 'Mission and discipleship are social action … Personal salvation is found in community redemption' (Life on the Breadline online survey, 2020).

Other Church leaders, however, spoke in more ambivalent terms. A Church of Ireland bishop hinted at the withdrawal and communalism to which Beckford and Bretherton point, as well as alluding to an inward-looking understanding of spirituality, saying that the Church is still, 'rather "spiritual" in our approach and believes that most economic change can only be affected through government policy' (Life on the Breadline online survey, 2020). Other Church leaders pointed to an ecclesiological, theological and missiological dilemma – 'Christians care but owing to demographics are isolated from the worst effects of extreme poverty' (Church of Scotland leader, Life on the Breadline online survey, 2020). A United Reformed Church leader from Lancashire summarized the challenge facing the institutional Church as it responds to poverty: 'Our congregations are often comfortably off. Some individuals are well informed. Often those who volunteer and spend time with those for whom poverty is a reality are themselves less well off' (Life on the Breadline online survey, 2020).

'Caring' in action – glimpses from Life on the Breadline

Snapshots from two Life on the Breadline case studies illustrate the features, strengths and dilemmas of 'Caring' Christian responses to austerity-age poverty: the work of B30 food bank in South Birmingham and the response of Notting Hill Methodist Church to the Grenfell Tower fire in June 2017. Established by the ecumenical network Churches Together in B30 in 2013, B30 food bank is part of the UK-wide Trussell Trust network and is one of largest food banks in the West Midlands. In its first 12 months, B30 gave out 2,581 three-day food parcels. Four years later in 2017–18 this number had more than trebled to 8,488 and by 2022–23 B30 distributed 13,703 food parcels annually, a rise of more than 400% in ten years.[5] One person who relied on B30 said to us, 'This is amazing. It really is. I don't know what I would do without this place' (B30 interview, 2019).

Reflecting a Matthew 25 model of Christian discipleship and a common-good ethic of solidarity, B30 implicitly reflects aspects of Catholic Social Teaching and social gospel movement thinking, and exemplifies the servant neighbour love that characterizes 'Caring' responses to austerity-age poverty. However, during the Age of Austerity, the Trussell Trust gradually shifted its philosophy and its approach. When it was established in 2000, the Trust's goal was to open a food bank in every town and city. Twenty years later, in the aftermath of the 2008 global financial crash and more than a decade of austerity policies, the Trussell Trust's focus had shifted towards a 'Campaigning and Advocacy' approach to poverty. Whilst still largely revolving around what might be called a 'Caring'-plus approach, the Trussell Trust is now publicly committed to ending 'the need for food banks in the UK'. B30 food bank reflects a similarly multidimensional approach in its 'Caring' response to poverty in Birmingham, reminding us that the various Christian responses to poverty that we identified during Life on the Breadline are not fixed or static but fluid and evolving. B30 volunteers recognized this ambivalence – committed to a pastorally focused 'Caring' Matthew 25 ethic, they nevertheless saw the need for structural change. Is 'Caring' enough? One volunteer summarized the dilemma: 'Are we just papering over the cracks?' (B30 interview, 2019). B30 volunteers appeared to be wrestling with the limited impact of food bank responses to austerity-age poverty and searching for a more politicized framing of 'Caring' that 'rammed a spoke' into the 'wheel' of austerity.

The Royal Borough of Kensington and Chelsea in North London is home to the Grenfell Tower block of flats. It is also one of the most unequal local authorities in the UK.[6] On average the life expectancy of people in North Kensington is 14 years less than for people just three miles away in South Kensington.[7] In the early hours of 14 June 2017, a refrigerator in a flat on the fourth floor of Grenfell Tower in North Kensington developed an electrical fault. Within a few minutes flames engulfed Grenfell Tower. Burning for more than 60 hours, the inferno took the lives of 72 men, women and children. Sitting just a few hundred yards away from Grenfell Tower, Notting Hill Methodist Church became a focal point for faith-based responses to homelessness and housing justice in the months and years that followed the traumatizing fire. The church building was opened as Grenfell Tower burned and people fleeing the fire were offered a place of unconditional welcome and sanctuary. On the face of it, sparks from faulty wiring in an old fridge caused the Grenfell Tower fire. We need to look deeper, however, for the real cause of the tragedy, which resulted from decades of under-investment in social housing in poor communities, deregulation, public spending cuts and the slow violence of ideologically inspired austerity (Shannahan, 2022). Our Life on the Breadline case study of Notting Hill Methodist Church's response to the Grenfell Tower fire, homelessness and housing injustice showed that the church was trusted locally because of its history of solidarity with people living in poverty in North Kensington (Plender and Oldfield, 2018, p. 9ff). Notting Hill's response to the fire and its subsequent campaigning for housing justice as part of the major 2019 consultation into social housing led by the homelessness charity Shelter exemplifies the convergence between 'Caring', 'Campaigning' and 'Advocacy'-focused Christian social action that is needed if the Church is to address the intersectional impact of multidimensional poverty.

Dubbing 'Caring' as pastoral politics

As I have indicated in this chapter and in my summary of our fieldwork in Chapter 2, most of the Church leaders with whom we spoke during Life on the Breadline articulated a clear commitment to the view that in a structurally unjust society God, necessarily, has a preferential option for the poor. A large majority, however, clearly framed the Church's engagement with poverty as a pastoral response to the damage wrought by austerity and an expression of servanthood and neighbour love intended to foster an egalitarian vision of the common good within which all people can flourish. Many Church leaders expressed a clear hesitation about moving beyond welfare to politics or from generalized advocacy to sustained grassroots 'Campaigning' for systemic political change for fear of appearing to be partisan.

And yet, I want to suggest that it might be possible to re-frame such common-good-focused 'Caring' as a form of pastoral politics. In a structurally unjust society within which policy and political practice undermine affirmations of human dignity, solidarity and the common good, 'Caring' for those who have been most damaged by a decade of austerity can be seen as a form of countercultural relational political praxis, an intervention in the public sphere. The 'Caring' for people whose lives have been torn apart by austerity and the affirmation of innate human dignity and worth is not only a reflection of the core of Catholic Social Teaching and the social gospel, not just an example of servanthood and neighbour love, but an embodiment of the relational *'politics of empathy'* to which Revd Al Barrett, the Vicar of Hodge Hill Church in Birmingham, refers in Chapter 6. It is important to stress that most of the Church leaders with whom we spoke during Life on the Breadline did not speak in this way about 'Caring' responses to poverty. I do not, therefore, want to imply that they did or put words in their mouths. However, I do suggest that the radicalism of 'Caring' in an uncaring socio-political context needs to be recognized. In this regard we can, for example, like the human geographer Sarah Marie Hall (2020), the political scientist Joan Tronto (2020) and the pastoral theologian John Swinton (1999), speak about the politics of 'Caring' or the politics of pastoral care. Drawing on insights from feminist theory and pastoral theology can help us to re-imagine the, often gendered, act of caregiving as an affirming and empowering activity that has the capacity to foster human security and well-being and subvert those forces that undermine, devalue or marginalize. As I show in this book, the relational solidarity of the Street Connectors in Bromford and the 'Community Building' of Hodge Hill Church's Asset-Based Community Development influenced missiology; the patient Incarnational hospitality and 'Community Building' social 'Enterprise' of the Inspire Centre in Manchester; the meeting of physical and emotional hunger at B30 Food bank in South Birmingham, and the ways in which Notting Hill Methodist Church has welcomed, cared for, sat alongside and 'Campaigned' on behalf of all damaged and torn by the Grenfell Tower fire exemplify 'Caring' as long-term empathetic politics.

However, it is important to recognize that politicized 'Caring' is not inevitably liberative. Indeed, as the concern of the B30 Food bank volunteer that 'we are just papering over the cracks' and Gaston and Shakespeare's (2010) critique of David Cameron's encouragement of Big Society good neighbourliness imply, even seemingly apolitical 'Caring' can underpin, mask or collude with structural injustice. The question to be answered, therefore, is not if Christian 'Caring' for people with direct experience of poverty is a political activity (even if it is unconscious), but whether the politics of 'Caring' are reactionary, reformist or liberative.

To help us to respond to this question, we need to draw on the hermeneutical tools that I discussed in Chapters 1 and 2: the hermeneutics of suspicion (Segundo, 1976), the nitty-gritty hermeneutics developed by Pinn (1999) and dub hermeneutical practice (Beckford, 2006; Shannahan, 2010). We need to dub 'Caring' by bringing it into a dialogue with a hermeneutics of suspicion on the basis of a holistic emancipatory ethic if it is to enable the building of liberative praxis. Such a hermeneutical process can enable greater critical self-reflection within the

Church and provide theologians with the kind of analytical clarity that will be needed if an austerity-age theology of liberation is to be rooted, reflective, critical, sharp and creative enough to enable the fashioning of a pattern of holistic liberative praxis that is capable of 'transforming structural injustice'.

This 'Caring' dub necessarily begins by drawing on a nitty-gritty hermeneutics in order to develop an unvarnished, honest and multi-dimensional understanding of the character of the particular expression of poverty to which the social action responds, the values and the motivations of the volunteers involved and the form that the 'Caring' action takes. Once this has been established a use of the hermeneutics of suspicion can site the expression of poverty and the act of 'Caring' in relation to wider social systems and structural injustice and hierarchies of power. As part of this reflective process, we need to ask a series of questions. What form does such 'Caring' take? Who is helped and who is volunteering? Does the activity meet one specific need in isolation from other issues or a variety of different needs? Does the 'Caring' activity address the symptoms of poverty or its causes? Is the agency of the person with experience of poverty enhanced or diminished? Such questions can help us to understand more about the systemic causes of the poverty to which 'Caring' responds. This is what Freire (1970) refers to as critical awareness or conscientization. At this point we can begin the reconstructive phase of this 'Caring' dub. Guided by the spirituality of liberation that Gutiérrez (1974) discusses, we can begin to ask how it might be possible to translate a kind of palliative care approach to 'Caring' into a prophetic *Shalom*-shaped politics of care intended to foster existential and economic liberation.

Conclusion

In this chapter I have discussed and analysed the 'Caring' approach to poverty that we identified during Life on the Breadline and noted how this represents the most widespread Christian response to social exclusion. 'Caring' represents a broad and evolving approach to social ethics, theology, missiology and the role of the Church in the public sphere, rather than a tightly defined 'model'. As such expressions of this approach to poverty converge with, incorporate and are complemented by other approaches, such as 'Campaigning and Advocacy'. I have summarized the theological foundations of 'Caring' in theologies of the common good, servanthood and neighbour love and in Catholic Social Teaching, the social gospel and aspects of liberation theology. I have drawn on case studies, interviews and survey responses from Life on the Breadline to illustrate the 'Caring' approach to austerity-age poverty, its depiction of the Church as a servant community fostering the common good and a society within which all people can flourish. I have discussed the strong tendency of the approach to prioritize welfare over politics and shown how most of the Church leaders with whom we spoke during our research express a theological reticence and a nervousness about moving beyond common-good responses to poverty to engage proactively in the politics of civil society. I have illustrated the immense value of 'Caring' responses to contemporary poverty and the physical, pastoral and emotional support it provides. However, I have argued that, unless we dub 'Caring' as a form of pastoral politics and infuse it with aspects of 'Campaigning and Advocacy', 'Enterprise' and 'Community Building' it will continue to tend the wounds of those broken by austerity, rather than transforming the structural injustice that gives poverty life. I turn now, therefore, in the next chapter, to 'Campaigning and Advocacy'.

Notes

1 See Anglican Communion, https://www.anglicancommunion.org/mission/marks-of-mission.aspx, accessed 3.07.2024

2 See Church of Scotland, https://www.churchofscotland.org.uk/about-us/our-faith, accessed 3.06.2024.

3 Methodist Church, 'Our Calling', see https://www.methodist.org.uk/about/our-calling/, accessed 31.05.2024.

4 See https://jpit.uk/about-us'; https://www.methodist.org.uk/for-churches/evangelism-growth/discover-church-at-the-margins/; https://www.methodist.org.uk/for-churches/social-justice/walking-with-micah/; https://www.methodist.org.uk/for-churches/social-justice/a-justice-seeking-church/ and https://letsendpoverty.co.uk/, all accessed 31.05.2024.

5 See the September 2023 B30 Foodbank newsletter at https://b30.foodbank.org.uk/wp-content/uploads/sites/55/2023/09/Newsletter-Sept-23-final.pdf, accessed 6.11.2023.

6 See Amelia Gentleman, 2017, 'Grenfell Tower MP highlights huge social divisions in London', *The Guardian*, 13 November, https://www.theguardian.com/inequality/2017/nov/13/grenfell-tower-mp-highlights-huge-social-divisions-in-london, accessed 28.05.2021.

7 Hatch Regeneris. May 2019. Westway Trust Socio-economic and Community Research, Final Report, available at https://www.westway.org/wp-content/uploads/2025/10/Westway-Trust-Socio-Economic-and-Community-Research-Baseline-Economic-and-Social-Data.pdf, accessed 27.10.2025 and London Councils, Kensington and Chelsea Demographics, available at https://directory.londoncouncils.gov.uk/demographics/rbkc/, accessed 16 July 2021.

4

'Campaigning and Advocacy'

Introduction

The 'Campaigning' approaches to challenging systemic austerity-age poverty that we uncovered during Life on the Breadline are motivated by a vision of the Church as a liberative movement that embodies God's preferential option for the poor in its own life and in its engagement in the public sphere. The companion tradition of 'Advocacy' reflects a similar missiological commitment to the primacy of social justice, rather than charity, in the Church's social action. This response to contemporary poverty is the inheritor of a centuries-old tradition of Christian radicalism, as I note below (Bradstock and Rowland 2002). However, this perspective has often found itself marginalized – a prophetic irritant to the more conservative institutional Church.

Theological foundations – poverty as systemic sin and multidimensional violence

Approaches to austerity-age poverty that acknowledge the social implications of Christian faith whilst insisting that it ultimately revolves around an individualized personal relationship with God sidestep the inherently political nature of Jesus' teaching. 'Campaigning' models of Christian social action are rooted in the theological conviction that poverty is not a reflection of moral inadequacy or individual weakness but the consequence of systemic sin and structural injustice. As I noted in Chapter 1, the pioneering liberation theologian Gustavo Gutiérrez (1974, p. 175) implied that the embeddedness of endemic poverty within social structures, policy initiatives and political discourse resembles a form of systemic sin, what Johan Galtung (1990) describes as structural and cultural violence. In his theoretical analysis of globalized power in a digital age Castells (1998) echoes aspects of the theological argument developed by Gutiérrez, suggesting that poverty is built into the fabric of capitalism. The Anglican theologian Kenneth Leech (1997, p. 135) makes a similar point, suggesting that 'the oppression of the lowly, the promotion of hunger and poverty, the persistence of concentrated wealth are not accidental aberrations within capitalism but are central to its character and vital to its success.' The systemic sin of poverty can be seen as a multidimensional form of traumatizing slow structural violence (Shannahan, 2018) as our Life on the Breadline Grenfell Tower and B30 cases studies revealed. The incremental damage of what Galtung (1969 and 1990) called the structural violence of poverty is exemplified by the roll-out of Universal Credit from 2013 onwards – the flagship Conservative welfare reform that brought a deepening of poverty and an increase in food bank use in its wake in community after community as it rolled six benefits into one (Shannahan, 2018; Shannahan and Denning, 2023). For Gutiérrez, the poverty that Galtung tells us is 'silent', showing up 'as unequal power and life chances' (Galtung, 1969, pp. 173 and 170–71), 'means death: lack of food and housing, the inability to attend properly to health and education, the exploitation of workers, permanent unemployment, the lack of respect for one's human dignity' (1988, p. xxi).

Drawing on the tradition of Catholic Social Teaching, Gutiérrez argues that the Bible makes it plain that poverty destroys the inherent dignity of all people and, therefore, subverts the will and nature of a loving creator God (1974, p. 291). He points out that, 'In the Bible poverty is a scandalous condition inimical to human dignity and therefore contrary to the will of God' (1974, p. 291). It is, therefore, 'an expression of sin ... a negation of love' (1974, p. 175). 'Campaigning' Christian responses to ballooning food bank use, persistent low pay, ever-rising numbers of zero-hours contracts, endemic food insecurity and housing injustice offer a twenty-first-century echo of the debilitating systemic sin of structural poverty to which Gutiérrez pointed half a century ago. The theological heritage upon which 'Campaigning' approaches to austerity-age poverty draw highlights the systemic and multidimensional nature of poverty. To date, however, with too few exceptions (Radford, 2022a, 2022b; Shannahan, 2018, 2022), contemporary theologians have barely explored its slow and traumatizing violence in any critical depth. Correcting this oversight could reconnect theologians with our political and social science colleagues and deepen our theological engagement with contemporary poverty. The nagging tentacles of the octopus of poverty don't just squeeze the life out of us, they slither into every corner of our lives and our communities. They sap our being (Tamez, 1982).

The 'Caring' Christian social action and the policy initiatives intended to reduce poverty that we encountered during Life on the Breadline tended to address symptoms rather than causes or one expression of poverty in isolation from other inherently interconnected challenges. Kimberlé Crenshaw's (1991) penetrating analysis of the multiple forms of intersecting oppression that were experienced by African American women highlighted the ways in which sexism, racism and classism combine in a perfect storm. Intersectional experiences of multidimensional oppression can be seen, Crenshaw (2017) suggests, as 'a metaphor for the ways in which multiple forms of inequality combine and compound themselves'. Crenshaw writes about the experience of structural racism, classism and sexism in the USA and not about systemic poverty in the UK. However, as I have argued elsewhere (Shannahan, 2022; Shannahan and Denning, 2023), her perceptive insights can help us to grasp the importance of understanding our intersectional experience of the multidimensional jigsaw of austerity-age poverty. Many of the Church leaders who participated in Life on the Breadline suggested that most Christian congregations have been cushioned from the everyday grind of austerity because of their relative affluence. Who we are and where we live shapes the dramatically different ways in which we experience austerity. The methodological and theoretical implications of the concept of intersectionality are beginning to be explored within aspects of contemporary theology (Ji-Sun Kim and Shaw, 2018). However, to date, neither 'Campaigning' approaches to poverty, nor explorations of austerity within political theology have fully grasped the ways in which intersectional theoretical frameworks can enrich theological analysis and Christian actions intended to 'transform' the 'structural injustice' of poverty.

God's preferential option for the poor

At the heart of 'Campaigning' Christian responses to poverty is the unswerving theological conviction that social systems built upon structural injustice contradict the doctrine of Creation, which declares all people to be of equal worth because everyone is made in the 'image of God' (Genesis 1.26–27). The systemic inequality that characterized the austerity policies of successive Conservative governments following the 2010 General Election hit people already left out or left behind harder than others and deepened pre-existing poverty. The slow structural violence of poverty was rationalized and justified through the cultural violence of a narrative that implicitly blamed people experiencing poverty for the 2008 financial crash and for being poor. In such a context a loving God who created all people in the divine image necessarily has a preferential option for the poor. Gutiérrez summarizes, 'The poor deserve preference not because they are morally or religiously better than others but because God is God, in whose eyes the "last are first"' (1988, p. xxviii). The term 'God's preferential option for the poor' was first publicly adopted by the Catholic Bishops of Latin America in Medellin in 1968 and has formed the cornerstone of liberation theology for more than half a century. Tamez suggests that in the face of structural poverty the God of the Bible 'identifies himself with the poor to such an extent that their rights become the rights of God himself' (1982, p. 73). Ivan Petrella (2006), however, perceptively warns us of the dangers of mimicking Latin American liberation theology in a twenty-first-century context that is very different from the one that gave birth to the movement in the 1960s. We need to heed this warning. Indeed, I have argued elsewhere (Shannahan, 2010) that early attempts to forge a British liberation theology fell into this trap. A contextually authentic struggle needs to form the basis of an austerity-age British liberation theology if it is to gain traction and attain credibility. As our Life on the Breadline research has shown (Shannahan and Denning, 2023), the converging of a decade of ideologically inspired austerity, deepening poverty and pre-existing systemic inequalities provides contemporary Christians with this new arena of struggle. Ours is the challenge of forging a new and contextually resonant theology of liberation that can resource the struggle to 'transform' the 'structures of injustice' that impoverish life in breadline Britain after more than a decade of ideologically motivated austerity.

It would be misleading, however, to imply that the assertion of God's preferential option for the poor has been confined to liberation theology. The conviction has also been a key feature of other theological movements that shape contemporary Christian responses to poverty, such as the tradition of Catholic Social Teaching, particularly since Pope Leo XIII's 1891 encyclical *Rerum Novarum*. As I noted above, Rowlands has brought traditional Catholic Social Teaching into a dialogue with the rupturing violence of austerity, and the structural injustice it embodies (2021, p. 239ff). Rowlands' emphasis on Catholic Social Teaching's focus on the inherent human dignity that flows from the doctrine of Creation and a solidarity with all who are oppressed that arises from the conviction that God becomes our brother in Jesus can enrich the fashioning of a contemporary theology of liberation. However, it is the reference to God's preferential option for the poor within Catholic Social Teaching that resonates most clearly with the theological values that underpin 'Campaigning' responses to austerity-age poverty. Whilst it would be unreasonable to reduce Catholic Social Teaching to the reflections shared within Papal Encyclicals, they do provide its doctrinal framework and ecclesiological foundation. In *Rerum Novarum*, Pope Leo XIII challenged the deepening poverty, inequality and abuse of workers that marked nineteenth-century industrialization. Almost 80 years later in 1967, Pope Paul VI's *Populorum Progressio* argued that structural poverty undermines efforts and policies intended to build the common good. Whilst his Papacy was characterized by a strong critique of Latin American liberation theology, John Paul II's 1987 encyclical *Sollicitudo Rei Socialis* built on *Populorum Progressio* in its critique of the 'structures of sin' (1987, paragraph 36ff) that embed poverty and inequality in policy and practice. Most recently, in his 2015 encyclical *Laudato Si'*, Pope Francis expressed a renewed commitment to the centrality of God's preferential option for the poor in his meditation on the ethical, theological and political challenges posed by the intersection of structural injustice, systemic poverty and climate crisis, and on the calling to become a Church of the poor:

> In the present condition of global society, where injustices abound and growing numbers of people are deprived of basic human rights and considered expendable, the principle of the common good immediately becomes, logically and inevitably, a summons to solidarity and a preferential option for the poorest of our brothers and sisters. (2015, paragraph 158)

Such theological resources remind Christian anti-poverty activists in an Age of Austerity of the contemporary significance of Catholic Social Teaching. However, at the same time it is important to ask if the apparent tendency within aspects of Catholic Social Teaching to depoliticize the preferential option for the poor by broadening it to embrace all experiences of vulnerability makes it more difficult for the Church to agitate for fundamental systemic change in the face of structural poverty. When such appeals to the common good fail to stimulate policy change, we need to ask if the institutional Church is too tied to the establishment to transform structural injustice – a question, as our Life on the Breadline research makes plain, that needs to be answered by the leaders of all major Christian denominations and not just Roman Catholicism.

Jesus' solidarity with the oppressed

For Gutiérrez, 'Only authentic solidarity with the poor and a real protest against the poverty of our time can provide the ... context necessary for a theological discussion of poverty' (1974, p. 302). Jesus' solidarity with oppressed communities in the Gospels exemplifies God's preferential option for the poor. Laurie Green views Jesus as an organic intellectual who embodies the radical message he preaches and 'shares the betrayal, the degradation, the vulnerability and the marginalisation of [the] urban poor' (2013, p. 113). The pioneering urban theologian John Vincent argues that in the Incarnation Jesus makes what he calls a 'journey downwards' into solidarity and a ministry of radical servanthood (1982, pp. 110–12). For Vincent, it was only when Jesus turned away from the religious elite that he discovered, 'a new kind of law going on among the poor … the unloved, the outcasts' (1982, p. 86). Vincent argued that there is an existential connection between people experiencing oppression today and the Jesus whom we read about in the Gospels because, as a Galilean, he too lived on the margins, within touching distance of political and religious power, but on the outside looking in (1981, p. 36ff). Going further, Vincent suggests that 'by placing himself alongside the abnormal and unacceptable', Jesus 'manifests … the living God' (1982, p. 26). As a result of such subversive solidarity, says Vincent, 'The poor are sinned against and Jesus sides with them, so that he too, by his solidarity with them, is himself sinned against and excluded' (1982, pp. 44–5).

Vincent's argument represents a prophetic challenge to the institutional Church but runs the risk of stigmatizing people experiencing poverty, by seemingly suggesting that their only hope lies in conscientized middle-class Christians making a 'journey downwards' to stand in solidarity with them. Such a perspective can perpetuate the objectifying and disempowering saviour myth that we critiqued in our Life on the Breadline case study of inside-out Asset-Based Community Development Christian social action in Hodge Hill in East Birmingham, which I discuss in Chapter 6. However, the force of Vincent's argument, that Jesus' liberative significance lies in his complete solidarity with all who are demonized, oppressed or diminished by the slow violence of poverty, should not be forgotten. It still remains a prophetic word to the institutional Church in the UK and echoes other liberative Christologies, such as Jon Sobrino's depiction of a Jesus at one with the struggles of the oppressed in Latin America (Sobrino, 1978, p. 358ff), James Cone's argument that in a systemically racist society the Jesus whom we read of in the Gospels must be Black if the gospel of God's solidarity with the oppressed is to be meaningful (Cone, 1975, p. 133ff), or Robert Beckford's suggestion that Jesus is Dread – the 'one who sides with all oppressed people in their struggle against all that denies them their full humanity' (Beckford, 1998, p. 73).

On the eve of the 2010 UK General Election that signalled the beginning of what was to become a decade of austerity I argued that Jesus' 'prioritising of insignificance' and practice of 'liberative reversals' that we read about in the Gospels provides us with a paradigm that has the potential to resource the development of a new ecclesiology of liberation (Shannahan, 2010, p. 240). Fifteen years later, as austerity-poverty continues to scar British society, Jesus' preferential option for the marginalized, demonized, excluded, impoverished and oppressed resonates ever more deeply. It is this vision of a Jesus in solidarity with people living in poverty that underpins 'Campaigning' Christian social action in breadline Britain. How then might this vision be translated into a liberative ecclesiology that embodies these values and enables the Church to live up to its calling to 'transform structural injustice'?

Church as prophetic truth-teller and liberative movement

The 'Campaigning' Christian responses to poverty that we encountered during Life on the Breadline emerge from this understanding of Jesus' solidarity with all who are oppressed and the conviction that in a structurally unjust society God necessarily has a preferential option for the poor. The Anglican theologian Andrew Davey reflects on the ecclesiological implications of this vision: 'God's new order is celebrated and claimed among ... the unemployed, the underpaid and those caught up in debt ... Christians are called to live a real presence through transnational communities that include, strengthen and give integrity to those on the margins' (2001, pp. 106–7). Gutiérrez suggested that the adoption of a preferential option for the poor needs to be accompanied by an equally important existential emancipation (1974, p. 205). Such a Church, says Gutiérrez, will be characterized by 'a commitment to solidarity with the poor ... to witness to the evil which has resulted from sin and is a breach of communion' (1974, p. 299). Writing out of an Anglo-Catholic Christian Socialist tradition, Leech echoes Gutiérrez' call for a spirituality of solidarity and radical servanthood and Jesus' washing of his disciples' feet in John 13, suggesting that the calling of the Church is to, 'wash the feet of Christ in the poor and oppressed of the world' (1981, p. 10). Leech goes on to explore the implications of this ecclesiology of liberative solidarity, arguing that it demands a conscious and consistent turn away from a Christendom mindset revolving around the valorisation of strength, size and power and an embrace of the Church's true calling to be a countercultural, agitating 'creative minority within society' (1997, p. 40).

There is an edge to Leech's ecclesiological vision. Whilst he affirms and exemplifies the liberative theological vision of the Christian gospel,

Leech argues that the Church has, too often, colluded with power elites, sanctified inequality and allowed its caring for the poor to objectify people living in poverty and diminish their agency (1997, p. 248ff). The Anglican theologian Ann Morisy offers a similar word of caution, suggesting that, 'the Church has found it easier to 'speak up on behalf of the poor than to confront the mainstream culture which forms us so extensively' (2004, p. 96). During our Life on the Breadline research, we witnessed this dilemma, which, as I showed in the previous chapter, continues to inhibit Church leaders. Might it be the case, as I have argued previously, that the institutional Church is 'too entwined with systems of power to subvert the structural violence of contemporary poverty' (Shannahan, 2018, p. 10)? This question is not new, but it has assumed an even greater significance during the Age of Austerity as the Church has become an increasingly important player in the struggle against deepening levels of poverty and inequality.

Methodism's *Justice Seeking Church* report and the Anglican Communion's Marks of Mission reflect the conviction that, in the face of the systemic sin of poverty, the Church is called to become a prophetic truth-teller, even though neither denomination has yet, I would suggest, translated this commitment into consistent sustained practice or strategic policy. Although many of the Church leaders whom we interviewed during Life on the Breadline expressed a nervousness about such an engagement in the public sphere, the speaking of truth to power was widely cited as an essential aspect of the Church's response to the structural injustice of poverty. Such austerity-age advocacy echoes an ancient tradition of speaking truth to power that stretches back as far as the preaching of the Hebrew prophets who denounced systemic injustice, inequality and political corruption more than 2,000 years ago, as we see, for example, in Amos 5.11–27, Micah 3.1–12 and Isaiah 58.6–12. Within the Gospels, Jesus' challenge to the religious and political elite exemplifies this Prophetic tradition of speaking truth to power. Perhaps the starkest example of this is Jesus' 'Cleansing of the Temple', which we read about in John 2.13–21. Jesus challenged the economic manipulation of people in poverty who visited the temple in Jerusalem, by moneychangers selling sacrificial animals at inflated prices, telling them to 'Get out of here! Stop turning my Father's house into a market!' (John 2.16). Whilst in its early centuries the Church was, to a large degree, an underground social movement, Christianity became the religion of Empire following the conversion of the Emperor Constantine in 312 CE. As the interconnection between Christianity and State power became more symbiotic in the centuries that followed, the tradition of speaking truth to power and advocacy on behalf of marginalized social groups was increasingly seen as a threat to the social position of the Church and an irritant to Church leaders. Nevertheless, we can still trace a subversive thread of such challenges to power running through Christian history, that form the backdrop to contemporary 'Campaigning' critiques of austerity-poverty. This subversive tradition has included seventeenth-century Levellers like John Lilburne who advocated for equality and human rights and Diggers leaders like Gerard Winstanley whose *New Law of Righteousness* pamphlet drew on the early Christian communism of Acts 2 to challenge those with power to see the earth as a 'common treasury' to be shared by all people. The nineteenth-century Tolpuddle Martyrs who formed the first agricultural labourers' trade union in 1834 led by the Methodist lay preacher George Loveless; the mid-Victorian pamphleteering of Anglican Christian Socialists such as F. D. Maurice, Charles Kingsley and Henry Scott Holland; and the preaching, agitating and publications of later nineteenth-century social gospel pioneers Washington Gladden and Walter Rauschenbusch exemplified this tradition of 'Advocacy' on behalf of people living in poverty and speaking truth to power as a means of raising awareness and transforming structural injustice. Much of this agitating tradition has existed on the margins of the institutional Church. However, it is important to recognize that the role of the Church as prophetic truth-teller has, on occasions, been exemplified by senior Church leaders through their interventions in the public sphere offering critiques of government policies that have caused or deepened poverty and inequality. Speaking from within the establishment, bishops, archbishops and popes have occasionally used their pulpits and profile to exemplify the tradition of advocacy from within the system – speaking on behalf of, rather than in solidarity with, those who have direct experience of poverty. Our Life on the Breadline research raises questions about the 'Advocacy' of a caring but largely disengaged institutional Church in the face of grinding poverty, as I show in Chapter 6 in my exploration of a 'Community Building' Asset Based Community Development Christian response to austerity poverty. However, at this point it is important to note the political significance and public value of such interventions by senior Church leaders. Three brief examples illustrate this point. First, just as he became Archbishop of Canterbury in 1942, William Temple published a short but seminal book that exemplified Anglican social theology and the thrust of Christian Socialist thinking. *Christianity and Social Order*, which Temple wrote when he was Archbishop of York during the Great Depression, offered a theological critique of poverty and inequality and played an important part in paving the way for the establishment of the Welfare State in 1945 by Attlee's incoming Labour government. Second, a key moment in the evolution of the Church's political engagement in the public sphere that, to a degree, has served as a template for senior Church leaders for the last 40 years, relates to the 1985 publication of the Church of England's *Faith in the City* report in the face of the growing unemployment, inequality and social unrest that characterized the Thatcher decade. In the report the Archbishop of Canterbury's Commission on Urban Priority Areas developed a strong critique of the social policies of the Thatcher government. This was not a generalized social commentary on government in abstract terms but a clear and targeted theological critique of the particular policies of a specific Prime Minister. With some justification, Adam Dinham notes that the publication of *Faith in the City* 'caused a political storm' (2008, p. 2166). Indeed, as Dinhan reminds us, Norman Tebbit, senior Conservative Minister and ally of Margaret Thatcher, dismissed the report as 'Marxist theology' (2008, p. 2166). Third, in the decades that followed the *Faith in the City* row, the Church became increasingly visible in the public sphere, particularly in the Age of Austerity that followed the 2010 General Election. In 2013, as Universal Credit was being rolled out following the 2012 Welfare Reform Act, the Archbishop of Canterbury publicly critiqued the Conservative government, suggesting that their welfare reforms would deepen poverty, hurt those who were already left out or left behind and damage the common good (see Siddique, 2013). Just a year later, soon after Roman Catholic leader Cardinal Vincent Nichols described austerity as a 'disgrace', an ecumenical group of more than 40 senior Church leaders signed an open letter critiquing the Cameron government's policy agenda (see Beattie, 2014; Weaver, 2014).

During Life on the Breadline it became evident that in spite of a widespread affirmation of God's preferential option for the poor, attitudes towards the Church's engagement in advocating structural and political change were mixed. A Baptist Church leader from the North of England exemplified the position of those who were nervous about moving beyond welfare-based 'Caring' into the more explicitly political and potentially divisive 'Campaigning' and 'Advocacy'. He depicted the Church's response to poverty as an unconditional example of common-good-oriented servanthood and neighbour love (Life on the Breadline online survey, 2020). Such a perspective summarizes the welfare-based implicationism of the 'Caring' response to poverty that is dominant in austerity-age Britain, just as it has been throughout Christian history. This Baptist leader's reflection embodies a person-centred approach to poverty that 'bandages up the wounds' of people damaged by austerity, while stopping short of ramming 'a spoke into the wheel of injustice'. The Church is envisioned as a 'Caring' but ultimately disengaged institution, responding to the urgent needs of people living in poverty and advocating on 'their' behalf, without taking the next step into long-term solidarity.

A Church of God of Prophecy bishop from Northern England pointed to a theological challenge that inhibits action on contemporary poverty and engagement in the public sphere – 'Our theology, which focuses less on earthly matters, contributes to us not fully grasping the issues at hand' (Life on the Breadline online survey. 2020). A similar reticence amongst other Church leaders appeared to be pragmatic rather than principled. Senior Pastor Adegoke of the Church of the Cherubim and Seraphim exemplified this view: 'Smaller churches have no voice. It is difficult for us to demand protests or a march on Downing Street' (Interview 2020). John Fulton, the Moderator of the United Free Church of Scotland voiced a similar view, expressing a sense of fragility and powerlessness – 'We're a small denomination. Why should the government be bothered about anything that comes from us? If the Church of England or the Church of Scotland make a noise, they're big enough to have clout' (Interview 2020).

When we spoke to him during Life on the Breadline, the Revd Dr Richard Fraser of the Church of Scotland articulated a very different view of the Church's calling and pointed to the systemic injustice that led to the financial crash of 2008, suggesting that it had been 'paid for by the poorest in society' (Interview 2020). Fraser spoke of the Church's calling to be a prophetic truthteller and liberative social movement that translates a commitment to God's preferential option for the poor into social action intended to 'transform unjust structures' as the Marks of Mission put it. 'Our campaigning,' said Fraser, 'is driven by our reading of the Gospel and a recognition that Jesus had a particular bias to the poor and to the people who were inhabiting the margins of society.' In a similar vein some of the most senior Church leaders in the UK pointed to the vital importance of 'Advocacy'. The Anglican Archbishop of Wales, for example, suggested that, 'The Church has a duty to speak up on behalf of people who are unjustly treated ... There will always be those who say it's nothing to do with us but, frankly, they are wrong' (Interview 2020). One of the Church of England's senior bishops, the Right Revd Paul Butler (Bishop of Durham) argued that their presence in the House of Lords provides Church of England bishops with an opportunity to speak truth to power (Interview 2020). Bishop Paul suggested that this had given him the chance to translate his belief that 'Jesus was always on the side of the poor' (Interview 2020) into action in debates seeking to reform Universal Credit. In March 2023, Bishop Paul critiqued the government's introduction of a 'two child cap' preventing

Universal Credit claimants claiming for more than two children. Bishop Paul suggested that such a step would push up to a further 1.3 million children into poverty (Wilkinson, 2023).

Our Life on the Breadline research revealed a variety of views amongst senior Church leaders about the Church's 'Campaigning' and 'Advocacy' role in the public sphere. Almost all of the Church leaders whom we interviewed or who completed our Life on the Breadline survey expressed the conviction that responding proactively and consistently to poverty lies at the heart of the Church's mission. Most suggested to us that in an unjust society God necessarily has a preferential option for the poor and, in a reference to the Marks of Mission, that the Church is called to 'transform unjust structures'. This ministry of 'Campaigning' and 'Advocacy' and the Church's calling to speak truth to power is central to the thinking of many Church leaders. However, the leaders of smaller and weaker denominations tended to be far more hesitant. It is clear, as I indicated above, that speaking truth to power has formed an important tradition of Christian social action for centuries. It might be, however, as some of our research participants implied, that 'Advocacy' – speaking on behalf of people in poverty – reflects the fact that, as Revd Micky Youngson, former President of the Methodist Conference, suggested, the Church is caring but largely removed from the raw edge of austerity (Interview 2020). This reflection was repeated by a number of Church leaders from different Christian traditions. However, it is important to set this critique against the theological vision articulated to us by a Baptist leader from the North-West of England: 'God is a God of justice … We have a prophetic voice and are in a place to tackle the causes of poverty whilst not losing sight of the symptoms' (Life on the Breadline online survey, 2020). The following glimpses of 'Campaigning' responses to poverty drawn from our Life on the Breadline ethnographic case studies wrestle with these challenges.

'Campaigning and Advocacy' in action – glimpses from Life on the Breadline

Our Life on the Breadline case studies uncovered many examples of Christian 'Campaigning and Advocacy'. In many cases the terms 'Campaigning' and 'Advocacy' were used interchangeably. However, I suggest that they refer to related but slightly different arenas of Christian social action. In brief, I use 'Advocacy' to refer to the public speaking of 'truth to power', often by senior Church leaders, that is the inheritor of the truth-telling traditions of the Hebrew Prophets, as discussed above. I use the term 'Campaigning' to reference long-term grassroots or strategic interventions in the public sphere that are directly intended to challenge and transform particular forms of structural injustice. Such campaigning often takes place within ecumenical networks like the Joint Public Issues Team, anti-poverty NGOs such as Church Action on Poverty or broad-based community organizations like Citizens UK. Three of our Life on the Breadline case studies illustrate the ongoing importance of 'Campaigning and Advocacy' as a strand of Christian engagement with austerity-age poverty and inheritor of the tradition of Christian radicalism.

Church Action on Poverty has become one of the UK's leading Christian anti-poverty NGOs since its establishment in 1982. Drawing much of its strength and energy from a dispersed ecumenical support base and a coalition-focused network-based approach to challenging UK poverty, Church Action has been at the forefront of 'Campaigning and Advocacy' Christian responses to growing poverty during the Age of Austerity. Church Action describes its approach in its own values statement: 'We speak truth to power, campaigning nationally and locally for policies that will loosen the grip of poverty on people's lives.'[1] When we interviewed him during Life on the Breadline, Niall Cooper, the Director of Church Action on Poverty from 1997 to 2025, spoke extensively about their nuanced approach to 'Campaigning and Advocacy'. Cooper praised the key role the Church played in responding to contemporary poverty, 'Over the past ten years churches have stepped up to the plate ... doing a whole host of social action projects, including food banks and debt advice' but also highlighted an unease, '... we felt we had to do this but we don't think in a rich country it's something we should be doing ... handing out emergency aid and offering a sticking plaster' (Interview 2020). While suggesting that not 'many institutions have done more than churches' because 'they've got institutional capital ... buildings and people', Cooper's assessment of national Church leaders' engagement with contemporary poverty appeared to hint at a frustration that more progress had not been made – 'At a national level it feels like it's an issue among many others ... What we've had so far is a one off statement, speeches and reports for church audiences that haven't cut through to public debate.'

Cooper went on to discuss the ambivalent relationship between welfare-based 'Caring' social action and 'Campaigning and Advocacy' – 'When we're talking about local churches it's much easier to open a food bank than it is to tackle structural causes. Churches were very successful in developing and rolling [food banks] out, the whole franchise is in a box. You don't have to learn how to do everything from scratch' (Interview

2020). Hinting at the nervousness about political engagement that we encountered amongst Church leaders, Cooper suggested that, in his experience, 'Churches are uncomfortable about political debate.' However, it is in the 'uncomfortable' engagement with politics and policy that systemic change occurs, according to Cooper, and it is in these liminal spaces where the Church is called to fulfil its calling to 'transform structural injustice'. Cooper referred to Church Action's joint publication with Oxfam of the hard-hitting report *Walking the Breadline* (Cooper and Dumpleton, 2013) to illustrate their model of collaborative 'Advocacy', but also the contentious nature of such Christian 'Campaigning'. Cooper suggested that 'any mention of food banks was immediately seized on as a proxy attack on austerity ... The government saw anybody talking about food banks as aligned with the opposition', going on to suggest that 'the Churches were reticent to be in the debate where it's so hot' because 'They don't find that comfortable.'

Three examples illustrate Church Action on Poverty's collaborative 'Campaigning' and 'Advocacy' activism. First, Cooper pointed to Church Action on Poverty's co-leadership of the End Hunger initiative between 2016 and 2019. As Liam Purcell from Church Action told us during Life on the Breadline, 'We need to talk about the root causes of poverty ... It's not enough just to do local social action' (Interview 2020). The End Hunger UK alliance drew together approximately 40 faith-based organizations, united in their determination to challenge food insecurity, holiday hunger and the damage caused to people experiencing poverty by delays and cuts in Universal Credit welfare payments.[2] A second example of such collaborative 'Campaigning' and 'Advocacy' is Church Action's support for the living wage campaign and leadership of the more focused Living Wage Church initiative intended to ensure that everyone who is employed by the Church is paid the living wage. Cooper argued that the living wage campaign 'was about getting employers to shoulder their share of the burden' (Interview 2020). Whilst the broad-based community organizing network Citizens UK has played a key role in living wage campaigns, Cooper implied that Church Action was 'the major living wage foundation' and 'the main campaigner' and that their 'Advocacy' 'created a public awareness about the living wage'.[3] Third, Cooper pointed to Church Action on Poverty's active support for Poverty Truth Commissions as an example of their commitment to grassroots long-term anti-poverty 'Campaigning' and 'Advocacy', which is largely led by people with direct experience of poverty.

Since the first Poverty Truth Commission (PTC) was established by Faith in Community Scotland in Glasgow in 2009, this bottom-up grassroots movement has grown into the UK-wide Poverty Truth Network.[4]

Cooper suggested that 'Poverty Truth Commissions are about trying to drive local change, about getting experts by experience in a room with power holders and policymakers.' Local Poverty Truth Commissions bring people with experience of poverty together in a purposive long-term dialogue with representatives from community development and anti-poverty NGOs, business leaders and local policymakers to fashion contextualized programmes of action intended to challenge poverty. Cooper highlights three important features of such 'Campaigning' and 'Advocacy' that I suggest need to inform the forging of a liberative theology of austerity-age poverty (Interview 2020). First, the PTC is built on a patient process of education, dialogue, awareness-raising and conscientization: identifying the source of the structural injustice of poverty in a town or city. Second, as a result of this relational awareness-raising, the PTC has the potential to become an empowering initiative that can begin the process of healing the trauma and stigma induced by systemic poverty. Third, the PTC moves from welfare to 'Advocacy' and from 'Caring' to 'Campaigning' as Poverty Truth Commissioners care for each other and learn together to 'speak truth to power'.

The gradual development of Church Action on Poverty's work has been accompanied by a growing emphasis on the need to foster the development of a grassroots working class-led Church on the Margins, which I return to in Chapter 6. This commitment has led Church Action to foster the development of small 'Communities of Self-Reliance'. These small grassroots communities offer an echo of the 'Community Building' Asset-Based Community Development model of engaging with stigmatizing poverty that we encountered in our Life on the Breadline case study in Hodge Hill, which I discuss in more detail in Chapter 6. Church Action's move towards social movement anti-poverty activism (Cooper, 2021) echoes the sentiments of a number of the regional and national Church leaders with whom we spoke during Life on the Breadline and presents a timely challenge to the institutional Church.

A second example of the 'Campaigning' and 'Advocacy' tradition of Christian engagement with poverty that is drawn from our Life on the Breadline research relates to our case study of Notting Hill Methodist Church's response to the Grenfell Tower fire and particularly the work of the Revd Mike Long. As I have noted elsewhere (Shannahan, 2022 and Shannahan and Denning, 2022), it was not coincidental that people fleeing the flames that had engulfed Grenfell sought sanctuary in Notting Hill Methodist Church, given its deep roots and long-term commitment to standing with marginalized people in North Kensington. As far back as the 1958 'race' riots in the area, Methodism established a team ministry, led by Revd Donald Soper, to work for reconciliation in

North Kensington. In the decades that followed, Notting Hill Methodist Church became a key player in struggles for racial justice. It was against this backdrop of half a century of rootedness in the neighbourhood surrounding Grenfell Tower that Revd Mike Long's response as Notting Hill's minister needs to be understood. As Grenfell still burned, Long, together with members of Notting Hill's congregation, exemplified the 'Caring' response to poverty as they met the urgent pastoral, physical and emotional needs of people fleeing from the fire. In the weeks and months that followed the fire, in the face of an inadequate response by Kensington and Chelsea Borough Council, cuts to welfare benefits during the Age of Austerity and local housing budgets and decades of under-investment in social housing Notting Hill Methodist Church became a focal point for local community meetings with local councillors and housing providers, as well as what have become annual candlelit vigils. As a result of Notting Hill's 'Caring' response to the tragedy and rootedness in North Kensington, Mike Long became a key community leader and increasingly visible advocate for housing justice in the absence of proactive local and national government responses to the homelessness caused by the fire and the housing injustice it highlighted. In 2018, Long became the chair of the public commission launched by the national homelessness charity Shelter to explore the crisis in social housing in the UK. Exemplifying the Christian tradition of 'Advocacy', Long (Shelter, 2019, p. 5) wrote in the 2019 Shelter *Building for our Future* report that social housing in the UK had been 'devalued and neglected'. 'Everyone,' he wrote, 'no matter their income, deserved a decent place to live … The time for the government to act is now.'

The third of our Life on the Breadline case studies that exemplifies the 'Campaigning' and 'Advocacy' Christian approach to contemporary poverty is the South London youth empowerment charity Power the Fight, which was established in 2019 to support and empower teenagers and young adults impacted by the growing problem of serious youth violence that had grown exponentially during the Age of Austerity. Drawing much of its support from evangelical and Black Pentecostal churches, Power the Fight cannot be squeezed into just one of our models of Christian engagement with poverty, illustrating the fluid and evolving nature of Christian action on poverty and the need for researchers and policymakers to avoid reductionist analyses that pigeonhole or try to pin down approaches. Power the Fight's work exemplifies a 'Self-help and Enterprise' approach to contemporary poverty, which I discuss in Chapter 5. However, their particular approach to 'Campaigning' should also be noted because of the combination between 'Advocacy', research-informed therapeutic 'Caring' and pragmatic 'Campaigning'. Power the

Fight's founder and chief executive Ben Lindsay drew on his many years as a youth worker and inner-city pastor in the establishment of a reflective organization that was characterized by an ethic of solidarity and a recognition that an effective faith-based response to serious youth violence needed to address the multidimensional nature of traumatizing social exclusion, poverty austerity-age cuts, and cultures of violence and abuse. By drawing on the spiritual and religious capital of Black Pentecostal and evangelical churches in London, Power the Fight exemplifies a faith-based use of linking social capital (Szreter, 2002) in its 'Advocacy'-oriented 'Campaigning' to transform the 'unjust structures' of austerity-induced poverty and inequality that have deepened the traumatizing impact of knife crime on socially excluded young people and communities. Soon after founding Power the Fight, Ben Lindsay told us of the need to see serious youth violence as an issue of social justice, rather than social welfare (Interview 2020). Speaking in 2019, Lindsay argued that 'Serious youth violence is always a sign of something bigger. We as a Church need to understand that. We've got to start challenging the structures, go upstream to find out why kids are dying. We've got to understand that it is because of austerity that we're facing this issue' (Lindsay in NewDay Event, 2019). This approach is summarized in Power the Fight's action statement – 'We advocate for system change by engaging with policy makers such as the Mayor of London's Violence Reduction Unit (VRU) and Local and Central Government, as well as ensuring that communities and individuals within those feel safer, supported and are heard.'[5]

The 'Campaigning' and 'Advocacy' response to austerity-age poverty that we encountered during Life on the Breadline and which I have discussed in this chapter stands as the inheritor of the ancient and often marginalized tradition of Christian radicalism. A majority of the national and regional Church leaders with whom we spoke expressed a clear commitment, albeit in a variety of ways, to the view that the Church is called to 'transform structural justice'. The approach, which prioritizes justice over welfare is no longer marginalized. It has, to a large degree, become almost mainstream, a litmus test of commitment to the common good. The impact that 'Campaigning' and 'Advocacy' responses to contemporary poverty have had has been immense. The approach has the potential to exemplify the Church's commitment in the Marks of Mission to 'transform unjust structures in society' and to shape a presence in the public sphere that embodies God's preferential option for the poor. However, as I have suggested in this chapter, the commitment to translating such a commitment into prophetic practice is patchy and piecemeal rather than sustained and strategic, in large part because of the Church's ongoing nervousness about appearing to stray from servanthood and neighbour love into liberative political action. We need to dub 'Campaigning' and 'Advocacy' if they are to fulfil their immense potential and play a key role in fashioning a credible austerity-age theology of liberation.

Dubbing 'Campaigning' and 'Advocacy' as holistic liberative praxis

The expressions of 'Campaigning' and 'Advocacy' that we encountered in our conversations with Church leaders and within our case studies during Life on the Breadline demonstrated the extent to which the public affirmation of God's preferential option for the poor reflects an ecumenical commitment to this cornerstone of Catholic Social Teaching and the social gospel, as well as liberation theology. During this chapter I have shown how our case studies exemplify the key features, sustained nature, approach to engagement in the public sphere and impact of grassroots 'Campaigning' and strategic networked 'Campaigning' and 'Advocacy'. I have pointed to the way in which the affirmation of God's preferential option for the poor has been adopted across the ecclesiological spectrum at national Church leadership level, from charismatic post-evangelical networks like Jubilee+ to the Church of Scotland, Methodist Church, United Reformed Church, the Church of England and the Roman Catholic Church, as well as within nationwide ecumenical bodies like Churches Together in Britain and Ireland. I have explained how this theological and missiological commitment has been articulated and disseminated through the adoption of international and national statements such as the Anglican Communion's 1984 Marks of Mission or Methodism's 2023 adoption of its *Justice Seeking Church* report. Such affirmations and commitments have helped to identify the theological and missiological underpinning of 'Campaigning' and 'Advocacy' and articulate a presence and a social justice-focused purpose for the Church in the public sphere in relation to poverty and inequality.

However, if we are to assess the extent to which the 'Campaigning' and 'Advocacy' approach to contemporary poverty can resource an austerity-age theology of liberation we need to adopt a nitty-gritty hermeneutical perspective so that we can honestly reflect on its weaknesses, as well as its strengths. The following reflections can help in this task. First, I have shown that the wording and adoption of different denominations' affirmation of God's preferential option for the poor has often been tentative, apolitical and its impact, I suggest, weakened, through qualification and a broadening to 'all who are excluded' as seen, for example within the Methodist *Justice Seeking Church* report. This apparent nervousness characterized the responses of most of the Church leaders with whom we spoke during Life on the Breadline. God's preferential option for the poor was affirmed but usually in generalized and apolitical terms. A number of participants spoke of needing to avoid being seen as 'partisan'. This institutional nervousness hinders the extent to which the formal Church can 'transform structures of injustice', given its relative affluence and varied links with the cultural, political and economic establishment. Second, our conversations with Church leaders revealed a tension related to the social location and relative strength of different Christian denominations. Those denominations that were larger and interconnected with the cultural and political establishment tended to be strong supporters of strategic 'Campaigning' and an 'Advocate's' speaking of truth to power. Other, smaller, historically marginalized denominations that articulated a feeling of being overlooked and fragile expressed a clear sense that their voice would not be heard by people in power. Might it be that large-scale top-down 'Campaigning' and 'Advocacy' is the privilege of the socially included? Third, as many Church leaders recognized, Christian 'Campaigning' and 'Advocacy' can be unconnected from the everyday realities of austerity because whilst local churches are 'Caring' they are often largely disengaged from the rawness of life in breadline Britain. In Chapter 6, where I discuss the 'Community Building' approach to poverty, Al Barrett of Hodge Hill Church in Birmingham critiques the tendency to wait for and rely on outsider 'saviours' to fix things, thereby objectifying local people and diminishing their agency. Fourth, the work of Notting Hill Methodist Church in London, the Inspire Centre in Manchester, and Hodge Hill Church in Birmingham demonstrate the importance of long-term presence and solidarity. One of the weaknesses of external 'Campaigns' or high-profile 'Advocacy' by Church leaders is that such actions can be short-term in nature and fail to reflect a contextualized understanding of local communities. Only by sitting with people and staying with them can the debilitating slow violence of poverty be understood and challenged. Fifth, a focus on the need for existential as well as economic transformation is of fundamental importance. Only where spiritual conversion accompanies economic and political transformation can the cultural violence that normalizes poverty be subverted and structural injustice be consigned to history. For such change to occur we need to dub 'Campaigning' and 'Advocacy' if it is to resource holistic liberative praxis.

As we begin to dub 'Campaigning' and 'Advocacy' the first question we need to ask is how specific actions and activists relate to existing systems of power. Does the campaign or act of advocacy agitate for the transformation of the structural injustice that gives rise to the systemic poverty that damages and destroys, or is it intended to simply dull the pain and make life bearable? Does the campaign recognize and address the multidimensional and systemic nature of poverty? Using a hermeneutics of suspicion can help us to clear the decks so we can begin building a new and holistic approach to 'Campaigning' and 'Advocacy'. Drawing on an *a priori* emancipatory ethic and the twin concepts of *Shalom* and human security as the theoretical drivers of our dub practice will enable the fashioning of a holistic and liberative approach to 'Campaigning' and 'Advocacy' that draws on the strengths of the entire ecosystem of Christian responses to poverty – 'Caring', 'Community Building' and 'Self-Help and Enterprise'. Such reinvigorated 'Campaigning' and 'Advocacy' will integrate existential emancipation and economic liberation and will be marked by a focus on challenging relational poverty as well as austerity-age social exclusion. This dubbed 'Campaigning' will be shaped by a commitment to long-termism and solidarity and a politics of empathy and will be fundamentally collegial, prioritizing ecumenical and networked grassroots action over isolationist activities developed and run by a single denomination or congregation on its own. Woven through the new 'Campaigning' and 'Advocacy' will be a clear and foundational commitment to the vision of the Church as a Kingdom-focused liberative movement called to embody and enact God's preferential option for the poor in its own life, in local communities and in the public sphere. Only such a reframed 'Campaigning' and 'Advocacy' that is unafraid of forging a public prophetic politics will have the capacity to generate the liberative praxis needed to forge an austerity-age theology of liberation capable of enabling the transformation of structural injustice.

Conclusion

In this chapter I have introduced and analysed the 'Campaigning and Advocacy' approach to austerity-age poverty that we discovered during our Life on the Breadline fieldwork. The approach is the inheritor of a radical theological tradition that has often been hidden or marginalized, particularly during the long centuries of Christendom, and envisions the Church as a counter-hegemonic liberative social movement that is called to 'transform structural injustice'. I have discussed the theological foundations of the approach, particularly its framing of poverty as systemic sin and structural violence, its rooting in a radical reading of the Incarnation as an expression of God's preferential option for the poor and solidarity with all who are oppressed and the hermeneutical privilege of those with direct experience of poverty. I have shown how the approach, which was affirmed by many of the Church leaders who participated in Life on the Breadline and exemplified by our Church Action on Poverty, Power the Fight and Grenfell Tower fire case studies, rejects the implicationism of 'Caring' traditions and commits the Church to act within the public sphere to 'transform structural injustice'. However, our research made it clear that many of the Church leaders who affirm the approach are still hesitant to encourage local churches to engage more proactively in politics. The approach embodies many of the core values of Latin American liberation theology and Catholic Social Teaching on God's solidarity with the oppressed. It will, therefore, lie at the heart of efforts to fashion a new, austerity-age theology of liberation. However, as I have shown, 'Campaigning and Advocacy' can objectify people with direct experience of poverty and be removed from the trauma of everyday austerity. It can neglect the pastoral needs of people living in poverty and the vital importance of existential as well as economic change. We need, therefore, to dub 'Campaigning and Advocacy' on the basis of a holistic *Shalom*-centred spirituality and the embeddedness of 'Community Building' to ensure that it realizes its potential to 'transform structural injustice'. I turn now to 'Self-help and Enterprise' to ask if this approach can play a key role in the development of a contemporary theology of liberation.

Notes

1 See https://www.church-poverty.org.uk/who-we-are/vision/ for more details, accessed 17.04.2024.

2 For more details about the End Hunger campaign, see https://www.church-poverty.org.uk/whyendhunger/, accessed 27.04.2024.

3 For detail about the Citizens UK living wage campaign see https://www.citizensuk.org/campaigns/the-campaign-for-a-real-living-wage/, accessed 27.04.2024.

4 For further information about Faith in Community Scotland see https://www.faithincommunity.scot/, accessed 28.04.2024. To find out more about the Poverty Truth Network go to https://povertytruthnetwork.org/, accessed 29.04.2024.

5 See https://www.powerthefight.org.uk/about-us/, accessed 9.06.2024.

5

'Self-help and Enterprise'

Introduction

'Self-help' and 'Enterprise' approaches to contemporary poverty are motivated by a vision of the Church as an empowerer, nurturing individuals to realize their potential through business or social enterprise. Within Life on the Breadline, we encountered this ecclesiological perspective most widely in evangelical and Pentecostal churches and networks, but it was also evident in the advocacy and empowerment of Power the Fight, Church Action on Poverty's Local Pantry initiative and the Gear Up 'Community-Building' social enterprise in Hodge Hill.

Theological foundations: self-help, aspiration and enterprise

Many self-help and business enterprise-oriented Christian responses to contemporary poverty are rooted in the historical development of the Black Church, its encounter with historic and contemporary austerity and its relationship with the State. Drawing on his previous research (Beckford, 2000; 2006) and insights sharpened during the project, Life on the Breadline researcher Robert Beckford (2021) suggested that we can identify four theological phases in the articulation of a Black Church theology of emancipation as it relates to historic and contemporary austerity. Beckford reminds us that for Black Britons, austerity is not new. The Age of Austerity that followed the 2010 UK General Election is simply the most recent example of four periods of austerity stretching back to the slave trade and colonial era, each with its own historical, political and cultural context. As Rebecca Bramhall notes, in philosophical terms, austerity can be seen as a 'site of discursive struggle between different visions of the future' (2013, p. 1). Our Life on the Breadline research shone a theological light on this 'discursive struggle'. Beckford (2021) argues that the 'Self-help' and 'Enterprise' response to contemporary poverty within Black evangelical and Pentecostal churches needs

98

to be seen against the backdrop of an ongoing Black 'discursive struggle' for emancipation from physical, political and economic bondage. Four phases of austerity illustrate the Black Church's developing theological engagement with poverty.

Phase one – self-reliance

Beckford (2021) discusses the brutal and intense austerity of the slave trade and the colonial era. Drawing on the work of Black Marxists such as Cedric Robinson, Beckford points to the interwoven nature of racism and capitalism during the slave trade and colonial era and the intersection of the interconnected identity markers of 'race' and class within racialized capitalism (Robinson, 1983). Alluding to the systemic violence of austerity poverty (Shannahan, 2022; Shannahan and Denning, 2022), Beckford (2021) argues that racialized capitalism during the slave trade and colonial era sought to foster an ethos of dependency on 'master' and State by damaging, diminishing and dehumanizing Black men, women and children (Patterson, 1982). Against this backdrop, Kortwright Davis suggests that, 'Emancipation is the major thrust of Caribbean existence ... the common project of those whose lives have been constantly encumbered by structures of poverty, dependence, alienation and imitation ... Emancipation has been the vision of God in Caribbean history' (1990, pp. ix–x). Beckford (2021) argues that the confluence of racialized capitalism and the search for emancipation during slave-trade/colonial era austerity fed the development of a theology of self-reliance and an antipathy towards the State. In this theological context the State is not blessed by God (as in Romans 12) but is an oppressive beast (as in Revelation 13) to be avoided or resisted. Beckford (2021) suggests that in the face of the tension between the ethic of demoralised dependency fostered by racialized capitalism and the antipathy towards the state the theology of self-reliance led Black Christians to turn to the Church for sustenance and hope and away from engagement with the State.

Phase two – self-help

Beckford (2021) suggests that the second Black experience of collective austerity arose in the years following the docking of the *Empire Windrush* in Tilbury on 22 June 1948. He argues that in this post-war era the migration from the Caribbean to the UK was rapidly racialized. The 'colonial citizens' from the Caribbean, carrying their British passports were re-framed as 'coloured colonials' in the immediate post-Windrush years and as 'immigrants' by the late 1950s (Paul, 1997). Beckford (2021) suggests that alongside these changing descriptions of identity, specific policy-related strategies were used to discourage migration to the UK and to make life as uncomfortable as possible in relation to work and housing for Black people who settled in Britain (Harris and James, 1993). Beckford (2021) argues that during this period of Windrush-era social and economic marginalization Black churches drew upon Caribbean traditions of community-based financial self-help, setting up shared saving schemes and credit unions. The State is not to be relied upon. Beckford puts it this way, 'Self-reliance and self-help become the way in which you respond to austerity' (2021, minute 20:45). This theology of self-help views the Church and not the State as the source of emancipation from economic bondage. Poverty is responded to at a micro level within the local congregation and extended community, but the broader systemic factors that drive such social exclusion are, our Life on the Breadline research suggests, left largely untouched.

Phase three – aspiration

The third period of austerity to which Beckford (2021) points took place during the 1980s when Margaret Thatcher was Prime Minister (1979–90). In response to the economic problems of the late 1970s, the Thatcher government focused its energies on reducing inflation and introducing the neoliberal monetarism, deregulation and valorizing of free market entrepreneurs that has, to varying degrees, dominated British politics for the last 40 years. The casualties in Thatcher's war against inflation were people and communities who were already left out or left behind. Thatcherism, I suggest, led to an abandonment of people experiencing poverty and played an important role in the creation of an underclass of Black and White youth and the fomenting of urban unrest in inner-city communities across the UK in the early 1980s (Beckford, 2004). This confluence of the further abandonment of socially excluded Black communities, deep public spending cuts and the celebration of free market enterprise as the primary vehicle for social mobility had a significant impact on the theology and practice of the Black Church. Beckford (2021) suggests that the entrepreneurial political culture of the 1980s gave rise to what he calls a theology of aspiration within which personal faith and the energizing encouragement of the Church became a stimulus for individual empowerment. Set against the backdrop of a theological and ecclesiological orientation towards self-reliance and self-help, the theology of aspiration can be seen as a logical next step in the Black Church's theology of emancipation from economic bondage. Beckford (2021) suggests that an example of this theological framework in practice is seen in the emergence and growth of the Saturday school phenomenon of supplementary education as a driver of social mobility that became increasingly common in Black Pentecostal churches during the 1980s.

Phase four – enterprise and empowerment

The 2008 financial crash shook the foundations of the global economy and caused a recession that was as deep as anything since the Great Depression of the 1930s. Following the 2010 UK General Election, the David Cameron-led Conservative–Liberal Democrat coalition government, which was influenced by Thatcherite neoliberalism, introduced a wide-ranging and long-lasting package of austerity measures and sweeping cuts to public spending and welfare. As I noted in previous chapters, the Cameron–Osborne Age of Austerity was targeted at communities and groups who had already been hit hard by structural economic injustice, including many Black and Brown British communities. Alongside spending cuts, the period was characterized by Cameron's vision of a newly active but apolitical and localized 'Big Society' where neighbour looked after neighbour with little or no reference to the State. In this context, and in the face of a retreating State and shrinking welfare safety net, an ethic of self-reliance, self-help and aspiration within the Black Church coalesced into what Beckford calls a theology of enterprise. Poverty, suggests Beckford (2021), was seen as a curse, rather than the result of systemic economic injustice – an individual matter, not a collective challenge, in need of a spiritual cure, not a political solution. Enterprise that arises from a self-help and self-reliance-oriented theology of aspiration becomes the basis for spiritual and economic emancipation in an Age of Austerity.

In light of this understanding of emancipation and the ambivalence towards the State and engagement in civil society politics that is embodied by this theology of self-help, self-reliance, aspiration and enterprise, it is perhaps not surprising that prosperity-gospel teaching gained traction amongst Black Pentecostal churches during the Age of Austerity. Beckford argues that the prosperity gospel has captured the 'hearts, minds and wallets of African Caribbean Christians in the UK' (2006, p. 131). Given its resonance in breadline Britain, it is important to say a little more about the prosperity gospel and to ask if it has the capacity to turn the tide of growing poverty.

Holy entrepreneurs – poverty, enterprise and the prosperity gospel

The individualization of austerity poverty that has dominated public discourse since the 2008 financial crash, reflects a broader philosophical debate about neoliberalism and individualism. This discussion, in turn, is rooted in a much older theological and economic narrative about wealth and poverty that is rooted in the Protestant Reformation of the sixteenth century. Protestantism encompasses a wide spectrum of ideas about the Church, the Bible, ethics and doctrine. Consequently, it is important to avoid unreflective generalizations that imply that Protestantism and capitalism are simply two sides of the same coin. The reality is far more nuanced, although it is true that the teaching of some strands of Calvinistic Protestantism did form the ideological stimulus for elements of early capitalism.

In his seminal 1905 text *The Protestant Ethic and the Spirit of Capitalism*, Max Weber analysed the emergence of early capitalist economies in Europe. Weber's intellectual shadow is long and his thinking about the connections between Calvinism and the birth of capitalism remains influential. However, it is important to avoid falling prey to uncritical generalizations about early Puritanism. Ian Hart (1995, p. 202ff) and Donald Frey (1998, p. 1573ff) remind us that whilst Puritan pastors preached about the importance of individual entrepreneurship, they also taught that Christians had a spiritual responsibility to build the common good. Consequently, discussion about the roots of capitalism should not ignore this advocacy of social responsibility, as well as enterprise and entrepreneurship within early Protestant preaching. That said, Weber (1905/2011) argued, with some justification, that the understanding of salvation, grace and stewardship within ascetic Calvinism provided an ethical basis for early capitalism. Seventeenth-century Calvinism, and broader Puritanism, asserted that in response to God's saving grace, Christians should become conscientious stewards of what God had given them. Hard work was a way of giving thanks to God. This mindset, Weber argued, fostered the economic entrepreneurialism that formed the basis for early capitalism.

Weber argued that poverty resulted from the impact of unequal life chances and asymmetric power relations on individuals, rather than laziness or moral failure. However, some later evangelical re-workings of the Protestant work ethic did interpret wealth as a sign of God's blessing for the faithful and poverty as a form of punishment for a lack of faith – a perspective that is exemplified by the prosperity gospel. The roots of contemporary prosperity teaching lie in the ideas of the US

Baptist pastor E. W. Kenyon in the early decades of the twentieth century. Kenyon's emphasis on what he called 'positive confession' laid the ground for the emergence of the Word of Faith movement, established by Kenneth Hagin just after the Second World War. In essence, positive confession suggests that because the Bible represents God's covenant relationship with humanity, Christians can envision and name something they need in the expectation that they will receive what they have claimed as true believers. In her exhaustive exploration of prosperity teaching in the USA, Kate Bowler (2013) suggests that prosperity-gospel teaching asserts that through entrepreneurship, tithing, positive confession and a life of prayer, Christians can access the material blessing guaranteed to the faithful because of the salvation Jesus won for humanity on the Cross.

Two striking recent examples of prosperity gospel teaching within Pentecostal churches in the UK relate to the preaching of Matthew Ashimolowo, the leader of Kingsway International Christian Centre (KICC) and the work of the Salvation Proclaimers Anointed Church (SPAC Nation) in London. Established in Hackney in East London in 1992, KICC has become one of the largest churches in the UK, with possibly as many as 12,000 members, and was a focal point for the Black Church's engagement in civil society ahead of the 2015 General Election, as the then Prime Minister, David Cameron, recognized (Gledhill, 2015). SPAC Nation was founded in Peckham in South London in 2008, placing a strong emphasis on outreach in marginalized communities and alongside young adults caught up in gang culture. Leading Conservative and Labour Party leaders praised SPAC Nation's work alongside socially excluded young adults, particularly within the Black community in South London. In 2017, Prime Minister Theresa May's Chief of Staff, Lord Gavin Barwell, praised the church's work helping young adults to find accommodation in their 'safe houses' (White, 2019). In December 2019, the founding pastor, Tobi Adegoyega, won a Peace prize, sponsored by the Labour Mayor of London, Sadiq Khan, for SPAC Nation's work alongside gang members. Both KICC and SPAC Nation fashioned a model of missiology and a way of being church that provided a welcoming space, sense of direction, feeling of belonging and dignity for thousands of socially excluded people. Both congregations have drawn heavily on prosperity gospel teaching. Burgess (2009; 2020) notes that prosperity teaching is common in Nigerian diasporan churches such as KICC and SPAC Nation. Beckford suggests that 'Prosperity doctrines have nurtured a mostly constructive interest in responsible personal finance' within the Black Church and that in 'contexts that are blighted by social and economic marginalisation it makes good sense to direct people to the fact that the biblical text has something to say about financial needs' (2006, p. 137). However, as Beckford also recognizes, this aspirational theology becomes problematic when, 'need explodes into a legitimisation of materialism' (2006, p. 137). KICC and SPAC Nation connected with socially excluded communities, but also, I suggest, conflated need with greed and promoted the assertion that poverty represents God's curse and material wealth, divine blessing.

In recent years, both congregations have encountered growing criticism. Whilst it remains one of the largest and wealthiest churches in the UK, the Charity Commission found KICC guilty of financial mismanagement and fraud in 2016. Criticisms of SPAC Nation's use of prosperity teaching have been sharper still. The senior leadership of the congregation were strongly criticized for misleading, and taking financial advantage of, vulnerable socially excluded young adults to increase the church's wealth. SPAC Nation pastors gave emotional support to young former gang members and welcomed them into the congregation where they were encouraged to make 'seed offerings' and articulate what material blessing they were praying for, what is often referred to as 'positive confession'. It was widely reported that SPAC Nation then provided young adults with loans to establish small businesses, on the understanding that they would then invest more heavily in the congregation. In June 2022, SPAC Nation was closed down by the High Court, following a three-year fraud investigation.

In the face of paralysing poverty, the promise of social mobility and financial security embodied by prosperity gospel teaching can make the unbearable bearable. However, the promise of individual empowerment does nothing to transform the structural injustice that gives rise to systemic poverty. In a sense the prosperity gospel can be seen as a form of theological neoliberalism (Wrenn, 2021). Well-being, security and flourishing are all exclusively centred on me, my family and my relationship with Jesus. As Beckford notes, 'material success is grounded in an individualistic perception of the world' (2006, p. 137). Wealth becomes a sign of God's blessing and poverty, a curse, and both are uncoupled from economic and political processes. Salvation and teaching about the Kingdom of God are individualized, and faith becomes a gateway to individual financial success, not a stimulus to servanthood, neighbour love or a preferential option for the poor. We did not explicitly explore prosperity-gospel teaching during Life on the Breadline. However, the underlying ethic that wealth reflects the blessing of God was apparent in our exploration of the work of New Jerusalem Church in Birmingham, as I note below.

Church as enabler – empowering individuals to flourish

The 'Self-help' and 'Enterprise' approach to Christian social action has not previously been studied in a rigorous fieldwork-led manner by theologians seeking to understand the Church's response to austerity-age poverty. Our Life on the Breadline research sought to address this challenge in our exploration of a wide spectrum of Christian responses to poverty in the UK. Our research provided the first theological analysis to identify, discuss and critique a fluid typology of differing Christian approaches to austerity-age poverty. In this book, whilst I discuss the specific characteristics of each approach, I show that they evolve, converge, inform and critique each other. Consequently it would be a mistake to view 'Self-help' and 'Enterprise' in isolation from 'Caring', 'Campaigning and Advocacy' and 'Community Building'. That said, each approach reflects a broad but distinct strand of Christian ethics, ecclesiology and theology. What then might the 'Self-help' and 'Enterprise' approach have to say about the nature and calling of the Church?

Two contrasting lessons in relation to business enterprise and social enterprise can be learned from our Life on the Breadline research which offer important insights for all who seek a holistic understanding of the Church's role in responding to poverty. First, the self-help, aspiration-focused ethos that promotes business enterprise as a source of overcoming, flourishing and emancipation frames the Church as a shelter, an equipper and an enabler in a hostile world. The Church and not the State becomes the source of human flourishing in an Age of Austerity, especially within marginalized communities. Particularly evident in our Life on the Breadline research into the Black Church and aspects of wider Pentecostalism, the Church becomes the crucible within which a theology of emancipation can be forged. In this context the Church becomes an informal anchor institution within marginalized communities; valuing, enabling and empowering individuals to overcome the debilitating constraints of poverty, rather than engaging proactively in the public sphere to transform structural injustice. Second, we encountered a focus on not-for-profit social enterprise as a Christian response to poverty within the work of Power the Fight, the Local Pantries initiative developed by Church Action on Poverty as seen at Hodge Hill Church, the Gear Up Cycle Repair enterprise, Church Action on Poverty's Self-Reliant groups and at the Inspire Centre in Manchester. Unlike the business enterprise approach, social enterprise tends to de-centre the institutional Church, which becomes an energizer, empowerer or facilitator – more like the images of salt and yeast to which Jesus refers in the Gospels than a mustard seed (Matthew 5.13 and 13.31–33). The social enterprise approaches to engaging with poverty that we studied were not neat and tidy ideal types and drew on aspects of the 'Advocacy' and 'Community Building' responses that I discuss in this book. The examples we studied provide a glimpse into the wider world of Christian social enterprise. In theological terms such social enterprise responses to poverty are characterized by a commitment to the transformative community building potential of common-good teaching, an emphasis on the empowering force of entrepreneurial hospitality as a means of overcoming stigma, fostering self-confidence and well-being and fore-grounding the fundamental importance of a commitment to dignity and agency to resource liberation.

Our experience in Life on the Breadline suggests that social enterprises like the Local Pantry network, Inspire, Power the Fight or Gear Up tend to be outwards-facing and faith-inspired rather than faith-based. Such expressions of social action implicitly reflect Christian teaching about poverty, inequality, structural injustice and the Common Good but in an inclusive and generative manner that is not tied to or confined by the institutional Church. In light of the ongoing splintering of the secularist orthodoxy amongst twentieth-century social scientists, it has become increasingly clear that the dichotomous binaries of secular versus sacred fail to capture the nuanced realities of everyday life in the twenty-first century. This third-space spirituality is reflected in such social enterprises. Faith has not withered away but become an increasingly visible player in struggles against structural injustice and systemic poverty. This is not a revival, but a recovery of the public and political significance of faith as a motivating energy in broader struggles for social justice (Graham, 2013; 2016). On this fluid new cultural landscape, social capital-rich faith communities, with their roots deep in, often socially excluded, local communities, can resemble informal anchor institutions. In this context, where Jurgen Habermas (2006, p. 10) argues that 'religious traditions have a special power to articulate moral intuitions, especially with regard to vulnerable forms of communal life', faith-inspired social enterprises have the potential to become liminal postsecular spaces of liberative hope in the struggle to defeat systemic poverty. It is critical, therefore, that if such faith-based anchor institutions are to fulfil this potential they translate their bridging capital into more politicized linking capital (Szreter, 2002) and overcome the widespread nervousness about engaging prophetically in the public sphere to embody a politics of *Shalom*-oriented liberative hope.

'Self-help' and 'Enterprise' – glimpses from Life on the Breadline

It is tempting to focus a discussion of 'Self-help' and 'Enterprise' responses to poverty on business development and economic entrepreneurship alone. However, our Life on the Breadline research makes it clear that we need to resist such a reductionist perspective if we want to see the whole picture. Three examples from Life on the Breadline illustrate the breadth of 'Self-help' and 'Enterprise' approaches to contemporary poverty.

First, we encountered examples of churches whose response to poverty revolved around the individual empowerment made possible through business enterprise. Our experience confirms the value of such an approach but also a tendency to adopt aspects of prosperity gospel teaching and a failure to engage with systemic poverty. During the project Beckford explored how, 'In response to historical austerity Black Caribbean and African Churches have developed economic resilience to the disproportionate impact' of the social policies of successive governments on Black majority communities (Beckford et al., 2022, p. 43).

The first example of this that we encountered during Life on the Breadline was at New Jerusalem Pentecostal Church in inner-city Birmingham as we detail in our project report for Church leaders. Beckford suggests that New Jerusalem represents an attempt to resist 'the binary opposition between serving God and wealth creation'. In his interview with us during Life on the Breadline, New Jerusalem pastor Karl George referred to his ministry and approach to pastoral care as his 'spiritual business practice' (Beckford et al., 2022, p. 43). He suggested that this focuses on 'promoting an enterprise culture within the congregation' to 'build financial resilience and resource amongst church members'.

Second, during Life on the Breadline we learned about the vision and practice of the Pentecostal Credit Union. Established in 1980 as a savings scheme within the Church of God in Christ in South London, the Pentecostal Credit Union had become one of the largest credit unions in the UK by the time it was rebranded as the Pentecostal Community Bank in 2024.[1] In conversation with Robert Beckford during Life on the Breadline, Elaine Bowes from PCU (Interview January 2020) discussed the development of the Pentecostal Credit Union, pointing to its roots within Pentecostal spirituality. The Credit Union provides members with the opportunity to save regularly within a trusted scheme that is rooted in the Church; makes low-interest loans to credit union members; offers advice that provides people with economic security and provides a vehicle through which the wider Black community can become economically empowered.

Beckford suggests that the Pentecostal Credit Union arises from and has been shaped by a history and culture of self-reliance, self-help and mutual support, underpinned by a theology of aspirational emancipation (Beckford et al., 2022, p. 43). Bowes pointed to the financial resilience of the Credit Union, suggesting that, in spite of almost a decade of austerity, 'very few members experienced the negative effects of austerity policies' (Interview January 2020). The so-called 'cost of living crisis' that followed the Covid-19 lockdowns from March 2020 to December 2021 in the UK was felt more keenly by Pentecostal Credit Union members and so it is unsurprising that the 2024 founding statement of the Pentecostal Community Bank strikes a less individualistic tone – 'We are the means by which the Pentecostal Faith community can pool its resources to build the economic health and strength of the community.'[2]

As we noted during Life on the Breadline the business enterprise responses to contemporary poverty exemplified by New Jerusalem Pentecostal Church and the Pentecostal Credit Union have been a source of strength for their members and their families, providing greater 'financial resilience' (Beckford et al., 2022, p. 43) within Black-majority communities that have been hit hard by successive waves of austerity and economic injustice. They reflect the spirituality of self-reliance, energized aspiration, mutuality and enterprise that characterizes the emancipatory theology to which Beckford points. Overcoming and empowerment arise from the Church, and not the State. However, these approaches frame poverty and wealth in exclusively individualized terms. Poverty is seen as something shameful. It is a moral and spiritual problem that needs a moral and a spiritual response, rather than a critical engagement with the structural injustice that causes it. Consequently, just as poverty is individualized, so too is empowerment. The approach exemplified by New Jerusalem and the Pentecostal Credit Union has enabled many people and their families to escape poverty. However, as Beckford notes, it has left unjust structures untouched and promoted the 'neo-liberal economic thought which has had adverse consequences for Black communities in Britain' (Beckford et al., 2022, p. 43).

Second, our Life on the Breadline case study of the Power the Fight youth and community organization exemplified the use of an 'Enterprise' ethic in its 'Caring' and 'Advocacy' work alongside young people hurt or impacted by knife crime and related gang culture. As I noted in Chapter 3, Power the Fight, which was established in south London in 2019, draws much of its support from evangelical and Pentecostal churches and works increasingly closely with the London Mayor's Violence Reduction Unit. As a former Pastor, Ben Lindsay, the founder of Power the Fight, recognizes the informal spiritual and pastoral importance of Pentecostalism within the wider Black community and the progressive potential of the Church's social capital, but also its reluctance to engage in civil society politics.[3] During our fieldwork, Lindsay alluded to the Church's bridging and linking capital, suggesting that, 'The church can make a very significant contribution to the issue by not just praying or burying young people but by intelligently offering their buildings, resources and volunteers to help combat the issue' (Interview July 2019).

Power the Fight exemplifies the self-reliance and self-help ethos of the Black Church's response to structural injustice, combining this with energetic empowerment-focused enterprise, 'Caring' and 'Advocacy' and a strong emphasis on training and education. Against the backdrop of the trauma of a decade of austerity, structural injustice and rising levels of knife crime, Power the Fight developed its 'therapeutic intervention programme' in 2020, alongside the Mayor of London's Violence Reduction Unit. Williams et al. (2020) argue that the traumatizing nature of the damage caused by knife crime, when compounded by austerity age spending cuts to youth and community services and the 'structural harm' caused by systemic marginalization, has created a perfect storm to which statutory authorities cannot adequately respond because of their remoteness and a lack of trust at grassroots level. As we discovered during Life on the Breadline research, Power the Fight have designed their pastoral, training and advocacy work around the conclusion that therapeutic interventions need to be carried out in the context of a long-term relationship of trust in a manner that is rooted, sensitive to and shaped by local cultural contexts. Power the Fight calls this 'culturally competent' support (Williams et al., 2020, p. 59ff). Their reflective approach resembles the cyclical nature of the pastoral cycle that is widely used within contextual theology.

Power the Fight's Community Empowerment Cycle points to the ongoing and iterative nature of their work alongside young people impacted by austerity-age knife crime. A little like the pastoral cycle within contextual theology, the Community Empowerment Cycle reflects a dialogical methodology. Therapeutic interventions, educational work, the development of resources and training and advocacy are contextual in nature and action oriented in design. Shaped by a context of serious youth violence that has deepened as a result of a decade of austerity cuts and the philosophical commitment to 'community empowerment', the cycle brings 'communities, ideas, voice and experience' into a purposive dialogue with 'strategy, policy, funding and decision makers' to 'co-design delivery' of therapeutic interventions and empowerment programmes.

A feature of Power the Fight's 'Enterprise'-oriented 'Caring' and 'Advocacy' is their recognition of the need to balance grassroots work with strategic engagement with key powerbrokers. Change needs to emerge from a long-term pastoral engagement that resembles aspects of the 'Community Building' approach to poverty that we identified during Life on the Breadline. As Figure 5 below shows, Power the Fight combines 'Air Engagement' and 'Ground Engagement' – policy and pastoral care; youth work and advocacy; mentoring individual young people and working alongside policymakers.

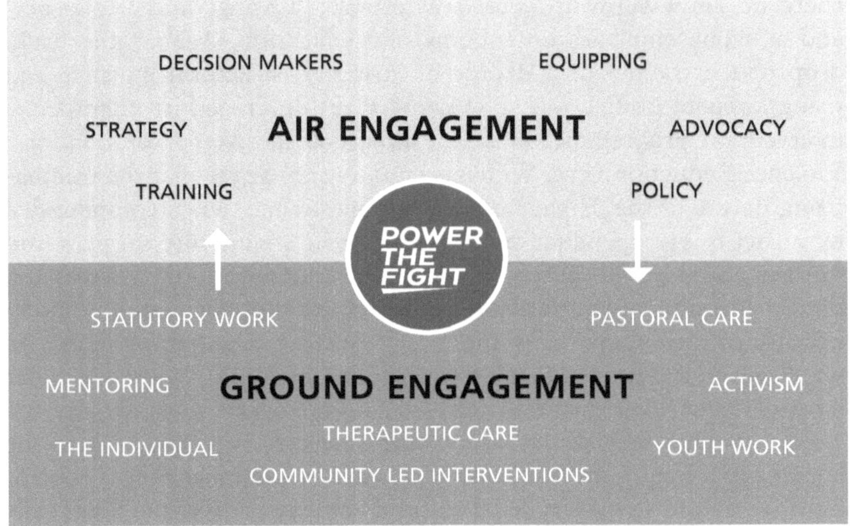

Figure 5. Power the Fight 'Air Engagement' and 'Ground Engagement', https://www.powerthefight.org.uk/about-us/

The self-reliant entrepreneurialism that Beckford (2022) describes in relation to the business enterprise approach of the Black Church and the Pentecostal Credit Union is apparent in the work of Power the Fight but gives rise to a very different theology of emancipation. Three features of Power the Fight's work that we discerned during Life on the Breadline underline their distinctive use of a combination of 'Enterprise', 'Caring' and 'Campaigning/Advocacy'. First, whilst a focus is placed on individual pain, trauma, need, aspiration and potential, Power the Fight's 'therapeutic intervention for peace' recognizes the systemic causes of serious youth violence, social exclusion and austerity-age poverty. Second, like other 'Enterprise' approaches to poverty, Power the Fight focus on the empowerment of socially excluded young people and the equipping of local churches to be spaces of affirmation, inclusion and healing. However, such empowerment is focused on the clear priority of forging greater collective human security and enabling the building of a just positive peace that can foster an egalitarian vision of the common good and not on the economic flourishing of individuals in isolation from wider society.

Third, Power the Fight emerges from the cultural context of self-reliance and self-help within the historical and contemporary Black Church, that Beckford describes. Power the Fight recognizes that the State is often absent and unable to offer the presence and empathetic empowerment that the Church can provide because of its enduring social capital within Black majority urban communities. However, rather than turning inwards and away from proactive engagement in the public sphere, Power the Fight draws on this experience to forge conscious, deliberate and purposive collaborations with a range of statutory authorities, from the Metropolitan Police to the Mayor of London and local Members of Parliament.

Third, during Life on the Breadline we encountered Christian engagements with poverty that revolved around an ethic of social enterprise. We explored three examples of such social enterprises – Gear Up in Hodge Hill in Birmingham, the Inspire centre in Manchester and the Local Pantry network. Gear Up is a bicycle service and repair social enterprise that was established by the Worth Unlimited faith-inspired youth work organization on the Firs and Bromford estate in Hodge Hill, East Birmingham in 2012. Built in the 1960s, about four miles from Birmingham city centre, Bromford has rarely benefited from waves of economic regeneration in the city and its relative isolation, poor public transport links, limited local shopping and lack of employment opportunities have, at least historically, hampered opportunities for local people, inhibited entrepreneurship and community empowerment and contributed to a sense of economic and political marginalization and social alienation (Shannahan, 2012).

As I have noted elsewhere (Shannahan, 2018, pp. 10–11), the depiction of poverty as a moral problem, rather than a systemic issue resulting from structural injustice, began to resurface within public discourse towards the end of the New Labour decade. Following the election of the David Cameron led Conservative–Liberal Democrat government in the 2010 General Election and introduction of a decade of austerity policies, this stigmatizing narrative became the dominant feature of Chancellor George Osborne's economic policies (Shannahan and Denning, 2022). In a speech to employers in April 2013, Osborne defended his spending cuts and the changes he had made to the benefits system as part of the 2012 Welfare Reform Act, dividing people into 'strivers', whom the Government wanted to champion, and 'skivers', who were happy to live on benefits (Wintour, 2013). At the same time, in the aftermath of the global financial crash, discourse about the growing number of 16–24-year-olds who were Not in Education, Employment or Training (NEET) became increasingly debilitating (Shannahan, 2012). The House of Commons Children, Schools and Families Committee recognized that 'the term "NEET" is imperfect … its use as a noun to refer to a young person can be pejorative and stigmatising' (2010, p. 9). As the recession that followed the financial crash lingered on and austerity began to bite, such young adults became exemplars of what David Cameron, called 'broken Britain'.[4] This dominant narrative was characterized by widespread use of pejorative and largely inaccurate images about people experiencing poverty – 'lazy', 'doing drugs', 'on the fiddle', 'not really looking for work'. Poverty and youth unemployment were individualized and moralised, not least in television programmes like the Channel 4 documentary *Benefits Street* and the sitcom *Shameless*, but as the Joint Public Issues Team (2013) noted, none of the descriptors were based on any credible evidence. The political and public discourse that justified and framed austerity can be seen as a political myth. By permeating the popular imagination, the myth of austerity was able to justify the unjustifiable manner in which those with experience of poverty were stigmatized and held accountable for the failings of bankers on whose watch the global financial markets went into meltdown (Bottici and Challand, 2006).

In a similar vein, Tracy Shildrick speaks of the way in which 'poverty propaganda' (2018, p. 784) was used to stigmatize people in North Kensington in the decades preceding the Grenfell Tower fire in 2017. The stigmatizing of young men in Bromford who were unemployed and the ways in which they were implicitly labelled as 'lazy' or, to use Osborne's descriptor, 'shirkers', drew upon and amplified the political myth that people who experience poverty are, somehow, morally inadequate. This discourse, which was particularly resonant in the Age of Austerity, carries echoes of the much older binary narratives contrasting the 'deserving' and 'underserving' poor that I discussed in Chapter 1, and was painfully clear in Bromford as we worked alongside Hodge Hill Church during Life on the Breadline. Gear Up social enterprise has sought to respond to the ways in which this disempowering and stigmatizing discourse became a debilitating source of shame on the estate. Philosophically Gear Up draws on the Asset-Based Community Development model (ABCD) that I discuss in the next chapter on 'Community Building'. Gear Up combines a focus on the interests and gifts of the young people they work alongside with the energizing self-help entrepreneurial spirit I discussed earlier in relation to the Black Church.

Gear Up draws on these principles to counter the internalized shame that arises from the stigmatizing narratives used about young men in Bromford (and similar estates elsewhere) in order to foster and encourage them to realize their potential. First, as we discovered during Life on the Breadline, Gear Up uses the interest young men have in cycling to 'engage marginalised young people in positive activity, life skills education, training and apprenticeships which hopefully leads to employment'. Second, Gear Up seeks to address economic disempowerment and isolation by providing, 'affordable cycling to deprived local communities and marginalized groups through our recycle bike scheme'. Third, Gear Up responds to physical and mental health and well-being challenges by encouraging 'greater participation in cycling by providing access to our led rides and cycle training'. Fourth, Gear Up seeks to foster sustainable business development by 'providing Cycle 2 Work schemes and offering assistance to businesses seeking to improve cycling participation within their workforce'.[5]

A second social enterprise engaging with people who are experiencing poverty that we explored during Life on the Breadline was the Inspire Centre in Manchester.[6] Established in collaboration with the United Reformed Church in Levenshulme in 2010, Inspire has used the former URC building as the base for a faith-inspired social enterprise that works alongside marginalized groups and communities. Revd Ed Cox (Interview February 2020), the non-stipendiary minister of Inspire United Reformed Church and the founder of the Inspire Centre, told us that the URC asked him to work alongside the small congregation in 2000. After about a year of Ed being present in the space, following conversations with a person who ran a local community radio station, another who was looking for space to establish a local café and a contact at the Manchester Methodist Housing Association, Inspire began to take shape in an organic way. For several years the congregation dispersed and met in people's homes whilst the building was being redeveloped ahead of its 2010 re-opening.

In his conversation with us during Life on the Breadline, Ed Cox (Interview, 2020) shared three reflections about the role of the Church in the public sphere in an age of structural injustice. First, he made it clear that Inspire's work is not envisaged as an explicit response to economic poverty, but as a broader, holistic approach to empowering people in South Manchester who are marginalized in a variety of different ways. Cox told us that, 'In our vision and values we talk about material ... emotional and spiritual wellbeing ... So of your classic social policy categories we would be more about cohesion and community engagement and empowerment' than a welfare-based charity-approach. For Cox, engaging with poverty is one aspect of Inspire's holistic focus on 'Community Building' – a response to the challenge of 'living together in a diverse neighbourhood, rather than [asking] how are we going to help poor people'. Second, in light of this focus, Cox (Interview January 2020) made it clear that Inspire's approach is shaped by a social enterprise ethic that arises from their reading of Jesus' ministry of empowering marginalized people, as it is described in Luke's Gospel – not charity but empowerment. This perspective is expressed succinctly in Inspire's Vision and Values where the Centre suggests its goal is 'to be a thriving hub for all members of the community; providing opportunities to unlock potential' by providing a 'well-resourced and sustainable community facility', developing projects and partnerships and being 'a catalyst for positive change in the whole community'.[7]

The third example of the social enterprise model of Christian engagement with poverty that we explored during Life on the Breadline is the Local Pantry response to food insecurity that we encountered in our Hodge Hill Church case study and our work alongside Church Action on Poverty.[8] A Local Pantry is a member-based social enterprise, or community-based food shop, that provides good quality food to people experiencing poverty. Pantry members pay a small weekly fee (£3.50/week in 2024) and are then able to select ten items of food as regularly as they need to. The first Local Pantry in the UK was established in May 2013 in Stockport, Greater Manchester, by the Stockport Homes housing association. In 2017 Church Action on Poverty began to manage the emerging Local Pantry network as a social franchise, which by 2024 had 121 Local Pantries with a total of 13,000 members across the UK. During 2023–24 people made 270,000 visits to Local Pantries (Aitchison et al., 2024). Each Local Pantry serves a specific geographical area, is managed and run by local people, often in collaboration with a community organization or a faith group, like Hodge Hill Church. The entrepreneurial social franchise model has enabled Church Action on Poverty to fashion a broad framework of solid support that underpins the growing Local Pantry network that includes Stockport Housing, the FareShare food poverty charity and, since 2022, the Co-op Group. Aitchison refers to the political significance of Local Pantries:

> Pantry members have been at the sharp end of the cost of living scandal in recent years, and Pantries rely on supply systems that are fragile. Charity can never be a long-term answer to food insecurity. We need a national Government-driven commitment to ensure that all incomes

are enough to live on, so people are not swept into deep poverty. (Aitchison et al, 2024, p. 2)

Like other Life on the Breadline case studies, the Local Pantry network developed by Church Action on Poverty cannot be confined within a single Christian approach to responding to poverty. Local Pantries daw on 'Self-Help and 'Enterprise' to foster empowering 'Caring' and 'Community Building' that enables 'Campaigning and Advocacy'. Aitchison puts it this way: 'Pantries are based on the values of dignity, choice and hope' (2024, p. 11). Such a faith-inspired approach, they suggest, enables a holistic response to the debilitating damage of poverty that fosters greater human security – enhancing mental health, countering isolation, improving financial security, enabling friendships, renewing social connections and nurturing community.

When he spoke to us, Niall Cooper, the Director of Church Action on Poverty from 1997 to 2025, suggested that Local Pantries are, 'all about small groups of people taking action to empower themselves; to build their resilience and out of that then picking issues where we can influence public policy' (Interview, February 2020). A Local Pantry leader from Northern England (Interview, April 2020) told us about the ethos and value of the Pantry model but also of the challenges it embodies for individuals, the Church and political engagement. Speaking of food banks, she said, 'I think food banks should be for emergency use only, but they've become a solution to long-term or chronic poverty.' Pantries, she suggested, can be 'the next step and hopefully a model that could support families who are in chronic poverty, long term unemployment or on zero-hours contracts'. Local Pantries, she said, offer people 'a chance to get to know their neighbours and build positive relationships ... You're a member of the Pantry, not a client or service user ... it is about more than food, it's about relationships.' This ethos of sharing both food and a warm welcome is clearly central to the Local Pantry model for this leader. For her, the Local Pantry becomes a foundation for potential campaigning to bring about structural change – 'We meet and talk through their lived experiences and use those stories to challenge the system.' She recognizes that this poses a challenge for local churches who recognize the corrosive damage caused by the violence of poverty but find it difficult to commit to the 'Campaigning' and 'Advocacy' needed to 'transform structural injustice':

Ideally you want a church to be doing both, but I know in reality in some ways it is easier to respond to the human need in front of you. It's very clear and in the Bible that that is something we should be doing.

So it feels very practical, it makes you feel good. Whilst I guess challenging structures or campaigning against the policies is much more abstract from the lives of people in our congregation, I find it harder to grasp myself, because it feels so much more concrete thinking, I've sent that single mum home with loads of fresh fruit and veg that her kids might not have had otherwise.

During our Hodge Hill case study, we spoke with church members who opened a Local Pantry in April 2021, during the Covid-19 pandemic. As I discuss in the next chapter on 'Community Building', Hodge Hill Church draws heavily on Asset-Based Community Development as it seeks to challenge the debilitating nature of public discourses that stigmatize estates like Bromford. It is, therefore, not surprising that this emphasis was evident in our conversation about the development of the Hodge Hill Local Pantry. Allannah suggested that the Local Pantry 'gives [people] a better feeling about themselves … I think it's building people up' (Interview, October 2020). Speaking of a man he described as one of the 'hidden poor' who did not qualify for any benefits and regularly had just £7 a week to live on, a volunteer called Peter said of the man, 'he wanted respect and I think the Pantry will give him his self-respect as well as food'. Alluding to the shame that can arise from the stigmatizing of communities like Bromford, Peter went on, 'It's demeaning having to go to a food bank, but if you say you're going to a food club, which is what a Pantry is, that's different' (Interview, October 2020). Paul, who is a senior youth and community worker in Bromford, as well as a member of Hodge Hill Church, suggested that the Local Pantry

> opens up an opportunity for the church to be a welcoming open space and for things to grow off the back of the pantry. I think for all of us we see this as the way to open the door of the church more … becoming an even more welcoming space for the parish.

In a similar vein, Steve summarized, 'The Pantry will be a catalyst' (Interview, October 2020).

Church leaders' reflections

Only a small number of the national and regional Church leaders with whom we spoke during Life on the Breadline talked to us about the Church's support for business or social enterprise as part of their response to poverty. The overwhelming majority focused on 'Caring', 'Campaigning' and 'Advocacy'. What became clear during our fieldwork, however, is that an 'Enterprise' ethos is a key feature of contemporary evangelical and Pentecostal engagements with poverty and social exclusion. A senior Church leader from the Salt & Light network of independent evangelical and charismatic churches illustrated the point, suggesting that 'The best way to bring about lasting change is by financing workers. Increasingly we are releasing workers into social enterprise schemes' (Life on the Breadline online survey, 2019). Similarly, the District Superintendent of the Wesleyan Holiness Church in the UK suggested that the 'Enterprise' model has been increasingly used by local Wesleyan Holiness Pastors to support people who have become trapped in a cycle of personal debt (Interview, November 2019). A further example of the use of the 'Enterprise' approach that we encountered during Life on the Breadline is found in the work of the Jubilee+ network that arose from and is loosely connected with the New Frontiers network of charismatic churches. Jubilee+ supports its member congregations to engage with poverty in their neighbourhoods in a variety of ways.

When we spoke with Martin Charlesworth (Interview November 2019), the founder of Jubilee+, during Life on the Breadline, he told us about the network's creation in 2012 and its use of the energy of the 'Enterprise' ethos as the basis for its development of a wide range of partnerships, educational resources, courses and conferences intended to support local churches in responding to poverty locally and its commitment to a model of 'Advocacy' intended to 'promote campaigns that tackle structural poverty and injustice'.[9] Our conversation with Martin Charlesworth served as a further reminder of the need to develop rigorous fieldwork-led theological research into the Church's response to contemporary poverty if theologians are to resist perpetuating simplistic stereotypes about evangelical Christian attitudes towards poverty. The most developed traditions of Christian engagement with poverty are rooted in liberative readings of Catholic Social Teaching, the social gospel and liberation theology. However, the work of Jubilee+ illustrates the emergence and increasing visibility of socially engaged evangelical and post-evangelical Christian responses to contemporary poverty. Its Theory of Change, whilst aspirational and difficult to substantiate, communicates the network's entrepreneurial energy and drive. Through talks and stories; accessible and challenging resources; supporting 'Campaigns' and enabling 'Advocacy'; creating mission-oriented 'Networks' and 'Partnering' with local churches, Jubilee+ suggests that it changes churches, lives and communities. It argues that their work fosters more viable social action ministries, increased training for Church leaders on responding to structural poverty, more people with direct experience of poverty helping to shape social policy, people being empowered to bring about transformative change in their own lives and local church buildings becoming inclusive neighbourhood social justice hubs. Such changes, it claims, will generate 'social policy based on compassion and justice' and 'more individuals empowered to break the cycle of poverty'.[10]

Influenced much more by social gospel teaching and Liberation Theology, the Revd Richard Frazer spoke to us about his role as the Church of Scotland's Faith and Society National Secretary and his work alongside the Greyfriars Kirk in Edinburgh (Interview, November 2019). Frazer suggested that Greyfriars has placed an emphasis on 'providing a space where the community can come together for enterprise, well-being, support and reimagining the place of the Church in the local community'. Greyfriars, according to Frazer, embodies this commitment to entrepreneurship as a vehicle for engaging with poverty through offering space and support to three networks intended to foster social enterprises. First, Greyfriars supports the HeartEdge ecumenical network, initially developed by St Martin-in-the-Fields Anglican church in London in 2017. HeartEdge provides Greyfriars with an opportunity to foster and resource well-being and social inclusion-oriented social enterprises in Edinburgh. Second, Greyfriars provides space for and supports the Grassmarket Community Project's social enterprises alongside people who are experiencing poverty or struggling with substance abuse – Coffee Saints café and the Wood Workshop. Third, Greyfriars expresses its commitment to an enterprise ethos through its support for the Charteris Centre, which hosts the Edinburgh Social Enterprise Network.[11]

Dubbing 'Self-help' and 'Enterprise'

I have shown in this chapter that 'Self-help' and 'Enterprise' (business and social enterprise) approaches to contemporary poverty are a response to histories of racialized oppression, abandonment or exclusion by the State and wider establishment and stigmatizing public discourse. The theology of self-reliance, aspiration and enterprise that has arisen, particularly, as Beckford (2006; 2021) shows, within the Black Church, but also within a wider evangelical and post-evangelical context, roots existential and economic emancipation in a vision of the Church as empowerer. This ecclesiological vision has enabled people experiencing poverty to overcome exclusion, marginalization, recover a sense of their own agency and strengthen individual and localized resilience. However, I suggest that the approach is limited and problematic for the following reasons. First, 'Enterprise' responses to poverty tend to reduce human flourishing to individual material wealth. We could, with some justification, view the approach as a theological companion to neoliberal capitalism, particularly where the approach is strongly influenced by prosperity gospel teaching. Second, such an approach separates the individual from community and revolves around individualized economic emancipation, resting on a conservative behaviouralist ethic of self-improvement, whilst neglecting systemic poverty. Third, as a result, whereas individuals flourish, structural injustice is left untouched and, arguably, systemic inequality is deepened. Individuals overcome poverty but the communities from which they come remain largely unchanged. Like Beckford (2021), therefore, I suggest that, whilst 'Self-Help and 'Enterprise' can enable and empower, the theology of aspiration and emancipation that they exemplify runs the risk of reinforcing the alienating binary of 'deserving' 'strivers' versus 'undeserving' 'skivers', of individualizing poverty, and can blind the Church to its deeper systemic nature. Consequently, I argue that such an approach cannot play any significant role in an austerity-age theology of liberation, unless we draw on the dub hermeneutical practice I have discussed in this book.

What, then, might an 'Enterprise' and 'Self-Help' dub look like? As with other dub interventions, the process begins with a use of Pinn's (1999) nitty-gritty hermeneutics as the basis for an honest description of the 'Enterprise' and 'Self-Help' approach. Use of nitty-gritty hermeneutics, when informed by engagement with the hermeneutics of suspicion (Segundo, 1976), can help us to sketch an unvarnished holistic picture of the assumptions, drivers and character of the approach. Furthermore, we are able to understand the way the approach privileges individuals over community and material emancipation over collective liberation, the ways in which it can affirm existing economic power relations and lead the Church to collude, if only unconsciously, with structural injustice. Once this process of theoretical deconstruction has taken place it becomes possible to reimagine 'Enterprise' and 'Self-Help' within a conscientized liberative framework. This 'Enterprise' dub will be premised on an *a priori* emancipatory ethic that rests on an affirmation of God's preferential option for the poor and an egalitarian vision of a common good within which all people can flourish. By drawing in this manner on the emancipatory potential of the approach's focus on self-reliance, aspiration, enabling potential, empowerment of repressed individuals, cultures and communities, and energetic social entrepreneurship it becomes possible to see a valuable role of a dubbed 'Enterprise' and 'Self-Help' as part of a multidimensional and holistic austerity-age theology of liberation.

Conclusion

This chapter has broadened the analysis of Christian engagement with contemporary poverty to encompass a perspective that has rarely been critically studied by theologians seeking to respond to structural injustice. The 'Self-help and Enterprise' approach to poverty that I explore within this chapter frames the Church as an enabler that empowers individuals who are trapped by poverty or other forms of social exclusion to develop a sense of resilience and self-reliance that can foster aspiration and emancipatory business or social enterprise. During our Life on the Breadline research it became evident that the 'Self-help and Enterprise' approach to poverty is widely supported within evangelical and Pentecostal churches and has a key influence on Black Pentecostal churches in particular. I have shown how this approach to poverty is rooted in a theological commitment to human flourishing, self-reliance, aspiration, resilience and emancipation and in the historic experience of the Black church as a space of affirmation, empowerment and overcoming in a hostile world and in the face of excluding racialized capitalism and an absent State. Drawing on examples from our Life on Breadline fieldwork relating to business enterprise and individual resilience (New Jerusalem Church and Pentecostal Credit Union) and social enterprise and communal resilience (Local Pantries, Gear Up and Power the Fight), I have shown how the 'Self-help' and 'Enterprise' approach can enable and empower individuals to overcome the economic and existential exclusion that is caused by ongoing poverty. However, I have also clearly demonstrated that the approach can deepen inequality by addressing individual poverty without challenging the structural injustice that causes it. I have shown how the approach is hindered by an exclusively materialistic and individualized understanding of human flourishing that resembles aspects of neoliberal capitalism. Aspects of the 'Self-help and Enterprise' approach are emancipatory, energizing and empowering, particularly the positive change wrought by social enterprises. The 'Self-help and Enterprise' we encountered during Life on the Breadline was largely empowering, holistic and community focused. However, the approach can be characterized by problematic prosperity gospel teaching that frames poverty as spiritual curse and wealth as spiritual blessing and pays no attention to its systemic causes or the political realm. It is, therefore, only by engaging in an iterative form of dub practice that we can identify potentially liberative elements of the approach that can feed into a holistic austerity-age theology of liberation.

Notes

1 For more details about the Pentecostal Credit Union/Pentecostal Community Bank see https://pcbank.co.uk/about-us (accessed 30.10.2024).

2 See https://pcbank.co.uk/about-us, accessed 30.10.2024.

3 See Ben Lindsay's talk at NewDay event, 2019, '#YC19 — Ben Lindsay (Power the Fight UK)', *YouTube*, 27 February, https://www.youtube.com/watch?v=gd8VrLV5nlo&t=1549s, accessed 9.06.2024, accessed 31.10.2024.

4 The term 'broken Britain' has characterized the social policy of the British Conservative Party since its use by David Cameron in the Glasgow East by-election in July 2008 and the publication of Conservative social policy initiatives in June 2008. See https://www.theguardian.com/politics/2008/oct/01/davidcameron.tory conference1. See also his speech following the 2011 'riots' in a number of English towns and cities: https://www.gov.uk/government/speeches/pms-speech-on-the-fightback-after-the-riots, accessed 5.11.2024.

5 For more information about Gear Up, see https://www.gearupbirmingham.co.uk/.

6 For more information about the Inspire Centre in Levenshulme, see https://www.lev-inspire.org.uk/.

7 https://www.lev-inspire.org.uk/about-us/ accessed 8.11.2024.

8 See https://www.yourlocalpantry.co.uk/ accessed 8.11.2024.

9 Jubilee+ Theory of Change, https://jubilee-plus.org/docs/TOC-Doc.pdf, accessed 12.11.2024.

10 See https://jubilee-plus.org/, accessed 12.11.2024.

11 For more about the Greyfriars Centre and its Edinburgh Social Enterprise Network, see https://greyfriarskirk.com/; https://www.heartedge.org/; https://grassmarket.org/ and https://www.charteriscentre.com/; https://www.charteriscentre.com/enterprisehub, accessed 12.11.2024.

6

'Community Building'

Introduction

The final approach to Christian engagement with austerity-age poverty that we identified during Life on the Breadline focuses on 'Community Building'. The other approaches that I have discussed can be decontextualized external interventions, designed and delivered by other people who may have very little direct experience of poverty. 'Caring', 'Campaigning and Advocacy' and 'Self-help and Enterprise' can be disconnected from the life of the local community within which an action is taking place. Shaped by an Incarnational ecclesiology and a vision of the Church as a bottom-up grassroots companion and an inclusive space of affirmation, 'Community-Building' responses to austerity-age poverty are characterized by a relational approach to social action and a long-term model of holistic engagement and presence. As we discovered during our Life on the Breadline research, 'Community Building' approaches to contemporary poverty complement but also diverge from 'Caring', 'Campaigning and Advocacy' and 'Self-Help and Enterprise' in a nitty-gritty fashion. This is a fluid and iterative form of relational Christian engagement in the public sphere that grapples with the slow violence of austerity-age poverty, but from quite a different perspective that foregrounds community development, rather than short-term intervention or explicitly challenging systemic injustice.

'Community Building' draws on similar theological traditions to the other Christian approaches to contemporary poverty that we identified during Life on the Breadline, not least because of the emphasis it places on an Incarnational spirituality of presence, a pastorally focused affirmation of God's preferential option for the poor, and the focus on inherent human dignity, agency and the common good within Catholic Social Teaching and the social gospel. However, its integration of theological thinking and the community development resources found within Asset Based Community Development (ABCD) is original. Might such an approach to austerity-age poverty have the capacity to resource the forging of a new relational theology of liberation and enable the

Church to 'transform structures of injustice'? It is this question that runs through this chapter.

Theological foundations

In considering 'Community Building' approaches to contemporary poverty it is important to explore the theological themes and questions that give it life. What might they teach us about the extent to which the approach can resource the development of new liberative models of Christian discipleship and the transformation of structural injustice?

Damaged lives, spirits and communities

'Community Building' responses to poverty are radically contextual and inherently relational. Such an approach is forged in the crucible of pain, damage, stigma and trauma, which become the stimulus for its relational approach to ecclesiology and missiology. 'Caring' and 'Campaigning and Advocacy' perspectives reflect the views of most of the Church leaders with whom we spoke. Such approaches are immensely valuable and yet, in spite of common references by Church leaders to God's solidarity with humanity in the Incarnation, they can reflect a disengaged, top-down form of social action; critiquing austerity from a safe distance, rather than feeling the havoc it wreaks and sensing the damage it causes. The journalist Nick Davies summarizes the slow violence of poverty, 'Poverty kills with subtlety and skill ... Poverty will use the damaged emotions of its victims as a deadly weapon, driving them to violence against each other' (1998, p. 187). Grassroots 'Community Building' approaches to contemporary poverty respond to the slow violence of such damage in an engaged developmental manner that is rooted in the everyday realities of austerity. The violence of austerity is not critiqued second-hand; it is experienced and responded to in an organic manner.

'Community Building' Christian social action emerges from long-term engagement with the traumatizing damage wrought by the violence of poverty. I suggested in Chapter 1 that Galtung's (1969) discussion of the three-dimensional nature of violence can help us to capture the multifaceted character of contemporary poverty. Within their 'web of poverty', the Church Urban Fund (2014) point to the interwoven nature of poverty, highlighting the psychological and spiritual impact of what they call a 'poverty of relationships' and a 'poverty of identity' that are characterized by a lack of self-worth, diminished well-being and poor mental health. Speaking to us during Life on the Breadline about his experience as vicar in Hodge Hill, Revd Al Barrett amplified this point, suggesting that 'poverty of identity collectively has a huge impact on identity individually' (Interview June 2020). Barrett reinforces the need to grasp the existential, as well as the economic aspects of austerity-age poverty. From our experience during Life on the Breadline this perceptive interconnection of individual emotional well-being and macro patterns of structural injustice and the interplay between the two was often neglected within 'Caring', Campaigning and Advocacy' and 'Self-help and Enterprise' approaches to contemporary poverty. These approaches either tended to place the welfare of individuals at the heart of their action, while neglecting systemic poverty, or focus on strategic campaigns challenging structural injustice, rather than the pain of people experiencing such social exclusion. As we forge a new austerity-age theology of liberation such interconnection is vital if we are to fashion a holistic emancipatory ethic. Given the multidimensional characterization of contemporary poverty, we need to envision austerity as a form of slow burning violence (Shannahan, 2022) if we are to fully comprehend the debilitating damage it continues to cause. It is to this challenge that 'Community Building' seeks to respond.

Slow violence, stigma and shame

Rob Nixon's (2011) exploration of the incremental degenerative damage wrought by slow, seemingly imperceptible violence can inform theological analyses of austerity. In Chapter 4, I spoke about the ways in which the creeping slow violence of decades of housing deregulation and a decade of austerity policies paved the way for the Grenfell Tower fire in 2017 and the collective trauma that followed in its wake. Such slow burning but long-lasting and, often, unresolved, traumatic damage is also seen in the sapping and disempowering impact of hegemonic public discourses that stigmatize marginalized groups, communities and neighbourhoods. Not a visual spectacle like the fire that engulfed Grenfell Tower but debilitating and life-limiting, nevertheless.

As I showed in Chapter 1, the political myth of austerity was used by Cameron and Osborne to underpin their 'skivers' versus 'strivers' discourse. Whilst such a moralising attempt to name, blame and shame individuals who are experiencing poverty and to cast some as 'deserving' and others as 'undeserving' owed more to ideology than real life, the narrative took hold and gained significant cultural traction during the Age of Austerity. Reality-TV documentaries like *Benefits Street* painted a picture of lazy and feckless people who didn't want a job and were living a good life on welfare benefits were prime-time viewing. Kayleigh Garthwaite (2016, p. 278) and Wren Radford (2022b, p. 321ff) point to the stigmatizing impact of such narratives, suggesting that they perpetuated the political myth of austerity and reinforced the presuppositions of the 'deserving' versus 'undeserving' dichotomy. Imogen Tyler suggests that stigma is best understood as a material force that has psycho-political power (2020, p. 9).

In their 2024 Joseph Rowntree Foundation report, Campbell and Tyler discuss the weaponizing of stigma, describing it as 'something which is done to people ... acts of harm' (2024, p. 11). Campbell and Tyler (2024) argue that the act of stigmatizing individuals, groups or communities is a conscious and deliberate form of hegemonic cultural violence. Stigma is 'a powerful glue that holds poverty in place' (2024, p. 4) that is evidenced in conscious actions and 'embedded in social systems' (2024, p. 14). Campbell and Tyler argue that 'Poverty stigma is cumulative. It wears down people's self-esteem and self-worth over time. It ... narrows people's horizons and diminishes their hope for a better future' (2024, p. 34). Such stigma, they suggest, can elicit debilitating feelings of shame when it is internalized – 'Shame is an intensely powerful negative and disabling emotion that can arise from experiences of being stigmatised ... Shame scars people' (2024, p. 10). Campbell and Tyler suggest that

> Poverty stigma leads to rich people feeling like they have a right to keep their wealth whilst people in poverty need to be kept poor to teach them to behave better ... Stigma excuses people with power from having to act and enables them to shrug off their responsibility. (2024, p. 19)

Consequently, as they note, 'Loosening the grip of stigma is a key lever of wider social change' (2024, p. 4). In Chapter 4, I discussed how we discovered during our case study of Christian responses to the Grenfell Tower fire that the public discourse that stigmatized communities like North Kensington infected community relations, and deepened the collective trauma of the neighbourhood in a manner that would have been unthinkable if an apartment block in South Kensington had caught fire (Shannahan, 2022).

During Life on the Breadline, Revd Al Barrett (Interview June 2020) alluded to the impact of such stigma on the people alongside whom he lived and worked on the Bromford estate. Barrett suggested that 'neighbours in communities like ours feel doubly stigmatised ... somehow they're made out to be the problem; they're a drain on the state, whilst at the same time being punished through punitive benefits sanctions and the removal of vital services.' Writing about his experience growing up on the Pollok housing estate in Glasgow, Darren McGarvey (2017) makes a similar point, suggesting that multigenerational experiences of social exclusion and the negative stereotyping of outer city housing estates become internalized and reinforce the moralistic public discourse that blames people who are living in poverty for being poor. Stigmatizing public discourse that demonizes marginalized communities and people experiencing poverty is a form of epistemic violence that can foster debilitating shame and the internalization of feelings of worthlessness (Chase and Walker, 2012) as our Life on the Breadline studies of B30 food bank (Chapter 3), Grenfell Tower (Chapter 4), Power the Fight (Chapter 5) and Hodge Hill Church in Birmingham demonstrate.

Drawing on Michel Foucault's (2019) exploration of the construction of knowledge and the nature and exercise of power, the postcolonial critic Gayatri Spivak (1988) argued that the hegemonic valorization of Eurocentric discourse and modes of thinking during the colonial era was weaponized and used to diminish, devalue and silence the witness, voice and agency of the 'subaltern', or oppressed class. Such epistemic violence damages the soul – it stigmatizes those considered 'other' or 'less than' and, like some hegemonic form of slow violence, fosters the internalizing of shame. The political myth of austerity painted people on estates like the Firs and Bromford as 'other'. 'Community Building' rejects this narrative and the stigma it promotes. In a very different context, arising from his ministry in the East End of London, the political theologian Kenneth Leech suggests that deep-seated and enduring marginalization can fester, like an unhealed wound, over time, into 'emptiness, void and loss of meaning' (1997, p. 90).

The language of stigma has a long history that can help us to re-imagine, or 'Dub', the term and its resonance in an Age of Austerity. In the ancient world the word 'stigma' referred to the physical marking, burning or tattooing of slaves, criminals or people with mental health problems as a mark of ownership or shame. To be stigmatized was to be marked as unworthy. Within early Christian tradition emphasis was placed on the marks, or stigmata, of Jesus as he hung on the Cross. These wounds were viewed as signs of Jesus' solidarity with humanity and especially those whom society stigmatizes and see as unworthy. At the heart of the witness of liberation theology is the testimony that those who are oppressed are especially close to the God who has a preferential option for the poor (Gutiérrez, 1983, p. 204ff). Those who are stigmatized and considered unworthy stand, therefore, in a place of hermeneutical privilege. Those who bear the mark of stigma are better placed to understand the gospel than the included or the powerful. By drawing on the affirming methodology of ABCD and the transformative potential of a liberative dub hermeneutics we can re-frame the understanding of the experience of shame in communities like Bromford and, in so doing, take a tentative, nitty-gritty step towards existential emancipation.

Collective trauma and theological reflection

Standing in solidarity with people experiencing systemic poverty and the damage of the shame-inducing stigma of slow epistemic violence represents the first step on the journey towards an austerity-age theology of liberation. More than that, however, this liminal third space can be seen as a place of hermeneutical privilege. Such a perspective reflects the thrust of the Incarnation, characterizes the 'Community Building' Christian responses to poverty we identified during Life on the Breadline and resonates with the methodological approach of the first generations of liberation theologians (Gutiérrez, 1983). As we discovered during Life on the Breadline, if theology and Christian engagement are to be liberative forces there is an urgent, but often overlooked, need to sit in long-term solidarity with those whose lives are scarred by stigma and the slow violence of traumatizing poverty and shame. Such embeddedness remains all too rare, as we learned during our research, in spite of the centrality of the Incarnation in the reflections of almost all of the national and regional Church leaders who spoke to us during Life on the Breadline.

The emergence of pastoral trauma theologies in the early years of the twenty-first century, especially in the US and the UK, has begun to provide political theologians with a new way of envisaging systemic poverty and seemingly unending austerity. Drawing on insights from a multi-disciplinary range of trauma theorists such as Cathy Caruth (1996), Kirby Farrell (1998) and Susannah Radstone (2007) and pastoral and practical theologians such as Shelly Rambo (2010) in the USA, Karen O'Donnell and Katie Cross (2020; 2022) in the UK have fashioned a liberative feminist model of trauma theology. This has begun to inform and enrich theological analyses of the slow epistemic violence of systemic poverty, as seen in my own (2022) reflections on our Life on the Breadline Grenfell Tower fire case study and housing injustice in austerity-age Britain, and Wren Radford's (2022b) discussion of the work of the Poverty

Truth Commissions in Glasgow and Greater Manchester. Trauma theologians such as Rambo, O'Donnell and Cross offer three important insights to all of us who are striving to find a contextually credible liberative theological response to austerity-age poverty and the damage it causes. First, as Rambo (2010; 2019) notes, trauma theory can help theologians to sit with people in the mess, lament and unresolved pain of oppression far more honestly than classical approaches to theodicy that seek to rationalize suffering or reframe it within ill-fitting redemptive clothing. As I have noted, the nitty-gritty hermeneutics of Pinn (1999) can help us to sit within such pain and see it as a source of unkempt revelation, rather than rushing to fashion it into a new liberative discourse. Austerity-age theologies of liberation that integrate the kind of 'Community Building' approach to poverty that we encountered during Life on the Breadline need to ensure that lament, anger and trauma are not spiritualized or explained away. There can be no true emancipation if we rush past pain. Second, O'Donnell and Cross remind us that trauma rumbles on and its damage is not easily overcome (2022, p. 335). It is, therefore, essential for austerity-age theologies of liberation to prioritize long-term solidarity. Third, as a result, when engaging with the trauma of austerity-age poverty, theologians and faith-based activists need the faith and the patience to stand with people, to listen before they speak and to build community in collaboration with others. Only then does it become possible for 'Community Building' to earn the trust and credibility needed for the Church to play an important role fashioning a *Shalom*-centred spirituality of holistic liberation and egalitarian human security that can gain traction in marginalized communities.

Trauma can often be individualized, but it has the capacity to rupture collective well-being, as our Life on the Breadline Grenfell Tower fire study demonstrated (Shannahan, 2022). Gilad Hirschberger describes trauma as 'a cataclysmic event that shatters the basic fabric of society' (2018, p. 1). Such collective trauma can rupture the narratives of meaning, belonging and truth that bind us (Sewell and Williams, 2002, p. 205ff). It is within such a context that 'Community Building' Christian responses to poverty are forged as we discovered in relation to homelessness and Grenfell Tower, and the evolving ministry of Hodge Hill Church in East Birmingham. Such approaches are characterized by a vision of the Incarnation that is synonymous with solidarity as I discuss below.

Incarnation – presence and solidarity

Arising from the anguish of diminishment, exclusion and marginalization, 'Community Building' responses to poverty are rooted in a relational bottom-up Incarnational theology. In theological terms the Incarnation is scandalous and politically revolutionary in its insistence that the God who created the universe becomes our brother in the person of Jesus of Nazareth – salvation through solidarity. Such a conviction has the potential to energize, sharpen and shape liberative 'Community Building' responses to contemporary poverty. Too often, however, framings of this fundamental Christian doctrine and the assertion within John 1.14 that God becomes one of us, with us – our brother – are individualized, spiritualized and depoliticized.

Common-good thinking and Catholic Social Teaching framing of the Incarnation is evident, if not always acknowledged, within 'Community Building' responses to austerity-age poverty. In particular, the emphasis within Catholic Social Teaching on the inherent dignity and worth of all people, the gospel calling to conscious long-term solidarity with marginalized and oppressed communities (Gutiérrez, 1974; 1983) and the pivotal importance of recognizing that our interdependence is the basis of shared human flourishing and the common good shape 'Community Building' praxis (Rowlands, 2021). Viewed in this way, the Incarnation becomes a challenge to isolation, atomization, individualization, separatism and hierarchy. 'The Word becomes flesh and lives among us' (John 1.14), challenging the Church to commit to a comparable radical presence as the building block for transforming the 'structural injustice' of poverty and building sustainable community. 'Community Building' rests on a theology of presence, solidarity, companionship and trust – a commitment to patient, long-term 'inside-out' relationship-based mission, rather than a reliance on short-term social action by top-down activists and a vision of the Church as a rooted and contextualized Kingdom movement. Al Barrett speaks of the importance of a quiet, convivial but determined Incarnational presence on the Firs and Bromford estate (2018, p. 84). Church becomes an open-ended and inclusive gathering, often taking place way beyond the traditional notion of a gathered congregation, as evidenced by the Bromford Passion Play and the Real Junk Food Kitchen that take place on the estate. Barrett suggests that the 'Community Building' vocation of public theology

> … takes flesh in the Firs and Bromford in … finding and sometimes creating and convening, 'micro-public' spaces, 'bumping spaces where

people from diverse ethnicities, ages, genders, backgrounds and abilities encounter each other, grow in trust … and learn to engage with each other in conversations about what we share, where we differ, and what we might do together to further deepen our connections to each other and within the wider world. (Barrett, 2018, p. 88)

Community building as holistic missiology

The Incarnational 'Community Building' responses to austerity-age poverty that we explored during Life on the Breadline arise from long-term engagement alongside stigmatized communities scarred by the multidimensional trauma and slow violence of structural injustice. This approach to engagement in the public sphere is characterized by an intersectional missiology focused on building communities of solidarity within which the dignity and worth of all people is affirmed, stigma and social exclusion are resisted, and an alternative vision of inclusive community is nourished. By engaging honestly with the messy pain of shame-inducing public discourse and resisting the temptation to rely on top-down 'Campaigning' interventions intended to challenge structural injustice because of the ways in which they can further disregard, demean and disempower people experiencing poverty, 'Community Building' missiology enables a refocusing on gift, hospitality, reciprocity, possibility, potential and holistic justice. In this vein, Al Barrett and Ruth Harley (2020) dare the institutional Church to re-balance its perspective and re-define its understanding of centre and margins. Change, they suggest, comes from the outside-in. Those whom we define as marginalized are the ones who have a word of wisdom to share – if we have ears to hear and eyes to see.

Drawing on the lessons that the concept and practice of intersectionality (Crenshaw, 1989; May, 2015; Ji-Sun Kim and Shaw, 2018) can teach us about the complexity of context, the plurality of our experience and the multidimensional nature of poverty and its overcoming, 'Community Building' approaches to structural injustice remind us of the liberative potential of the Hebrew concept of *Shalom*. The term *Shalom* is mentioned more than 500 times in the Bible. Whilst the word is often translated as 'peace', it is, in truth, a far richer idea than such a one-dimensional translation implies. We need to avoid the temptation to adopt a reductionist mindset when reflecting on this multidimensional concept. Within the Hebrew Scriptures the term is better translated as 'wholeness', comparable in some senses to Christian understandings of the common good, or even its secular counterpart human security. The concept of *Shalom*, therefore, can refer to the 'peace' and 'wholeness' of individuals, communities or whole societies. The Anabaptist theologian Perry Yoder suggests that *Shalom* within the Bible can best be understood as a description of the intersectional and multi-dimensional nature of social justice (1997, p. 5ff). *Shalom* speaks to us of the building of inclusive, egalitarian communities characterized by an attention to holistic individual and communal well-being. Engaging with *Shalom*-based thinking reminds us that the 'Community Building' response to austerity-age poverty should not be seen in isolation from its broader integrated approach to multiple political, economic and existential patterns of oppression and fashioning individual and collective wholeness, flourishing and the common good.

Church as companion on the journey

'Community Building' approaches to austerity-age poverty paint a picture of the Church as an empathetic companion and are rooted in an unconditional and long-term pastoral commitment to people who are experiencing poverty. The expressions of this approach that we identified during Life on the Breadline reflect an Incarnational and contextual understanding of ecclesiology and a liberative Christology that foregrounds Jesus' radical solidarity with marginalized communities. Many of the church leaders with whom we spoke during Life on the Breadline articulated a clear commitment to the Church's calling to 'transform structures of injustice' and become what Pope Francis called 'a poor Church for the poor'.

Three of our ethnographic case studies offer glimpses of such embedded ecclesiology. First, as I demonstrated in Chapter 4, the role Notting Hill Methodist Church played as a space of support, unconditional hospitality and sanctuary following the Grenfell Tower fire and as an informal anchor institution in the struggles for housing justice that followed resulted from its half-century long embeddedness as companion to marginalized communities in North Kensington. Second, as I noted Chapter 5, the United Reformed Inspire Centre in Manchester has reflected a social enterprise influenced 'Community Building' ethic in its organic development since its inception. Third, as I show in this chapter, Hodge Hill Church in Birmingham exemplifies the multidimensional nature of 'Community Building' missiology and liberative ecclesiology through its perceptive use of ABCD. However, many of the Church leaders with whom we spoke during our research acknowledged that such embedded solidarity is all too rare and admitted that the institutional Church in the UK is often cushioned from the raw pain of debilitating poverty and the traumatizing damage it causes.

During Life on the Breadline, a Church of England vicar from Lincolnshire told us that 'Church leaders are removed from day-to-day contact with poverty. People in church see it and experience it every day' (Life on the Breadline online survey 2020). Revd Micky Youngson, the former President of the Conference of the British Methodist Church (Interview 2020) reflected on this lack of engagement and understanding when we interviewed her: 'John Wesley suggested that the reason the rich don't help the poor is because they don't spend any time with them. They don't understand their living conditions.' Speaking of the Methodist Church, she suggested that –

> The demography of the Methodist Church … is of people who are relatively protected if only by their age … I think the Church has continued to respond to the needs of the communities that we're in. The problem is we're less in the communities of abject need than we are in more comfortable communities.

Youngson's nuanced reflection pinpoints the nature of the dilemma facing a declining institutional Church that 'Cares' but is removed from key centres of pain and struggle. How can the Church respond to the *Kairos* challenge? I reflect further on this question in the closing two chapters of this book.

'Caring', 'Campaigning and Advocacy' and 'Self-help and Enterprise' Christian approaches to poverty, while valuable in different ways, can be semi-detached and distant from the everyday realities of austerity. Commitment to transforming structural injustice, providing vital emergency support and pastoral care, and enabling people experiencing poverty to realize their entrepreneurial spirit are vital aspects of the Church's calling. However, in the face of the grinding slow violence of austerity a caring, campaigning and empowering top-down Church 'for the poor' is not enough. Pinn's nitty-gritty hermeneutics can enable theology to engage with the messy and multidimensional nature of poverty in an honest manner that does not smooth away the raw realities of violating austerity and the Church's ambivalent record in embodying the liberative gospel it proclaims.

In a similar manner, a bottom-up contextualized 'Community Building' approach can teach us about the importance of sitting with people in the mess, stigma and trauma of contemporary poverty as a companion. Such an approach to ecclesiology can help us to begin to fashion a credible vision of what a Church 'of the poor' might look like. A generation ago, in his critique of what he called 'progressive theology', Gutiérrez argued that the Church needs to re-orient itself and re-imagine theological reflection (1983, p. 92ff). Instead of focusing on the so-called 'non-believer', he argued that we need to focus on the experiences, fears and hope of those whom society sees as 'non-persons'. 'Community Building' approaches to contemporary poverty invite us to look afresh at the way we think and act as Church – to foreground the experience of people whose lives are scarred by austerity and to place those whom society treats as worthless at the heart of the Church's life. On the margins no longer, but centre-stage.

'Community Building' places an emphasis on a holistic theological anthropology which highlights the agency and dignity and potential of people experiencing poverty – active subjects with experience and gifts and not passive objects in need of rescuing by people who don't share their experience. This perspective is often accompanied by a missiology that draws on the concept of *Shalom* to address the multidimensional nature of individual and communal life and our intersectional experience of poverty.

The *Shalom* oriented missiology and Incarnational theology that characterize 'Community Building' responses to poverty give rise to holistic contextualized understandings of ecclesiology (Barrett, 2018, p. 87ff; 2020). Al Barrett sketches a brief outline of some of the features of a 'Community Building' ecclesiology (2018, pp. 88–9). He offers three short reflections that are relevant way beyond Hodge Hill. First, there is a need to resist the top-down temptation to implicitly assume that the Church creates, owns or governs spaces of liberative encounter and life-enhancing mutuality. Such liminal spaces are shared and emerge when, and only when, the Church learns to be what Barrett calls 'radically receptive' (2018, p. 89). Second, there is a need to de-centre the institutional Church and to place those who are perceived to live on the margins at the centre of new life-giving communities of faith because 'in the borderlands giving and receiving are mutual'. Third, ABCD 'Community Building' challenges the Church to engage in what Barrett calls 'penitential listening' (2018, p. 89) as a step on the journey to the shared building of inclusive egalitarian communities and a dynamic movement-shaped Church. Before a liberative Christian movement can arise, the institutional Church needs to shake itself free of old habits that hem it in, hinder its capacity to forge organic liberative praxis and 'transform structural injustice' and tie it to hierarchical welfare-based reformist visions of the common good.

Gutiérrez (1974, p. 205) speaks of the need for conversion and Freire (1970) for conscientization as preludes to the fashioning of credible theologies of liberation. Segundo (1976) urges us to adopt a hermeneutics of suspicion and Pinn (1999) to resist the temptation to smooth away contradiction in the name of liberation and adopt, instead, a 'nitty-gritty' hermeneutics that engages honestly with untidiness, mess, plurality and traumatizing pain. In the context of more than a decade of austerity and a so-called 'cost of living crisis' in breadline-Britain and a 'Caring' but distant institutionalized Church, Barrett's (2018) perceptive and timely call for humility, repentance, engagement and a willingness to learn from people with experience of poverty builds on this tradition and needs to play a role in the dub hermeneutics needed to fashion a contemporary theology of liberation. But is the Church ready to listen?

'Community Building' – glimpses from Life on the Breadline

The 'Community Building' approach to contemporary poverty was particularly evident in three of our Life on the Breadline case studies and in the reflections of a number of regional and national Church leaders. In all three case studies it is important to note that the use of the 'Community Building' approach was combined with elements of the 'Caring' and the 'Campaigning' forms of Christian engagement with austerity-age poverty as well as aspects of the 'Enterprise' response.

Community building in Hodge Hill

The 'Community Building' response to austerity-age poverty and structural injustice characterizes Hodge Hill Church's engagement in the public sphere and is built around the framework provided by Asset-Based Community Development (ABCD). During Life on the Breadline, Al Barrett (Interview 2020) spoke of the way in which the Hodge Hill Church saw an ABCD informed ecclesiology of presence and solidarity that resists any use of what he termed 'rescuer language' as a way of responding to what he called 'a deficit in empathy'. ABCD is rooted in the community work research of John McKnight and John Kretzmann (1993) alongside socially excluded communities in the United States. In recent decades, Cormac Russell has sought to develop a UK-focused approach to ABCD, which the people of Hodge Hill Church have drawn upon in their own work (Russell and McKnight, 2022).

On the basis of their experience, Kretzmann and McKnight (1993) argued that dominant community development perspectives were premised on deficit-based assumptions that revolved around top-down institutional interventions intended to address what were perceived as social problems. Such an approach, they argued (1993), disempowered local people by beginning with the weaknesses and absences within a community, rather than people's strengths and experience. I discuss the principles of ABCD, as well as its possible limitations and critiques towards the end of this chapter. At this point, it is sufficient to recognize the way in which the perspective informs 'Community Building' Christian responses to austerity-age poverty. As I have already noted, in statistical terms, Hodge Hill, and the Bromford estate in particular, is one of the most multiply deprived neighbourhoods in England and Wales. However, in its Street Connecting, Common Ground Community and Worth Unlimited children's and youth work, Hodge Hill Church paints a contrasting, much more nuanced, picture of a community that is enriched by the ways in which people share their gifts, experience and skills (Denning et al., 2021). 'Community Building' in Hodge Hill is premised on Cormac Russell and John McKnight's (2022) argument that ABCD enables holistic liberation because it begins with what is strong in a community, rather than what is wrong.

At the heart of Hodge Hill's approach to 'Community Building' lies the Street Connectors initiative within which local people seek to connect neighbours, foster relationships and build an inclusive community as one way of subverting the negative self-image of residents that has been fostered by the stigmatizing public discourse that paints Hodge Hill as a neighbourhood of 'skivers' and 'scroungers'. By affirming people and fostering empathetic connections between them, Street Connectors implicitly challenge the 'poverty of relationships' and 'poverty of identity' that Al Barrett suggests damage the social fabric of Hodge Hill by encouraging a relational 'politics of empathy' and a shared commitment to building community (Interview 2020). Such 'Community Building' is built on a foundation of 'Caring' and 'Social Enterprise' and can pave the way for localized 'Advocacy' and illustrates both the way in which Christian approaches to poverty interweave and the argument I made in Chapter 3 that it is possible to see 'Caring' as a form of relational empathetic politics (Tronto, 2020) in an uncaring and structurally unjust society that disregards the social importance of the common good.

Community building in the work of Church Action on Poverty

As I discussed in Chapter 4, the work of Church Action on Poverty exemplifies the 'Campaigning and Advocacy' approach to engaging with austerity-age poverty. However, it is important, as I noted in Chapter

2, to recognize the porous and evolving nature of the ecosystem of Christian approaches to poverty that we uncovered during our Life on the Breadline research. These are evolving approaches, not fixed ideal types. Consequently, it is not surprising that Church Action's activism includes aspects of the 'Community Building' approach to responding to poverty. Two of Church Action's programmes offer varying examples of their approach to 'Campaigning' informed 'Community Building'. First, as an expression of its determination to emphasize the dignity, agency and power of people experiencing poverty, Church Action has supported the grassroots development of small Self-Reliant Groups (SRGs), largely in the North-West of England. Self-Reliant Groups reflect elements of the 'Self-Help and Enterprise' model of Christian engagement with poverty, as well as the 'Community Building' approach. SRGs are small groups of friends, often, but not always living in the same community, who meet together regularly in a purposive manner to save small sums of money, offer mutual support and share their skills and experience to develop ideas for localized small-scale social or business enterprise as a means of enhancing their own dignity, agency and power. Such small SRGs revolve around an ethic of solidarity and mutual care and are similar, in some respects, to the Small Powerful Groups developed by the Wevolution network in Scotland.[1]

When we spoke with him during Life on the Breadline, Niall Cooper, the Director of Church Action on Poverty from 1997 to 2025, reflected on what he suggested is the power of 'small groups of people if they use their power and are willing to speak out' (Interview 2020). Cooper spoke about Church Action's SRGs as 'people taking action to empower themselves [building] their own resilience and out of that picking issues where they can influence public policy' (Interview 2020). For Cooper, therefore, SRGs utilize 'Community Building' and 'Self-Help and Enterprise' approaches to 'Campaign' and 'Advocate' for policy change. Church Action's Sarah Purcell spoke about the SRGs in more detail as forms of empowering 'Enterprise' influenced 'Community Building':

> Small groups of people, usually women, come together and maybe learn a skill and then try to create some kind of enterprise between them ... each member puts in, maybe a pound a week, to a general pot ... Then the group decides what to do with that money; whether it goes to each member, or whether it goes towards the group and they can put it towards training and education and various things. So ... I suppose we're trying to identify practical responses to poverty. (Interview 2020)

Whilst it is important to recognize that Self-Reliant Groups are not specifically faith-based, they do bear some similarities with the Base Ecclesial Communities that paved the way for the development of Latin American liberation theology. Church Action is, at the time of writing, working alongside a Welsh NGO called Purple Shoots to develop training for local churches wanting to establish faith-inspired SRGs.[2]

A second, quite different, example of Church Action on Poverty's 'Community Building' work relates to its Church on the Margins initiative, which was established in 2020 in response to the challenge that Pope Francis laid before the Church when he was elected to the Papacy in 2013 to become a Church of and for the Poor. Pope Francis spoke publicly about the Church's calling to embody its commitment to God's preferential option for the poor. In response to the Pope's statements, Church Action on Poverty developed a report of short reflections entitled *Church of the Poor?* (Purcell and Purcell, 2016). In the report's introduction, Niall Cooper asked three crucial questions: 'Do we really believe that God can be found at the margins; do we really believe in a countercultural church of and for the poor; are we prepared to let go of our own power?' (2016, p. 3). Church Action's Church on the Margins initiative arose from the 2016 report and was committed to challenging the institutional Church's withdrawal from poor urban communities and to 'ensuring the church is present in communities on the margins ... in ways which recognise that people in poverty have agency and dignity and leadership capacity' (Cooper; Interview 2020). Cooper views the Church on the Margins initiative in two ways. First, it is an attempt to ensure that churches 'create space for low-income people to exercise leadership' and second, part of a bigger commitment to 'building a social movement of people in poor communities who are able to exercise agency' (Interview 2020). At the time of writing, Church on the Margins remains largely confined to Greater Manchester and South Yorkshire. However, its commitment to fostering small 'communities of praxis', similar to the Base Ecclesial Communities of Latin American liberation theology, can challenge the Church to embody its verbal commitment to God's preferential option for the poor. Furthermore, the worship and educational resources it has developed had a strong influence on the British Methodist Church's establishment of its UK-wide Church at the Margins programme in 2020, which also drew on our research within Life on the Breadline.[3]

Community building at Inspire

In the previous chapter, I spoke about our Life on the Breadline case of the URC Inspire Centre in South Manchester and its use of holistic social enterprise as a means of responding to poverty and broader structural injustice. An important feature of Inspire's use of the 'Enterprise' approach to austerity-age poverty is its commitment to Incarnational long-term presence and 'Community Building'. This perspective was summarized by Ed Cox when we spoke to him during our fieldwork:

> From the outset we've recognised that everyone has something to give, even if it's not financial … [You can] address people's needs through a charitable model, a model around education and then there's a model around empowerment. We chose the empowerment model … So we are much more about enabling the community to stand on its own two feet. Material poverty is part of that because you can't stand on two feet unless you can feed yourself, but that's not our primary objective. (Interview January 2020)

Cox implicitly picks up on the language of ABCD in his description of the way in which Inspire models its approach to 'Community Building' on the conviction that gifts (or assets) and social entrepreneurship are present in local communities that can provide the foundation for inclusive and egalitarian communities within which all people can flourish. The focus at Inspire is on 'Enterprise'-oriented 'Community Building' and empowerment as Cox made clear in conversation: 'The majority of stories of Jesus' ministry were about setting people on their own two feet – tackling the injustices that were holding them down' (Interview January 2020). Inspire consciously seeks to avoid the 'sticking plaster stuff that goes on in the name of tackling poverty'. Cox spoke about the ecclesiological and theological vision that underpins and shapes Inspire's work. He articulated a bottom-up Incarnational ecclesiological vision characterized by a relational approach to 'Community Building', comparable to that we discovered in Hodge Hill, and a strong sense that the Church is called to embody a commitment to reflecting God's active liberative presence in and through the whole of life (the *missio Dei*). Cox summarized:

> God is doing God's mission all of the time. In the café, in the interactions between people who wouldn't duck in the door of a church. But in the conversations that they have and the way they interact with one another, in the kind of ethos of what we're trying to do here; the spirit of God is moving. (Interview January 2020)

Church leaders' reflections

Very few of the national and regional Church leaders who participated in Life on the Breadline spoke specifically about 'Community Building' approaches to the Church's engagement with contemporary poverty. However, many did allude to such a perspective in their reflections on the holistic implications of the Incarnation for ecclesiology and mission. A United Reformed Church leader from South Yorkshire hinted at a holistic 'Community Building'-oriented understanding of the Incarnation as the basis for the Church's commitment to the common good and to challenging the structural injustice that damages and destroys: 'The incarnate Christ is at the heart of the world, its people's lives, relationships, societies and cultures, communities and nations. Therefore, all that damages the well-being, peace and justice of these is at the heart of God' (Life on the Breadline online survey 2020).

Building on this, an Anglican leader from Liverpool (Life on the Breadline online survey 2020) offered an implicit critique of implicationist theologies of social action that separate an individual's relationship with God from community development and social justice. She pointed towards the kind of integrated approach to which I have alluded in previous chapters. The existential and the economic are intimately interconnected: 'Mission and discipleship are social action … Personal salvation is found in community redemption.' Another Anglican respondent from Nottingham told us that, 'The gospel is about transformation and freedom – Impacting individuals, communities, nations and the world. It's the Matthew 25 agenda' (Life on the Breadline online survey 2020). A Methodist Superintendent Minister from the North-East of England summarized the challenge that this mindset poses to the Church: 'It will mean a change of attitudes and language, also a rethink of what church looks like and how faith is expressed. Congregations need to be able to reflect on what their words and actions actually say to the communities in which we live and worship' (Life on the Breadline online survey 2020).

These reflections from Church leaders who participated in Life on the Breadline highlight four insights that lie at the heart of 'Community Building' responses to austerity-age poverty, which can play a key role in the forging of a new theology of liberation. First, because of the Incarnation, God doesn't just become our brother in Jesus but sits at the heart of human life, at one with the struggles of oppressed individuals and communities. God becomes completely engaged, challenging a 'Caring' but disengaged Church. Second, because of this, the structural injustice of systemic poverty and all that damages the human security of marginalized communities damages God, who suffers with those who suffer. Third, the tendency on the part of some Church leaders to imply a separation, between personal faith and social action and the common appeal to an implicationist welfare-based common good, reflects a misunderstanding of a gospel within which personal and communal redemption are completely intertwined. Fourth, such a vision demands an ecclesiological revolution – a radical reimagining of Christian community in an age diminished by structural injustice.

Dubbing 'Community Building'

The examples of 'Community Building' that we identified during Life on the Breadline show that the approach can play a pivotal role in the development of a contextualized and holistic austerity-age theology of liberation. However, unless it is deployed in dialogue with aspects of the other Christian approaches to contemporary poverty that we explored during fieldwork and the limitations of the approach are addressed it will not fulfil this progressive potential. We need to dub 'Community Building'. A careful use of a nitty-gritty informed hermeneutics of suspicion can help us to identify the key questions that need to be asked about the approach's engagement with systems of power.

A use of 'Community Building' within an austerity-age theology of liberation needs to address three challenges. First, whilst the 'Community Building' that we studied during Life on the Breadline, exhibited a strong use of bridging social capital, its translation into the linking capital that is more capable of resourcing community development in systemically unequal contexts was sporadic. Second, whilst its grassroots approach, embedded ecclesiology and focus on the nuances of local communities is a strength of 'Community Building', it could be argued that this detailed attention to the specificity of a local context could lead to a localism that neglects the importance of wider power structures and broader systemic inequalities. Third, the empathetic focus on challenging paralysing stigma and enhancing individual agency is centrally important. However, it is possible that this pastoral focus on the individual might cloud a recognition of the need for systemic change in a structurally unjust society.

Once the use of a nitty-gritty hermeneutics of suspicion has enabled us to paint an honest and holistic picture of 'Community Building', helped us to recognize and understand the ways in which the approach engages with systems of power, and enabled us to ask and respond to these key questions it becomes possible to begin to engage with the reconstructive capacity of dub practice. Such a process, when premised on a clear emancipatory ethic, can interweave the strengths of 'Community Building' with the liberative, pastoral and empowering capacity of dubbed approaches to 'Caring', 'Campaigning and Advocacy' and 'Enterprise and Self-Help' to foster the development of a holistic theology of liberation that is rooted in a transformational *Shalom* spirituality that can help the Church to live up to its calling to 'transform structural injustice'. The focus within 'Community Building' on the relational radicalism of the Incarnation enables a dubbed approach to challenge not just isolationism, stigma, atomization and hierarchy but the systemic injustice and cultural violence that feeds these traumatizing phenomena. Furthermore, the development of an embedded ecclesiology of solidarity, a sitting with people in their trauma, pain and lament and the fostering of trust-based liminal spaces of shared action for change enables a dubbed and conscientized 'Campaigning and Advocacy' oriented 'Community Building' to articulate a liberative vision that revolves around the hermeneutical privilege of the stigmatized. Those who have been hurt the most become the authors of a new theology of holistic liberation.

Conclusion

This chapter has introduced and analysed the fourth Christian approach to austerity-age poverty that we uncovered during Life on the Breadline. I have discussed the deeply contextual and iterative nature of 'Community Building' and contrasted it with other Christian approaches to poverty. I have explored the ways in which 'Community Building' envisions the Church as a long-term companion committed to mutual learning and human flourishing. I have demonstrated the embeddedness that 'Community Building' has, largely because of its roots in a relational Incarnational spirituality, a holistic understanding of poverty, an inclusive vision of an egalitarian common good and its use of Asset-Based Community Development. Furthermore, I have argued that this approach enables the fashioning of a liberative ecclesiology of solidarity and presence.

I have drawn on examples from Life on the Breadline case studies, such as Hodge Hill's Street Connectors, the Self-Reliant Groups developed by Church Action on Poverty and the radical hospitality-focused 'Community Building' of the Inspire Centre in Manchester, to discuss the approach's emphasis on relational poverty, presence, affirmation and a focus on the gifts of people experiencing poverty, rather than the deficits in a community. I have shown how the approach, particularly in Hodge Hill, can help to challenge the existential damage caused by shame-inducing narratives of stigma and blame and how this experience has been transformed, so it becomes a space of hermeneutical privilege – the centre, not the margins. I have argued that 'Community Building' reconnects a 'Caring' but often disengaged Church with the raw everyday realities of austerity and that it can play a key role in the development of a re-imagined theology of liberation. However, I have also suggested that it can lack a clear focus on wider structural injustice and systemic economic and political causes of poverty and inequality.

By dubbing 'Community Building' on the basis of a careful hermeneutics of suspicion and drawing it into closer dialogue with aspects of 'Campaigning and Advocacy', the approach can realize its potential to play a key role in a theology that fashions the liberative praxis needed to 'transform structural injustice' and foster a holistic, *Shalom*-oriented vision of an egalitarian common good.

Notes

1 For more details about Wevolution, see https://wevolution.org.uk/, accessed 18.12. 2024.

2 For more details about Purple Shoots, see https://purpleshoots.org/church-partnerships/, accessed 18.12.2024.

3 For more information about the Church on the Margins initiative see https://www.church-poverty.org.uk/what-we-do/cotm/, accessed 24.10.2025. For more information about the Methodist Church at the Margins initiative see https://media.methodist.org.uk/media/documents/church-at-the-margins-leaflet_QsOB-BMl.pdf.

7

Theology's *Kairos* Moment

Introduction

Theologians have talked a lot about God's preferential option for the poor. Too often, however, such talk tends to be generalized, apolitical and book-bound – an affirmation of the core values of Latin American liberation theology, rather than a contextualized, empirically-based liberative theological analysis of poverty in breadline Britain. Our Life on the Breadline research modelled the iterative approach to fieldwork-led contextual political theology that can act as a resource for all seeking an austerity-age theology of liberation. In a seemingly unending Age of Austerity and debilitating poverty we need more than articulate articles, inspirational sermons and theological good intentions. Theology stands at a crossroads. This is a *Kairos* moment – a time of judgement and opportunity for theology and for the Church. The time has come for theologians to step up to the plate and to join our social science colleagues in responding to the clear and present danger that austerity represents.

In previous chapters I have introduced, illustrated and analysed the four broad approaches to the Christian engagement with austerity-age poverty that we identified during our Life on the Breadline fieldwork. I turn now, in the final two chapters, to an exploration of the implications of our research for the future of liberative political theology and for the Church's engagement with systemic poverty and structural injustice. In Chapter 8, I begin to sketch out some of the contours of a new contextualized austerity-age theology of liberation. First, however, in this chapter, I need to lay the foundations for such a fieldwork-led approach to liberative political theology by exploring four key themes – the nature of contemporary theology's *Kairos* moment; the need for a thoroughly interdisciplinary theological methodology; the importance of thinking in intersectional terms; and a re-imagining of the Church's role in the public sphere. Before I turn to these key themes, however, I should summarize the strengths and weaknesses of the 'Caring', 'Campaigning and Advocacy', 'Self-help and Enterprise' and 'Community

Building' approaches to austerity-age poverty that we identified during Life on the Breadline and which I have discussed in previous chapters.

Taking stock – Christian responses to austerity-age poverty

Life on the Breadline was the first major fieldwork led political theology project to identify, analyse and learn from four distinct but intersecting Christian responses to austerity-age poverty in the UK – 'Caring', 'Campaigning and Advocacy', 'Self-help and Enterprise' and 'Community Building'. It is tempting to view this interpretive framework as a typology of Christian social action during the Age of Austerity. The systematizing and analytical capacity provided by typological framing can enable rigour and greater structure to theological analyses of contemporary poverty. However, as I have shown in previous chapters, the structure that typologies appear to offer needs to be handled with care if we are to avoid ossifying living and evolving traditions of social action and Christian theology. Consequently, it is perhaps more useful to think of the differing approaches to the Church's engagement with systemic poverty that we identified during Life on the Breadline as distinct, but overlapping and still evolving traditions of ecclesiology, missiology and social ethics within a dynamic ecosystem of Christian social action. Such a nitty-gritty and provisional approach can help us to better understand the strengths and weaknesses of 'Caring', 'Campaigning and Advocacy', 'Self-help and Enterprise' and 'Community Building' engagements with austerity-age poverty, their relationship with each other and their capacity to provide the foundations for the new, contextualized austerity-age theology of liberation that is needed if the Church is to live up to its calling to 'transform structural injustice' and embody God's preferential option for the poor.

As I have shown in previous chapters these four approaches to the Christian engagement with austerity-age poverty meet immediate physical, financial, emotional and spiritual needs; challenge systemic injustice; speak truth to power; campaign for structural economic and political change; overcome shame-inducing stigma and enable, empower and build self-esteem and community. Each approach identifies the need for four kinds of change. First, such changes can relate to the empowerment of individual people and local communities in overcoming the internalized shame engendered by stigmatizing public, political or theological discourses. Second, change can relate to the development of life-enhancing skills, gifts or enterprise that enable personal flourishing and localized social transformation. Third, change can relate to the forging of new liberative spiritualities and deeper understandings of the transformative implications of the Bible's teaching about systemic poverty. Fourth, the change envisaged can revolve around the role the Church plays in the public sphere. Is the Church ready to move beyond welfare-based common-good social action to engage proactively and prophetically in civil society politics and ram a spoke into the wheel of structural injustice?

'Caring', 'Campaigning and Advocacy', 'Self-help and Enterprise' and 'Community Building' all respond to aspects of the damage wrought by more than a decade of traumatizing austerity, debilitating poverty and growing inequality. However, as I have argued in previous chapters, no single approach engages sufficiently holistically with our intersectional experience of the slow cultural, structural and direct violence of multi-dimensional systemic poverty to provide the basis for a new theology of liberation. Life on the Breadline demonstrated how these approaches can overlap and enhance each other, but localized illustrations of the liberative potential of such fieldwork-led holistic reflexive praxis can only take us so far. We need to translate organic holistic engagement with systemic poverty into consciously multidimensional sustained liberative praxis, dubbing 'Caring', 'Campaigning and Advocacy', 'Self-help and Enterprise' and 'Community Building' into a credible and holistic austerity-age *shalom*-oriented theology of liberation. Only such a step can begin to force debilitating poverty into retreat and enable the Church to fulfil its calling to embody God's preferential option for the poor and its commitment to 'transform the structures of injustice'.

In previous chapters I have indicated how a creative use of a process of emancipatory-focused dub hermeneutics can help us to strip these four approaches back to their foundations before rebuilding a new, reimagined approach that is premised on an *a priori* liberative ethic. Such theological dub practice can help us to draw on the strengths of 'Caring', 'Campaigning and Advocacy', 'Self-help and Enterprise' and 'Community Building' to fashion a new dialogical Christian response to austerity-age poverty that can pave the way for a creative, credible and contextual theology of liberation.

Theology's *Kairos* moment

Stretching back to the earliest Christian communities in Jerusalem, followers of Jesus have engaged with systemic poverty and structural injustice. In spite of the Church's collusion with power and money during the long centuries of Christendom, this liberative tradition has persisted, even though it has often been underground or marginalized. Since the nineteenth century, major theological movements such as the social gospel movement, Catholic Social Teaching and liberation theology have proclaimed God's preferential option for the poor. And yet, overwhelmingly such social and theological movements are either implicationist or are rooted in other times and places, rather than the here and now. As I have shown in this book, there are glimpses of such liberative praxis and theological reflection in breadline Britain. However, academic theologians have largely been found wanting during the Age of Austerity.

Since the global financial crash of 2008, whereas NGOs like Church Action on Poverty or think-tanks like Theos have produced important reports, there have been just a handful of studies of austerity-age poverty by academic theologians and only a tiny number of these papers have been rooted in extensive qualitative research (Gaston and Shakespeare, 2010; Cameron, 2014; Allen, 2016; Pemberton, 2018, 2020; Shannahan, 2019 and 2022; Shannahan and Denning, 2022). During the same period there have been numerous empirically based social science studies of austerity and of faith-based engagements with poverty since the global financial crash, particularly within human geography.

In the face of the traumatizing slow violence of systemic poverty and a decade of ideologically inspired austerity, theology has reached its tipping point. We stand at a moment of judgement, but also opportunity. This is theology's *Kairos* moment. It is time for theologians in the UK to recognize the urgent need to place austerity-age poverty at the heart of a new, liberative, interdisciplinary, intersectional fieldwork-led theology. Hesitation is no longer an option if the discipline is to retain contemporary resonance and cultural relevance – now is the time and this is the place. In the Bible, the Greek term *Kairos* is used to refer to a crisis point, or moment of opportunity. *Kairos* represents the moment when God acts to urgently challenge humanity to embody the liberative values of the gospel as seen, for example, in Mark 1.15.

The *Kairos* theologies of the late twentieth and early twenty-first centuries draw on this biblical impetus and, if only implicitly, on the existential theology of Paul Tillich (1948; 1949; 1968). Tillich served as a chaplain during World War One and was traumatized by what he witnessed in the trenches and in post-war Germany. In many respects his entire theological canon can be seen as a response to the existential crisis of these turbulent times. For Tillich, World War One and the resulting crises represented a *Kairos* moment for liberal Protestantism and for the Church's relationship with what he believed were the oppressive forces of nationalism and capitalism. Tillich's countercultural *Kairos* theology led to his embrace of democratic socialism and his opposition to the Nazis, who banned him from teaching in German universities soon after taking power in 1933. Tillich focused primarily on the existential dimensions of this *Kairos* moment. However, the critical correlation theological method he developed which brought the challenges of contemporary cultures in crisis into dialogue with core Christian teaching influenced the thinking and practice of Martin Luther King during the Civil Rights Movement in the 1960s and the later emergence of *Kairos* theologies, initially in South Africa and Palestine, but more recently in a range of contexts across the globe.

In July 1985, the government of South Africa declared a state of emergency intended to repress growing protests within Black townships, such as Soweto, against police violence and the increasing viciousness of apartheid policies. At the height of this crisis, activists and theologians gathered at what they believed was a *Kairos* moment for South Africa and for the Church in the face of racialized oppression. The resulting *Kairos Document*, which was signed by over 150 Christian activists, Church leaders and theologians, opened with these prophetic words:

> The time has come. The moment of truth has arrived. South Africa has been plunged into a crisis that is shaking the foundations and there is every indication that the crisis has only just begun and that it will deepen and become even more threatening in the months to come. It is the KAIROS, or moment of truth not only for apartheid but also for the Church. (Kairos Theologians, 1986, p. 1)

Forged in the fires of apartheid, the *Kairos Document* stimulated liberative theological reflection within oppressed communities in other contexts facing different, but comparable, crisis moments. Perhaps the most significant of these has been the 2009 *Kairos Palestine* report, initiative and movement, which arose as a response to the Israeli Occupation of Gaza and the West Bank. The report argued that the Occupation represented a *Kairos* moment. The Church, the report suggested, was called to stand in solidarity with the Palestinian people and to challenge the Occupation. In the aftermath of *Kairos* Palestine comparable initiatives have emerged in Canada (2010), the Netherlands (2011), the Philippines (2011), Brazil (2012), the UK (2013) and the USA (2011).[1]

Whilst particular contextual factors have shaped different initiatives, several common features characterize *Kairos* theologies globally that are of relevance in the UK as theologians and the Church face our *Kairos* moment after more than a decade of austerity. Three points need to be kept in mind. First, *Kairos* theology in breadline Britain should be seen as a model of public theology that articulates the progressive role of faith in the public sphere. *Kairos* theologies remind us that the Church is challenged to move beyond welfare to a political faith intended to meet the challenge of our times and 'transform structural injustice'. As such, *Kairos* theologies represent faith-based interventions in political and popular discourse about our common life. Second, *Kairos* theologies remind us of the foundational importance of what Freire (1970) refers to as 'conscientization'. As a crisis-oriented public theology, *Kairos* theology can provide us with the tools that can help us to read the signs of the times. The fashioning of such prophetic public *Kairos* theologies rests on the forging of a widespread liberative consciousness as part of what Gramsci (2007) calls the 'cultural war of position'. Writing out of his personal involvement in the anti-Apartheid struggle, Allan Boesak reflects on the nature and importance of *Kairos* consciousness: 'A *Kairos* consciousness will observe, experience and judge the world as seen through the eyes of the suffering, the poor and the marginalized, in so doing seeing the world through the eyes of Jesus' (2016, p. 18). Third, the witness of the South African *Kairos* Document and *Kairos* Palestine demonstrates the prophetic character of *Kairos* theology and *Kairos* ecclesiology. Looking back from the vantage point of a post-Apartheid South Africa, John de Gruchy argues that *The Kairos Document* should be seen as part of the prophetic tradition of speaking truth to power that stretches back through the ministry of Jesus to the socio-economic critiques and preaching of the Hebrew Prophets (2016, p. 1). For de Gruchy, prophets like Amos, Isaiah, Jeremiah and Hosea spoke out of specific contexts about particular social and political problems. As such, therefore, *Kairos* theologies are, by their very nature, always contextual, reading the signs of the times in specific places at particular moments of crisis.

De Gruchy argues that the potential liberative impact of such prophetic *Kairos* theologies lies in their capacity to generate and feed sustainable and impactful prophetic ecclesiologies (2016, p. 6). Unless the liberative intentions of *Kairos* theologies are translated into prophetic practice, therefore, it is unlikely that they will resource the transformation of structural injustice to which the Church claims it is called. Such prophetic practice is needed in breadline Britain as we stand at our *Kairos* moment.

Our Life on the Breadline research emerged in 2018, at the mid-point in a decade of traumatizing austerity and drew to a close in 2021 as the so-called 'cost of living crisis' that accompanied the Covid-19 pandemic lockdowns bit ever deeper. During our fieldwork it became clear in case study after case study, and in many interviews with Church leaders and practitioners, that the 'cost of living crisis' represented the almost inevitable result of ten years of austerity. This was not an unpredictable crisis but capitalism's perfect storm and a *Kairos* moment for theology and for the Church in the UK. Periodically, the Church has stood at an existential crossroads. In the face of slavery, colonialism, systemic racism in Apartheid South Africa and Jim Crow America, grinding poverty in the growing cities of Victorian England and the Nazi nightmare of Hitler's Germany. The history of the Church's response to such existential challenges reveals an ambivalent record. The Church has challenged but also colluded with and even blessed structural injustice. The debilitating violence of austerity poses a *Kairos* challenge to the twenty-first-century Church as it responds to contemporary poverty. In the face of the traumatizing violence of systemic poverty is the Church ready to ram 'a spoke' into the 'wheel' of structural injustice or will it be content to 'bandage up the wounds' of the broken?

Interdisciplinarity – more than a fad

Simple solutions to complex problems are very appealing because they do not disturb or challenge us. And yet, one-dimensional analysis, practice or policy inevitably fails to capture the breadth, depth and nuance of our three-dimensional world. It is disturbing, therefore, that theologians have, too often, implicitly assumed that we can provide those three-dimensional analyses without taking the time to see the whole picture. For too long, theologians and social scientists have tended to regard each other with varying degrees of suspicion. Secure in our disciplinary bunkers we have, too often, failed to recognize the ways in which insights from our disciplinary cousins can challenge, enrich and deepen our analysis and understanding of fundamental questions and social problems. On too many occasions social scientists still depict theology as book-bound, esoteric and disconnected from everyday life and theologians often tend to dismiss the importance of primary research and the intellectual significance of insights drawn from fieldwork in local communities.

In spite of developments in the geographies of religion and explorations of everyday theologies within the sociology of religion, there is still a tendency within the social sciences to skim over the 'Why' question and to underemphasize the pivotal importance of theological values and motivation. Whilst attention to the importance of social analysis within contextual theologies has grown, it is still the case that within theology there is little serious engagement with 'What' and 'Who' questions about context, culture and positionality. However, it would be disingenuous to suggest that nothing has changed. A number of leading researchers within practical theology, public theology, political theology, Black theology and womanist/feminist theology have adopted an increasingly interdisciplinary approach to their work.

The practical theologian Pete Ward (2012; 2022) has highlighted the importance of ethnographic methods in analyses of Christian community and is Chair of the Network for Ecclesiology and Ethnography. Within public theology, Elaine Graham has demonstrated the value of qualitative research methods within theological reflection (Graham et al., 2005; 2016), cultural studies within contextual theology (Graham, 2002; Graham et al., 2013) and sociological studies of secularization (Graham et al., 2013). Within political theology, Chris Baker (2009) has illustrated the importance of a critical dialogue with human geography and political philosophy. Robert Beckford (2000; 2006) has pioneered the extensive use of cultural studies, postcolonial criticism and diasporan studies within British Black theology, and Karen O'Donnell and Katie Cross (2020; 2022) have demonstrated the value of in-depth engagement with trauma studies within feminist theology. A growing, but still small, number of UK-based political theologians have also begun to model aspects of qualitative research, as seen, for example, in Beckford's (2000) use of case studies in his articulation of a liberative dread Black theology, Bretherton's (2010; 2015) use of ethnographic methods in his theological analyses of the involvement of faith groups in broad-based community organizing and O'Donnell and Cross's (2020) engagement with trauma studies in their development of new expressions of contextualized feminist theology.

This tentative shift signals a positive development within political, practical, Black, public and feminist/womanist theology. However, it needs to be recognized that most political theologians rarely engage in serious interdisciplinary study, beyond a critical dialogue with aspects of political philosophy or social theory. Interdisciplinarity, I would suggest, is talked about more often than it is practised. Even where political theologians adopt an interdisciplinary approach this can often be relatively selective, sporadic and superficial. At the time of writing the number of interdisciplinary analyses of austerity within political theology in the UK is tiny, as I noted in previous chapters. Several years after the conclusion of the research, it remains the case that Life on the Breadline is the only thoroughly interdisciplinary empirical theological study of the breadth of the Church's response to austerity-age poverty in the UK. As we continue to wrestle with the damage wrought by austerity, theologians need to engage far more proactively with the extensive theoretically informed empirical work of human geographers who have explored the roots and damage of systemic poverty, and the role faith-based organizations can play in responding to structural injustice. In particular, the work of Sarah Marie Hall (2019), Paul Cloke and Andrew Williams (Cloke, Williams and Thomas, 2009; Beaumont and Cloke, 2012; Cloke et al., 2019) can support the development of a more rooted, empirically rich and nuanced austerity-age theology of liberation.

At this *Kairos* moment, our Life on the Breadline research illustrates the need for challenge-led, nuanced, empathetic and thoroughly inter-disciplinary research to become the norm and not the exception within political theology. If this moment is not seized, theologians will find that we are increasingly talking only to each other and not the wider world. Our research within Life on the Breadline made it crystal clear that at the end of a decade of debilitating austerity the stakes are too high, and that academic isolationism is a luxury we cannot afford at this *Kairos* moment. Only an inherently interdisciplinary fieldwork-led political theology can provide the foundation for a culturally credible theology of liberation that has the capacity to resource a liberative ethic of *Shalom* and an egalitarian vision of the common good in breadline Britain. A deeper critical dialogue with multifaceted trauma studies (O'Donnell and Cross, 2020; Shannahan, 2022) and peace and conflict studies (Galtung, 1990) is needed if we are to fully grasp the depth and breadth of the unresolved collective suffering and systemic housing injustice that surrounds the Grenfell Tower tragedy, as I indicated in Chapters 3 and 4. Engagement with analyses of collective stigma (Garthwaite, 2016; Radford, 2022a) and its capacity to engender shame can enable a better understanding of the internalization of demeaning and debilitating tropes within public discourse that we encountered in our Hodge Hill case study, which I discussed in Chapter 6. In a similar vein a careful exploration of debates about the concept of human security (Martin and Owen, 2014) and multidimensional individual and collective vulner-abilities that originated in the work of the United Nations Development Programme can enrich analyses of structural injustice, the multifaceted impact of austerity and holistic *Shalom*-oriented explorations of the common good. I return to these debates in Chapter 8 and the ways in which they can enrich an austerity-age theology of liberation.

Life on the Breadline highlighted the tension between the Church's commitment to an egalitarian vision of the common good and a lack of everyday engagement with the traumatic realities of austerity-age poverty. Our B30 case study reveals the sincerity and value of 'Caring' but also the sense of stolen potential and repressed shame of depending on food parcels distributed by people with little direct experience of poverty. Our research suggests that the Church pays too little attention to the ambivalence of the 'Caring' approach to poverty. Whilst the Trussell Trust has become increasingly aware of such ambivalence and has moved increasingly towards an 'Advocacy'-focused approach, further attention needs to be placed on the unintended feelings of shame and dependency that can often become interconnected with 'Caring' responses to poverty. In Chapter 6, in relation to our case studies of Church Action on Poverty and Hodge Hill Church in Birmingham, I illustrated how faith-based engagements with the 'Enterprise' and 'Community Building'-oriented Local Pantry initiatives developed initially by Church Action are better placed to enhance the dignity and agency of people using them. Stuart was a client at B30 food bank and summarized the existential damage caused by poverty. His comment resonates with the reflections of Revd Al Barrett from Hodge Hill on the insidious impact of what he called a 'poverty of relationships' and a 'poverty of identity' and Tamez's (1982) argument that poverty attacks the divine image within each one of us. Stuart said, 'Poverty affects people's moods. Everybody seems to be miserable, depressed, anxious, worried, a lot of debt, struggling for food and … the basics of life' (B30 Interview 2019). As the Church seeks to respond to austerity-age poverty only an approach that sits with people in their lament and trauma will stand a chance of subverting the existential narratives that feed systemic poverty in the twenty-first century. As the Poverty Truth Network remind us, 'Nothing about us without us is for us.'

Contextual theology and the importance of fieldwork

It is important for all who are committed to the development of a credible interdisciplinary austerity-age theology of liberation to grasp the foundational importance of extensive fieldwork as an essential element of theological research. This is not, it should be stressed, to dismiss the insights gained through purely theoretical theological, philosophical or sociological research. The dismissal of the value of theoretical research as inherently derivative by some social scientists is as mistaken and myopic as the rejection of fieldwork as intellectually superficial by some theologians. If it is to achieve its potential to generate new theological perspectives, a multidimensional and intersectional critical consciousness and the breadth and depth of liberative praxis needed to 'transform structures of injustice' an austerity-age theology of liberation needs to embrace empirical and theoretical research in equal measure.

In Chapter 2, I discussed the central importance of extensive fieldwork within our Life on the Breadline qualitative research. Our commitment to the pivotal importance of primary research as an essential building block within an austerity-age theology of liberation reflected a conviction that contextual theology needs to become the normative methodological perspective within political, public and practical theology. The suggestion that theology somehow floats free, unconstrained and universal is, ironically, a deeply contextualized and ideologically informed claim that only those who enjoy the security and power borne of privilege tend to make. Theology has always been shaped by the socio-cultural context from which it arises, even if this is not recognized or acknowledged (Bevans, 1992). However, whilst all theology is shaped by context, not all theological reflection is consciously and proactively contextual. As a specific deliberative and iterative theological methodology, the sub-discipline of contextual theology first began to emerge in the late 1960s and early 1970s, at about the same time as Latin American liberation theology and Black theology in the USA.

The term 'contextualization' was first coined in place of the term 'indigenization' by the Taiwanese Presbyterian missiologist Shoki Coe in 1973 (Shenk, 2005) to reflect the need to engage critically and holistically with the breadth of a social, cultural and economic context, as opposed to focusing in a narrower sense on incorporating indigenous knowledge into, largely Eurocentric, theological and missiological frameworks. However, we need to distinguish between the recognition of the importance of contextualization and the proactive adoption of contextual theology as a specific theological method. As Pears notes, there is an important difference between the existential claim that all theology is subconsciously contextual because the way we think about and see the world is shaped by experience and social location and the conscious foregrounding of context as the primary source for particular and purposive situated theological reflection (Pears, 2009, pp. 7–9). The work of Robert Schreiter (1985), Bevans (1992) and, in a UK context, Laurie Green (1990) helped to shape the methodological contours of the emergent discipline of contextual theology, which we drew upon in Life on the Breadline. Consequently, it is important to spend a few moments summarizing their methodological insights.

Schreiter's (1985) reflections, which emerge from his experience leading a diverse Roman Catholic seminary in Chicago, played a pivotal role in shaping the philosophical tone of contextual theology in a manner that still resonates 40 years after his *Constructing Local Theologies* was published. He depicts the growing decolonizing and contextualization of Christian community within the global South and oppressed communities in the global North that began to emerge in the early 1960s as the philosophical companion of the liberation theology arising in Latin America (1985, p. 2ff). In methodological terms, theologies of liberation can be seen as expressions of the mindset and methodology found within contextual theology. Schreiter points to the central importance of rooting theological reflection in a deep analysis of the community within which we live – 'Without such an analysis, a theology can become irrelevant or a subtle tool of ideological manipulation' (1985, p. 4). Historically there has been a strong tendency for academic theology to be the individualized intellectual pursuit of privileged white men.

Schreiter suggests that contextual theology burst this bubble, emphasizing its collective, egalitarian and public nature – the context is the text from which contextual theology emerges as a communal, shared enterprise (1985, p. 16ff). 'Theology,' says Schreiter, 'is intended for a community and is not meant to remain the property of a theologian class' (1985, p. 17). Importantly, however, he warns against romanticizing the 'community as theologian' (1985, p. 17), which can, he wisely suggests, reduce theology to an ideological projection of the dominant discourses in a local community. I have argued elsewhere (Shannahan, 2010) that this was the trap that early iterations of a British liberation theology fell into during the 1980s and early 1990s. Contextual theology, for Schreiter, is a critical and empathetic dialogue between a community and those whom he calls 'professional theologians' that gives rise to a synthesis between the local and the global, the particular and the universal (1985, p. 18). The missiologist Stephen Bevans (1992/2002) builds on the foundations laid down by Schreiter, adding greater methodological clarity, thereby providing an invaluable resource for all who are committed to building an austerity-age theology of liberation.

Bevans describes six models of contextual theology that reflect a spectrum of theological standpoints from conservative perspectives to radical approaches. First, the 'translation' model seeks to identify and translate foundational Christian values into a contemporary context. Pears suggests that within Bevans' 'translation' model 'the gospel is prioritized over culture' (2009, p. 25). Second, the 'anthropological' model is premised on a positive and affirming engagement with culture, which is seen as the crucible out of which insight, discernment and revelation arise. Just as the 'translation' model appears, arguably unreflectively, to assume an unchanging Christian truth and to diminish the significance of context, the 'anthropological' model could be accused of romanticizing culture in an equally uncritical manner. Third, Bevans summarizes the 'praxis' model, which revolves around a process of social change-oriented action-reflection and has been closely aligned with a variety of theologies of liberation for more than half a century. Bevans summarizes: 'theology done in this way cannot be conceived in terms of books, essays or articles. Rather ... [it is] ... an activity, a process, a way of living' (2002, p. 74). Fourth, Bevans introduces the 'synthetic' model, which seeks to establish a dialogue between doctrine, Scripture and context. Such an approach is comparable to the correlation methodology pioneered by Paul Tillich (1951), whereby we bring our deepest existential questions into a critical dialogue with the heritage of Christian theology. Fifth, Bevans discusses the 'transcendental' model, which focuses particularly on our own spiritual quest for meaning. In a sense this approach is as much about self-realization and sanctification as it is about developing theological frameworks – theology as process, rather than project, praxis or product.

The sixth and final model that Bevans introduces is what he calls the 'countercultural' model, which he describes as a 'prophetic' model (2002, p. 119). The 'countercultural' approach is committed to social change, just like the 'praxis' model, but on the basis of a Scriptural critique of contemporary culture. Such a perspective has the potential to challenge what Galtung (1990) calls cultural violence, but can also, it should be noted, be reduced to an antagonistic conservative critique of contemporary culture. Bevans methodological survey provides an important tool for all contemporary political theologians. Considering our standpoint within Life on the Breadline and our commitment to fashioning a fieldwork-led austerity-age theology of liberation, the 'praxis' model and aspects of the 'synthetic' model were particularly useful. Furthermore, whilst it can collapse into a conservative anti-culture critique, the 'countercultural' approach can help to frame an emergent austerity-age theology of liberation where it is premised on an *a priori* counter hegemonic liberative ethic and interrogates dominant culture on the basis of a hermeneutics of suspicion.

During Life on the Breadline our case studies of Christian responses to the Grenfell Tower fire and wider housing injustice, Church Action on Poverty's End Hunger UK campaign and Power the Fight's educational and advocacy programmes, responding to the pain of growing knife crime in an Age of Austerity, shone a light on the interplay between localized trauma, systemic poverty and structural violence. Our research highlighted the dialogical (or synthetic) nature of contextual theology to which Schreiter refers. More particularly, as I have shown in previous chapters, our case studies illustrate Gutiérrez's argument that 'All through history there has been a repressed but resurgent theology, born of the struggles of the poor' (1983, p. 202) – what he calls, 'subterranean streams' that 'gush up unexpectedly from the living founts of poor persons' awareness of the God who sets them free' (1983, p. 202).

For Gutiérrez, this is 'a theology being done primarily by history's nameless ones' (1983, p. 204). This is what we might call a praxis model of contextual theology. We glimpsed raw, pain-filled hints of such a theology in the trauma-inflected reflections of people of faith responding to the burning of Grenfell Tower (Shannahan, 2022) as some of the photographs I took at the people's art gallery beneath the West Way overpass demonstrate:

Figure 6. Photographs taken at the Grenfell Tower People's Art Gallery

Our work within Life on the Breadline demonstrates not only the primacy of context but also the pivotal importance of praxis as the essential foundation for contextual political theologies in an ongoing Age of Austerity. Praxis is often translated as 'practice', which is a shame because the term is much more nuanced than that. While the concept of praxis emerges initially in the philosophical treatises of Aristotle, its contemporary use is largely rooted in Marxist theory where it is used to denote reflective critical human action that is intended to foster structural change within society. Within the pedagogy of Paulo Freire (1970), that paved the way for the emergence of liberation theology in Latin America, the concept of praxis was used to refer to the interplay between critical reflection on the conditions and causes of structural injustice, the process of conscientization and liberative practice. Marx's argument within his *Theses on Feuerbach* (2024) that philosophy has mistakenly focused on interpreting the world, rather than transforming it, informed and influenced the way in which the purpose of theology was understood as a transformative discipline within the early days of liberation theology in Latin America (Gutiérrez, 1974, p. 9).

The ideas of Marx and Freire are apparent, for example, in the early work of Gutiérrez (1974; 1983) and in Segundo's (1976) seminal discussion of the methodological basis of liberation theology. For both, truly liberative theology that has the capacity to generate transformational social change must emerge from praxis. Gutiérrez suggests that, 'Theology follows; it is the second step ... Theology does not produce pastoral activity; rather it flows from it' (1974, p. 11). For Gutiérrez, however, the biblical narrative, especially the preaching of the Hebrew prophets and the ministry of Jesus, is of far deeper theological significance than Marxist theory or Freire's pedagogy (Gutiérrez, 1983, p. 50). His pioneering *A Theology of Liberation* is filled with biblical references, whereas his citation of Marx is rare, as even a cursory glance through his iconic book attests. Such praxis-led theology, he argues, is, necessarily, 'subversive of a social order' that marginalizes the voices of people living in poverty. This subversive praxis, however, if it is to be rooted in the ministry of Jesus, must be a 'praxis of love of neighbour and of love for Christ in the neighbour, for Christ identifies himself with the least of these our brothers and sisters' (Gutiérrez, 1983, p. 50).

In methodological terms, as Segundo (1976), Bevans (1992) and Green (1990) point out, the foregrounding of praxis has become a defining feature of contextual theology. As we learned during Life on the Breadline, theology cannot be a force of progressive social change, nor can it provide people of faith with the resources to 'transform the structural injustice' of austerity-age poverty if it is not consciously rooted in liberative praxis and in the lives of those with direct experience of poverty. Life on the Breadline invites those political theologians who resist the call to engage in extended and wide-ranging fieldwork to get out of the library and root their analyses in the experience and praxis they reflect upon. The motivating principle of the UK-based Poverty Truth Network since its inception in Scotland in 2009 is summarized in the simple but powerful phrase, 'Nothing about us without us is for us.'[2] This deceptively simple mantra captures the promise and the challenge of contextual theology. During Life on the Breadline we learned that theologians can only credibly claim to be organic agents of liberative change (Gutiérrez, 1974, p. 18) if their reflections on the nature of poverty and Christian social action are rooted in and reflect the experience of those for whom this is a daily reality. Our engagement with the people who had lost family members in the Grenfell Tower tragedy, with women and men using the B30 Food bank, the experiential advocacy of Church Action on Poverty, the 'Community Building' of Hodge Hill Church and the Inspire Centre and the day-to-day work of Power the Fight alongside marginalized communities devastated by knife crime during Life on the

Breadline models the interdisciplinary, praxis-oriented, fieldwork-based approach needed if a genuinely liberative austerity-age theology of liberation is to emerge.

Life's complicated – the complexities of poverty

During our research a Baptist pastor from the North of England suggested to us that 'Poverty is complex … but most churches lack a bigger picture about the influences and changes which effect poverty' (Life on the Breadline online survey, 2020). Our research during Life on the Breadline confirmed this pastor's instincts that neither the Church nor contemporary theologians respond adequately to our varied experiences of the messiness of multidimensional structural injustice. Three insights from our research can help to enable theology to engage more holistically with the challenge implied in this pastor's concern.

First, the testimonies of people with direct experience of poverty are plural not singular, and messy not uniform. Such experiences can converge, diverge, complement or contradict each other. If it is to be authentic, an austerity-age theology of liberation needs to resist the temptation to tidy up, homogenize or systematize the plural, unsystematic and untidy rawness of contemporary poverty. As I noted in earlier chapters, the nitty-gritty hermeneutics developed by Pinn (1999), which seeks to reflect the unvarnished, unorthodox and uncensored ways which people engage with, interpret and make sense of structural injustice, can help contemporary theologians to fashion an honest and holistic austerity-age theology of liberation that takes trauma, stigma, anger, lament and despair seriously, rather than moving beyond such pain too quickly to a hope-filled liberative narrative.

If an austerity-age theology of liberation is to have emotional and ethical as well as analytical integrity, we need to paint an authentic picture of the context from which such theological reflection arises. Only then can a truly liberative theological analysis be fashioned. An example of this nitty-gritty authenticity from Life on the Breadline illustrates the point. As I discussed in Chapters 5 and 6, our Power the Fight case study shone a light on the traumatizing impact of rapidly rising levels of knife crime in London that accompanied the dramatic cuts to youth and children's services during the Age of Austerity. Power the Fight's multifaceted work exemplifies the kind of organic and nuanced praxis-driven approach that is needed if the Church is to respond effectively to the interwoven, traumatizing violent mess of contemporary poverty. An intimate understanding of the personal and collective struggles of young adults in South London, a pastoral concern for their well-being and that of their families, anger about the impact of austerity on children and young people in London and a commitment to the Church's calling to 'transform structural injustice' inform Power the Fight's multifaceted nitty-gritty response to knife crime. Power the Fight's therapeutic intervention programme, which I described in Chapter 6, exemplifies a nitty-gritty engagement with the pain and anger and trauma and violence and structural injustice that characterize the scourge of austerity-age knife crime. Whilst shaped by a commitment to liberative praxis as the heart of Christian faith, Power the Fight's therapeutic intervention programme meets young people in the midst of the mess and confusion of the sadness and fury of austerity-induced social exclusion and traumatizing violence without any political, pastoral or theological strings attached. If it is to gain cultural traction and reflect an authentic engagement with the raw realities of austerity-age poverty, an emergent theology of liberation needs to be embodied by a nitty-gritty, non-dogmatic liberative praxis that resists the temptation to systematize or smooth away untidiness.

Second, if they are to help to facilitate the forging of a holistic liberative praxis that exemplifies the biblical concept of *Shalom*, as well as reflecting the messy and plural nature of contemporary poverty, theologians need to resist the temptation of adopting reductionist definitions and analyses. As I have argued elsewhere (Shannahan, 2019; Shannahan and Denning, 2022), theological reflections on austerity-age poverty have, almost always, focused their gaze on food banks. The implicit reduction of contemporary social exclusion to food poverty concentrates our attention on just one piece of the poverty jigsaw. As Beth Waters' Jigsaw of Poverty illustration for Life on the Breadline in Chapter 1 makes clear, food poverty cannot be isolated from fuel poverty, poor housing, insecure employment, rising prices, static wages, zero-hours contracts and personal debt. During Life on the Breadline Church leaders from different Christian traditions spoke to us about the multidimensional nature of austerity-age poverty.

The Rt Revd Paul Butler, Bishop of Durham (Interview 2020), Nicola Jones (Interview 2020) of the Irish Council of Churches, Martin Charlesworth (Interview 2020) of Jubilee+ and Revd Micky Youngson (Interview 2020), the former President of the British Methodist Conference, all reflected on the need for the Church to wrestle with the multidimensional character of systemic poverty. Our case study of B30 Trussell Trust food bank in South Birmingham, which is described in detail in Chapter 3, illustrates the multidimensional and interwoven nature of austerity-age poverty and the need for activists and academics to adopt what Vivian

May calls a 'matrix worldview' (2015, p. 3), rather than a 'single-axis' understanding of structural injustice. The primary purpose of B30 food bank is to respond effectively and empathically to the damage caused by food poverty but volunteers recognize that this cannot be addressed in isolation from other expressions of marginalization, as I showed in Chapter 3. A three-day food parcel meets immediate need but is of limited value when somebody can't heat their food because they can't afford to pay the gas bill or because they are living in bed-and-breakfast accommodation with no kitchen facilities. As we discovered during Life on the Breadline, and as Beth Waters' painting illustrates, austerity-age poverty needs to be seen as a multidimensional expression of systemic injustice. The structural violence embodied by the converging of food poverty, poor housing, fuel poverty, low pay, insecure employment and personal debt represents a traumatizing perfect storm, what can be described in theological terms as a form of systemic sin. Such multi-dimensional, matrix-oriented and fieldwork-based analysis needs to become the norm within political theology if theological reflection on structural injustice is to resonate with the lives of people with direct experience of poverty. Furthermore, as our Life on the Breadline case study of the 'Community Building' that Hodge Hill Church is engaged in, which I explored in Chapter 6, demonstrates, the poverty wrought by austerity has existential, as well as economic impact. Theologians can draw on the Church Urban Fund's description of the Web of Poverty (2014) that I referred to in the previous chapter, as well as our own research, to enable a deeper reflection on the relational, spiritual and psycho-social impacts of poverty. Stigma, shame and social exclusion clash with and compound one another. An austerity-age theology of liberation needs to grasp this messy multidimensional picture if is to resource holistic patterns of liberative praxis.

Third, given the pivotal importance of context and social location, a contemporary theology of liberation needs to make it clear that who we are, what we look like and where we live shapes our experience of austerity. The concept of intersectionality can enrich our analysis of austerity and the contours of the liberative theology we attempt to fashion. Intersectionality refers to a liberative mindset, the relationships between social location and oppression and a methodological call to recognize and wrestle with complexity. Patricia Hill-Collins and Sirma Bilge (2020) see intersectionality as an analytical tool that helps us to address complex social problems in a holistic manner that resources the collaborative development of critical praxis that is able to respond effectively to the 'matrix of domination' (Hill-Collins, 2008) that underpins structurally unequal societies. For Crenshaw (2017), intersectionality is 'a metaphor for the ways in which multiple forms of inequality combine and compound themselves'. Writing about the use of intersectionality within feminist theory, May suggests that the concept can help us to subvert 'single-axis ways of thinking about subjectivity and power' (2015, p. 3). Such a perspective, May argues, can help us to understand identity 'interlaced' and 'systems of oppression as enmeshed and mutually reinforcing' (2015, p. 3). Grace Ji-Sun Kim and Susan Shaw suggest that 'for most of Christian history straight White male theologians have spoken for everyone else, as if their theologies do not reflect the bias of their own social locations and power. This has meant that our theologies have been partial, a reflection of only a very small slice of the whole of human experience' (2018, p. 3). They argue that an embrace of the 'kaleidoscopic' possibilities of an intersectional frame of reference can transform theology from a tool of the dominant into a means of liberation (2018, pp. 2–3).

I spoke in earlier chapters about the ways in which our Life on the Breadline partner, Church Action on Poverty, has embodied, albeit implicitly, an intersectional mindset in its development of initiatives that foreground the importance of class, gender, age and ethnicity as interlocking factors in the experience of and response to poverty. There are signs that Church Action is further emphasizing the need for a greater attention to intersectionality as a motivating force in the building of a broad-based anti-poverty social movement (Cooper, 2021). Academic theologians engaging with contemporary poverty or the role the Church plays in the public sphere can learn from the emerging intersectional liberative praxis of Church Action on Poverty. In Chapter 4 I discussed our Life on the Breadline case study of Christian responses to the Grenfell Tower fire and broader expressions of housing injustice in the context of austerity and systemic inequality. I have argued elsewhere (Shannahan, 2022) that a theological response to the Grenfell tragedy needs to be rooted in a fieldwork-informed wrestling with the messy and multidimensional intersectionality of slow structural violence. As I noted in Chapter 4, the deaths of the 72 men, women and children in the Grenfell Tower fire was more than a tragic accident. The tragedy resulted from decades of underinvestment in social housing and the neoliberal loosening of planning regulations under successive governments. Grenfell has become an iconic symbol of the traumatizing violence of austerity-age poverty and, at the time of writing, the tower's shell still stands as a grim monument to an economy built on systemic violence and structural injustice. I have argued elsewhere (Shannahan, 2022) that the enormity of the Grenfell disaster can only be captured by adopting an intersectional frame of reference.

Theological analyses of the housing injustice exemplified by the Grenfell Tower fire will be enriched if they pay close attention to the reflections of Ben Okri's poem 'Grenfell Tower – June 2017', which was published in the *Financial Times* just a week after the fire, and captured the fracture, violence and structural injustice of austerity-age Britain. Okri wrote of the Grenfell 72: 'They did not die when they died; their deaths happened long before … in the minds of the people who never saw them … in the profit margins … in the laws. They died because money could be saved and made'(Okri, 2018). By rooting theological analysis in the liberative praxis enabled by intersectional thinking theologians can better glimpse the 'matrix of domination' that fed Grenfell's harrowing perfect storm and resulting lament. The tragedy was years in the making. The life of people with direct experience of poverty, Black and Brown residents, asylum seekers and refugees, isolated older people and struggling families in North Kensington was dramatically different from that of wealthy neighbours in the private squares in Notting Hill and those just a few miles away in South Kensington. Geography, class, ethnicity and migration status allied to multigenerational inequality and a decade of austerity made the Grenfell tragedy possible, even likely, in a way that would have been impossible in other apartment blocks in wealthier parts of the Royal Borough of Kensington and Chelsea. If they are to gain traction and enable a new, more just and egalitarian future to emerge, austerity-age theologies of liberation need to engage in depth with the messy, multidimensional and intersectional realities of systemic poverty.

The Church and the public sphere

Life on the Breadline demonstrated that the Church has been in the vanguard of civil society engagement with deepening poverty during the Age of Austerity, largely as a result of its enduring social capital in socially excluded communities. As the State withdrew, the Church remained. The time has come for theologians to reflect again on the role the Church in the public sphere in a structurally unjust society. Scott and Cavanaugh suggest that 'Theology is politically important and those who engage in either theology or politics ignore this fact at their peril' (2004, p. 1). It has become clear that both the Church in the UK and those theologians interested in Christian responses to poverty stand at a *Kairos* moment. In Chapter 3 I noted the impact that the gradual shift towards a post-secular cultural landscape has had on the ways in which we envisage the role that the Church plays in an increasingly plural public sphere. Here, in light of the arguments I have developed in previous chapters on the basis of our Life on the Breadline fieldwork, I discuss the implications of this shift for the Church's engagement with systemic poverty and the forging of an austerity-age theology of liberation.

First, the renewed political significance of faith groups and their increasing visibility in the public sphere (Hoelzl and Ward, 2008) has profound implications for the ways in which we think about meaning and marginalization. Habermas argues that 'religious traditions have a special power to articulate moral intuitions, especially with regard to vulnerable forms of communal life' (2006, p. 10). He suggests that 'religious organisations are increasingly assuming the role of communities of interpretation in the public arena' (2008, p. 20). Our research during Life on the Breadline showed how, in the face of more than a decade of austerity policies in the UK faith groups have, as Habermas implied, become key points of trust, support and guidance as the State has withdrawn and they have remained. Such a development can grant local faith groups mobilizing power, if they are bold enough to grasp this opportunity. Second, the increasing visibility of the Church in civil society politics that we witnessed during Life on the Breadline should be read against the backdrop of a shrinking Welfare State. Soon after the 2010 General Election David Cameron championed the need for a reinvigorated but apolitical 'Big Society' as a corrective to what he called the 'broken society' that he suggested had arisen during the New Labour years. Third, the Church's increasing visibility within the public sphere during the Age of Austerity raises questions about its use of its social capital in local communities, which I summarized in Chapter 3.

In his exploration of the relationship between Christian faith and contemporary politics, Luke Bretherton points to the problematic use of the language of social capital to speak about the Church's social action, suggesting, with justification, that it can ossify and homogenize dynamic social relationships, reducing them to the static and instrumentalist language of economics (2010, p. 39ff). In spite of this reasonable critique, the use of the concept of social capital has become increasingly common within political theology and the strategic thinking of the Church over the last 20 years. It was widely used in the ecumenical report *Faithful Cities* (Commission on Urban Life and Faith, 2006), as a framework for articulating the 'faithful capital' that resources the engagement of the Church in the public sphere. Chris Baker and Hannah Skinner (2006/2014) argue that local churches possess significant levels of such social capital. What they call religious capital refers to the resources, networks, space and activities of local churches. Subject to the theological values (spiritual capital) that guide a local church, their religious capital can be used to facilitate introverted bonding capital, outward-facing bridging capital or the more politicized linking capital that fosters connections with other faith and community groups in networked campaigning for social justice (Szreter, 2002). A critical engagement with thinking about linking social capital and the spiritual capital that motivates it can enable a greater understanding of the ways in which the Church can address the asymmetric power that characterizes life in breadline Britain and help to resource the fashioning of an austerity-age theology of liberation. The work of Church Action on Poverty and Power the Fight exemplifies this interconnection between bridging and linking capital.

Bretherton argues that 'we are going through a period of de-construction and re-construction in which perennial questions about the relationship between religious and political authority are being asked again' (2011, p. 253). Elaine Graham suggests that in the emergent postsecular context, the Church is seeking 'a new voice in a public debate that is more fragmented, more global and more disparate' (2013, p. xvi). Habermas (2006) argues that, in this unstable new context, the Church has become an informal anchor institution for marginalized communities. Whilst recognizing this, Bretherton suggests that in seeking a consensual, policy-oriented role in the public sphere, the Church can become 'co-opted' or 'depoliticized' rather than offering a liberative counter-hegemonic vision of the common good (2010, p. 47). We observed this tension during our Life on the Breadline fieldwork, as I showed in earlier chapters. The Church's engagement with austerity-age poverty continues to be largely depoliticized and politics often remains a no-go area.

As it wrestles with its role in the public sphere, its renewed visibility in civil society politics and the extent to which it uses its social capital to resource the transformation of structural injustice, the Church has a decision to make. It stands at a crossroads, just as theology faces a *Kairos* moment. As I noted above, Gutiérrez argues that theologians are called to participate in the struggle for liberation (1974, p. 32) but are we ready to embrace this calling and the insecurity that might come with it? Is the Church ready to rise to Bonhoeffer's challenge to move beyond bandaging up the broken to thrust a 'spoke into the wheel' of austerity-age structural injustice – to embody an egalitarian vision of the common good (Bethge, 1995, pp. 316–17)?

In Chapter 3 I discussed the roots of the common-good teaching and social gospel ethic that shaped most of the Christian responses to contemporary poverty and the Church's engagement in the public sphere that we encountered during Life on the Breadline. Two broad approaches to the Church's engagement in the public sphere became evident in our survey of UK Church leaders. First, Church leaders from a small number of conservative evangelical or Pentecostal denominations, including the Wesleyan Holiness Church, the Church of God of Prophecy, the Independent Methodist Church, the Orthodox Church, and the United Free Church of Scotland, articulated a theological concern about moving beyond welfare-based 'Caring' to engage proactively in the public sphere. 'Campaigning' and 'Advocacy' were seen as problematic – partisan politics, rather than the biblically inspired servanthood exemplified by 'Caring'. An Anglican Mission Enabler from the South-West of England summarized concerns: 'Getting political is always controversial. It is so intertwined with party politics, and people are anxious about mixing party politics with faith' (Life on the Breadline survey, 2019). Second, however, a majority of Church leaders from the Evangelical Alliance, the Methodist Church, Jubilee+, the United Reformed Church, the Church of England, the Church of Scotland, the Church in Wales and the Irish Council of Churches suggested that their denomination's understanding of the common good and the mission imperative of 'transforming structural injustice' led them to develop both 'Caring' and 'Campaigning and Advocacy' responses to contemporary poverty. A United Reformed Church leader from the South-West of England typified this perspective – 'God's preferential option for the poor; a concern that justice and mercy go hand in hand; a sense that we cannot proclaim the gospel to someone without also meeting need and being Christ' (Life on the Breadline online survey, 2019). In his conversation with us, the Anglican Archbishop of Wales suggested that speaking truth to power, being an advocate for people robbed of their voice by debilitating poverty is a fundamental gospel mandate: 'a responsibility and a duty that we have to exercise' (Interview 2020).

As I have shown in previous chapters each of the approaches to austerity-age poverty that we uncovered during Life on the Breadline embodies a different understanding of the nature and calling of the Church and varying visions of the role it should play in the public sphere. The vision of the Church as pastor bandaging up the wounds of the broken, or as prophet speaking truth to power, or enabler empowering people in poverty to develop business or social enterprises, or as a companion in the building of inclusive communities in which all can flourish all embody different facets of common-good thinking. All have value but can any of the perspectives that we encountered during our research provide the Church with the resources needed to fashion an austerity-age theology of liberation that is capable of 'transforming structural injustice'? Many of the Church leaders with whom we spoke expressed a commitment to a vision of the common good that is shaped by a commitment to God's preferential option for the poor. Such commitment clearly sustains invaluable social action and should not be discounted. However, based on what we heard and saw during Life on the Breadline, it is clear that a hesitant depoliticized vision of the gospel call to 'transform structural injustice' and of the Church's role in the public sphere will leave structural injustice intact (Dorrien, 1990, p. 4ff). In the face of systemic injustice and ongoing austerity can the Church fulfil the potential of its social capital to feed the hungry and clothe the naked without agitating for structural change?

When we interviewed her during Life on the Breadline, Revd Mick Youngson (Interview 2020) pointed in graphic terms to the *Kairos* moment facing the Church: 'There's a theological gap between loving my neighbour and challenging Caesar.' Now is the time for the Church to overcome its nervousness and challenge Caesar. We need the imagination and the courage to fashion a counter hegemonic ecclesiology that dubs the strengths of the Christian responses to poverty that I have discussed in this book on the basis of a *Shalom*-oriented praxis driven liberative theological framework. Only then can a holistic austerity-age theology of liberation arise that is driven by a vision of the Church as a liberative movement agitating for transformative systemic and epistemic change begin to emerge. Only then will the Church be equipped to challenge Caesar.

Liberative praxis and the Church's role in an 'Age of Austerity'

Is the Church part of the problem or part of the solution to austerity-age poverty? The truth is that the Church has played an ambivalent role in relation to structural injustice since the Roman Emperor Constantine was converted to Christianity in the fourth century CE. The Church is part of the establishment, occasionally still blessing or spiritualizing inequality but, more often than not, bandaging the broken, whilst leaving systemic injustice intact. However, the Church is also part of an agitating movement subverting the hegemonic justification of austerity-age poverty and inequality, as our research during Life on the Breadline demonstrated. Our research highlighted the increasingly visible role the Church plays in the public sphere but also its nervousness, fragility, sense of impotence and deference to the establishment. How might our Life on the Breadline research help us to begin to sow the seeds of a liberative ecclesiology that can help the Church to live up to its calling to 'transform structural injustice'?

A cultural page has been turned in recent decades as we have begun to move beyond the secularist assumptions and assertions that characterized attitudes towards the sociological significance of faith throughout most of the twentieth century to fashion a more fluid and, I suggest, mature, postsecular cultural mindset (Davie, 1994; Berger, 1997; Habermas, 2006; Graham, 2013). Whilst many of the Church leaders who spoke to us during Life on the Breadline remain nervous about advocating a more proactive role for the Church in the public sphere, the stark challenges to the Church of England's critique of government policy in the seminal 1985 *Faith in the City* report, by Conservative ministers accusing bishops of being Marxists meddling in politics, are largely a thing of the past.

In light of the increasing recognition amongst policymakers of the value of the enduring social capital possessed by faith groups, this shift towards a postsecular settlement helps to explain the renewed engagement of faith groups in the public sphere (Shannahan, 2018), what Hoelzl and Ward (2008) called the new visibility of religion. During the Age of Austerity, as welfare spending was slashed by more than 30% and the State cut vital youth and community funding, the Covid-19 pandemic and the ongoing so-called 'cost of living crisis', the Church became an increasingly key player in the response to increasing levels of poverty and inequality. One simple example drawn from our research illustrates the point. In 2024, of the approximately 2,500 food banks in the UK, just over 1,400 were run in or by local churches as part of the Christian-inspired Trussell Trust. During Life on the Breadline we studied one of these (B30 in South Birmingham). The renewed and increasingly visible role of the Church in the public sphere can be seen as a direct consequence of the retreat of the State as cuts bit ever deeper during the Age of Austerity (Dinham et al., 2009; Hoelzl and Ward, 2008). Its enduring social capital and trusted status as an informal anchor institution combined with the Church's commitment to the common good made such a development almost inevitable. However, the renewed visibility of the Church in the public sphere has sharpened questions about its role within civil society and the purpose of its social action that continue to divide Christians.

It is not surprising to see the Church becoming the major provider of food banks in the UK given its historic involvement in comparable social action, from alms in the Middle Ages to soup kitchens in the Great Depression. In many senses such welfare-based action is written into the Church's theological DNA. The more difficult, and still unresolved, challenge relates to the extent to which a 'Caring' Church that is largely cushioned from the worst excesses of austerity-age poverty can credibly speak truth to power and become a vehicle for liberative social change, especially where it runs the risk of being 'co-opted' to deliver welfare services by a shrinking State. Life on the Breadline has focused attention on the emerging vision of Church as a grassroots liberative social movement and on examples of a proactive and prophetic use of its linking capital to fashion the liberative praxis capable of resourcing the transformation of structural injustice. It became clear during our research that a credible austerity-age theology of liberation rests on the willingness of the Church to turn away from its institutional past and embrace the possibilities of becoming a network of communities of faith and resistance, agitating for liberative social change.

Our Life on the Breadline research provided clear examples of the ways in which the Church used its social capital to respond to growing levels of poverty during the Age of Austerity. Since the election of Tony Blair's New Labour government in 1997, successive prime ministers have recognized that the Church retains significant localized social capital because of the roots and connections local churches have in local neighbourhoods, especially socially excluded communities where the Church is often one of the few anchor institutions not to have retreated to the suburbs. The 2006 ecumenical report *Faithful Cities* speaks of the Church's presence in socially excluded communities as a form of 'faithful capital' and Baker and Skinner (2006/2014) discuss how a congregation's spiritual capital (values or theology) shapes the way it deploys its religious capital (its people and building resource). The ecosystem of Christian engagement with austerity-age poverty that we identified during Life on the Breadline shines a light on the differing ways in which the Church uses such social capital in its response to poverty and inequality. In previous chapters I have discussed and critiqued overlapping 'Caring', 'Campaigning and Advocacy', 'Self-help and Enterprise' and 'Community Building' approaches to austerity-age poverty and spoken about the theological traditions they reflect. Each frames the Church, its missiology, its use of its social capital and its engagement in the public sphere in a distinct way – pastor; liberative movement; empowerer/enabler and companion on the journey. I have shown how valuable each approach is, but also demonstrated that none of these responses to poverty in isolation has the capacity to fully embody God's preferential option for the poor and generate the activism needed to 'transform structural injustice' and pave the way for a pattern of holistic liberative praxis that is shaped by a vision of God's *Shalom* ethic and an egalitarian vision of the common good.

Our research has shown that as the Church stands at this *Kairos* moment it is time to think again about its use of its social capital and to ask whether it's essentially welfare-based engagement with poverty is an adequate reflection of God's preferential option for the poor in a structurally unjust age. The pivotal question is not whether the Church uses its social capital to respond to poverty. Rather, the question that needs to be answered is whether the Church is willing and able to use its social capital to ram a spoke into the wheel of injustice. Such a shift has major implications for the ways in which the Church envisages its role in the public sphere and for its ongoing nervousness about being seen as 'political'.

The Commission on Urban Life and Faith speaks of the ways in which local churches have fashioned examples of bridging capital to develop intercultural and interfaith dialogue, aligning this with the more politicized linking capital that enables a step beyond understanding to racial justice (2006, p. 25ff). The term 'linking capital' refers to the development of purposive relationships between people or groups who are 'unequal in their power and their access to resources...' (Szreter, 2002, p. 579) as part of a shared struggle for social justice. Christiaan Grootaert et al. (2004, p. 4) compare bridging and linking capital: 'Where bridging social capital ... is essentially horizontal ... linking social capital is more vertical, connecting people ... across power differentials.' Such linking capital can, they argue, provide marginalized groups with a voice and a means of asserting their agency through the development of purposive alliances with other communities and socially included groups. They suggest that 'linking capital is demonstrably central to well-being, especially in poor communities' (2004, p. 4). Going further they argue that, 'Local leaders and intermediaries able to facilitate connections between poor communities and external development assistance constitute an important source of linking social capital.' The ways in which the Church uses its bridging capital to fashion broad-based networks of cooperation and trust can pave the way for the forging of the linking capital that enables local churches to foster the development of what Manuel Castells has called a social justice-focused 'project identity' (2010, p. 8) shaped by its commitment to God's preferential option for the poor. Linking capital, however, is not inherently liberative. Consequently, the fashioning of a pattern of linking capital that has the capacity to resource the Church's mission to transform structural injustice and forge a liberative presence in the public sphere needs to be informed by an emancipatory ethic and a clear hermeneutics of suspicion. Broad-based community organizing provides an example of the ways in which the fashioning of linking capital and the articulation of 'project identities' can provide relatively small and marginalized local churches with the opportunity to put their commitment to transform structural injustice into effective practice (Shannahan, 2014; Bretherton, 2015). Furthermore, our Life on the Breadline case studies of Church Action on Poverty's development of the End Hunger UK alliance as a challenge to debilitating food insecurity and Notting Hill Methodist Church's development of a network of faith and community groups campaigning for housing justice following the Grenfell Tower fire, which I discussed in Chapter 4, exemplify the liberative potential of such faith-based linking capital.

Conclusion

In this Chapter I have argued that we stand at a crossroads and suggested that this is a *Kairos* moment for academic theologians and for the Church. Fundamental choices need to be made, and harsh realities faced. I have shown that theologians need to move beyond an exclusively book-bound analysis, to escape our disciplinary bunker to fashion thoroughly interdisciplinary analyses that are informed in every way by extensive primary qualitative research. I have suggested that Life on the Breadline models the interdisciplinary, fieldwork-led approach that has the capacity to lay the groundwork for the development of a rigorous, holistic and credible austerity-age theology of liberation. I have argued that, whilst all of the Christian approaches to austerity-age poverty that we identified during Life on the Breadline have value, none are capable of resourcing a credible theology of liberation unless they are re-imagined using the dub hermeneutics I have developed in this book. Together, these dubbed approaches have the potential to provide the building blocks for this new form of liberative praxis-led theological reflection. I have shown that such a theology of liberation needs to be thoroughly informed by qualitative fieldwork and characterized by an openness to insights from a range of social science disciplines, but, in particular, cultural studies, human geography, peace studies, intersectionality studies and trauma studies. Such openness, I have shown, can resource a nitty-gritty intersectional theology of liberation that can reflect the messy plurality of life in breadline Britain. In the closing chapter I draw on the arguments I have made throughout this book to begin sowing the seeds of the austerity-age theology of liberation that is so badly needed if the Church is to fulfil its calling to embody God's preferential option for the poor and overcome its nervousness about engaging in prophetic politics.

Notes

1 For more information about Kairos movements globally see https://kairosusa.org/global-kairos-key-documents-and-resources/, accessed 7.01.2025.

2 See https://povertytruthnetwork.org/, accessed 6.02.2025.

8

Sowing the Seeds of an Austerity-Age Theology of Liberation

Introduction

Life on the Breadline arose directly from my personal commitment to the liberation struggle and my sense of vocation as an activist theologian. The project represented a search for a rigorous and culturally resonant, fieldwork-led austerity-age theology of liberation that has the capacity to transform structural injustice. In this final chapter, therefore, I respond to this sense of academic and spiritual calling and draw upon the insights that arose from Life on the Breadline to begin to sow the seeds of a theology of liberation that can meet the needs of this *Kairos* moment.

Dub hermeneutics and liberative praxis

The theology we fashion is forged in the fire of our experience but shaped by our vision of the world. If theology is to meet the challenge of this *Kairos* moment it is essential for theologians to nail our colours to the mast, to fulfil, what West (1985; 1999) calls our calling to 'shine a light on suffering' and to exemplify God's preferential option for the poor. Theology can only be a force for transformative progressive social change in breadline Britain if it is guided by such a praxis-oriented liberative hermeneutical perspective. Our Life on the Breadline research demonstrated the immense value but also the limitations of 'Caring', 'Campaigning and Advocacy', 'Enterprise and Self-Help' and 'Community Building' Christian responses to contemporary poverty. I have suggested that for an austerity-age theology of liberation that has the capacity to 'transform structural injustice' to arise it is necessary to fashion a model of liberative praxis and theological reflection that moves beyond consensual commitments to building the common good. At this *Kairos* moment we need to fashion an austerity-age Dub hermeneutics as a first step in building a credible theology of liberation that draws on the strengths of the approaches we identified during Life on the Breadline, as I indicate in Figure 7.

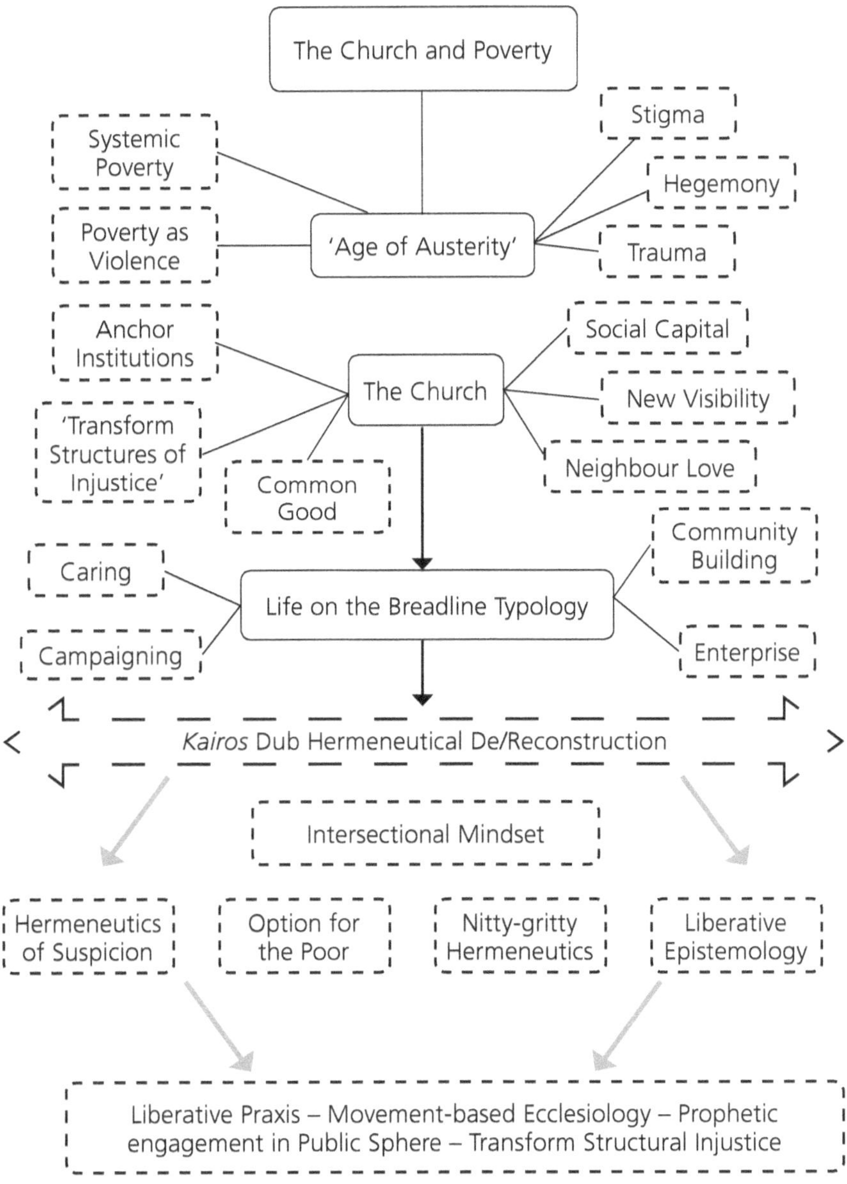

Figure 7. A Breadline Dub

The dub hermeneutical framework that I summarized above can make a creative contribution to hermeneutics, liberation theology and interdisciplinary analyses of Christian engagement with poverty. The features of this Life on the Breadline dub hermeneutics, which emerged directly from our fieldwork, have been introduced, critically discussed and brought into dialogue in previous chapters. Any linear depiction of such a dynamic reflective process runs the risk of presenting them in static, once-and-for-all terms. Like Reggae MCs or record producers, we need to fashion this new liberative hermeneutics on the foundations of the four Christian approaches to poverty that we identified during Life on the Breadline. Stripping back and building up as an ongoing iterative process that is always critically evolving – a Breadline spiral, more than a circular dub cycle.

Sitting with the pain and calling its name

There can be a tendency within Christian theology to skip straight from Good Friday to Easter Day. The anguish, confusion, pain and unresolved suffering of Holy Saturday is glossed over as we move smoothly from death to resurrection. People with whom we spoke during Life on the Breadline were concerned about the ways in which this mindset hinders the Church's engagement with austerity-age poverty. Al Barrett, of Hodge Hill Church on the Bromford housing estate in Birmingham (Interview 2020) gave voice to this frustration with a caring but disengaged and distant Church that seeks quick fixes to deep-seated structural injustice. Anglican, Church of Scotland, United Reformed Church and Methodist Church leaders from the North of Scotland and Northern England hinted at a similar frustration, describing the Church as 'isolated from the worst effects of extreme poverty', 'distinct from the community', 'comfortably off' and 'too distanced from the reality of poverty' (Life on the Breadline online survey, 2019–20). A volunteer at B30 Food bank in Birmingham (Interview 2019) implied that, whilst food banks meet people in their urgent need, 'Caring' without 'Advocating' systemic change runs the risk of unintentionally colluding with austerity rather than critiquing systemic injustice.

As I noted in Chapter 4 and have argued elsewhere (Shannahan, 2022), our Life on the Breadline case study of Christian responses to the tragedy of the Grenfell Tower fire shone a light on the slow traumatizing violence of austerity-poverty and housing injustice as well as the direct violence of the inferno that took the lives of 72 men, women and children in June 2017. I described the 'Caring' and the 'Campaigning and

Advocacy' of Notting Hill Methodist Church's response to the fire and the injustice it symbolized, just a stone's throw away from some of the wealthiest neighbourhoods in the UK and pointed to the quiet solidarity expressed by former Notting Hill Minister, Revd Mike Long. Too often, though, theological and faith-based responses to the Grenfell fire have moved on quickly from the raw rage of the tragedy to discussions about structural injustice, social housing and liberation. All are vitally important, but none can be credibly discussed if we are more interested in washing away the rage, dirt and despair of abandonment. In Chapter 2 I argued that an interdisciplinary and intersectional theology of liberation needs to adopt the nitty-gritty hermeneutical perspective developed by Pinn (1999) if it is to wrestle honestly in a non-dogmatic manner with the mess, complexity and raw pain of austerity-age poverty. No smoothing away uneven, ragged edges, no rationalizing rage, no fast forwarding to a just and egalitarian future minus the struggle. Such openness to the anguish and anger caused by austerity is a vital component in the Life on the Breadline dub hermeneutics I discussed above.

Two of the photographs I took during Life on the Breadline illustrate the theological importance of a nitty-gritty hermeneutical perspective. Both pictures capture the loss, traumatizing anguish, confusion, anger and sense of isolation of the survivors of the Grenfell Tower fire. Before there can be any credible theological analysis of structural injustice, or of God's preferential option for the poor or of the contours of an egalitarian common good, pain, rage, despair and the shaking of a fist at God need to be understood, honoured and grappled with as these two images attest:

Figure 8. Photographs taken at the Grenfell Tower People's Art Gallery

It is possible to read these images as urgent expressions of theodicy, but they point to something more visceral than that. These are austerity-age cries of anguished lament and abandonment that are infused with a subconscious hermeneutics of suspicion – 'Why do we the working class have to suffer again?' 'There ain't no sunshine now you're gone.' 'There's no justice, it's just us.' Only by sitting with such pain in intimate solidarity, naming it, acknowledging and wrestling with it can an authentic contextual liberative praxis emerge as the basis for an austerity-age theology of liberation.

The tradition of lament within the Hebrew Scriptures can be overlooked as we rush on in our search for liberation or the promise of salvation, and yet a recovery of this tradition of visceral painfully honest spirituality can provide an invaluable nitty-gritty resource as we forge an austerity-age theology of liberation. The Psalmist doesn't pull any punches but rails against personal and collective suffering, an unjust world and a seemingly absent God (See Psalms 22, 35, 44 and 137 for example) and the author of the book of Lamentations expresses the anguish, confusion and anger of the people of Israel exiled in Babylon in graphic terms (as we see, for example, in Lamentations 1). Lament has been used within faith-based activism and political theology in a variety of guises for generations, but is, arguably a neglected resource within contemporary theologies of liberation. Lament within political and liberation theology can root theological reflection in the pain of injustice as a form of nitty-gritty long-term solidarity, protest and a subversive call to liberative praxis.

As the Cameron/Osborne decade of austerity was beginning to bite, the human geographer Andrew Williams argued that the biblical tradition of lament provides a creative vehicle for anti-poverty protest. Williams suggests that lament offers an opportunity for a pain-filled emotional release that resonates with suffering, while at the same time resourcing liberative prophetic practice and political protest (2014, pp. 1–4). Williams challenges the Church – 'Failing to embrace and respond to the voices of lament in our congregation and beyond will more likely make us acquiescent partners in the political status quo – lulling ourselves into believing "everything is fine" when it is not' (p. 4).

In the face of debilitating austerity-age poverty, using the tradition of lament can provide theology with a creative means of sitting with the raw pain of traumatizing housing injustice, the slow and grinding violence of seemingly never-ending poverty and the internalizing of shame inducing stigma and corrosive narratives about people with direct experience of poverty. The cries of rage and anguish depicted in my photographs from the People's Gallery under the Westway exemplify the nitty-gritty postsecular lament, unconfined by formalized religious tradition, that arose from the smouldering ashes of Grenfell Tower and a community's unresolved collective trauma. The life-limiting relational poverty and poverty of identity in Hodge Hill that Revd Al Barrett

(Interview 2019) describes and internalized shame-inducing stigma that shuts out hope and feeds despair can be seen as expressions of systemic sin (Gutiérrez, 1974) and hegemonic cultural violence (Galtung, 1990). They are also the raw material of theological lament. Our Life on the Breadline research makes it clear that if it is to gain traction beyond the pulpit or the academy, an austerity-age theology of liberation needs to name and sit with anger, pain and shame and to lament with those who cry out in despair.

Where are songs of lament in breadline Britain? A hauntingly power-ful postsecular austerity-age lament was released by the West London rap musician Lowkey just a few weeks after the Grenfell Tower fire in 2017. Lowkey intoned, 'Oh, you political class, so servile to corporate power. Did they die or us? Ghosts of Grenfell still calling for justice, now hear them scream.'[1] Lowkey's lyrics were still graffitied on walls in North Kensington when I was visiting the community during Life on the Breadline in 2019 and 2020. We need more such austerity-age songs of lament. They represent the building blocks of a theology of liberation that can enable existential emancipation as well as a sung narrative to challenge the hegemony of structural injustice.

Apocalypse and conscientization

The political myth of austerity wove a narrative that justified a decade of impoverishment and pain whilst also masking the structural injus-tice that underpins systemic poverty. As I noted in Chapter 1, Bottici reminds us that the power of a myth is evidenced in its capacity to make itself invisible (2011, p. 41). Political and public discourse follow-ing the 2010 UK General Election framed austerity as an unavoidable economic necessity, which, as I noted in Chapter 1, David Cameron and George Osborne claimed was a corrective to what they suggested was New Labour's financial irresponsibility. Furthermore, Cameron and Osborne insisted that the pain of austerity would be felt by us all. We were told we were 'all in this together'. Our Life on the Breadline research demonstrated quite clearly that some of us were hit far harder than others and that austerity was, in fact, an ideologically motivated political choice. Nevertheless, the narrative woven into the public imag-ination was of shared economic sacrifice. In his analysis of ancient and contemporary prophetic practice and politics, biblical scholar Walter Brueggemann argued that, 'As long as the empire can keep the pre-tence alive that things are all right, there will be no real grieving and no serious criticism' (1978, p. 1). As I pointed out in Chapter 1, this ideological justification of injustice and poverty as natural and the result of individual inadequacy or laziness was described by Gramsci (2007) as hegemony and by Galtung (1990) as cultural violence. An austerity-age theology of liberation in the UK needs to facilitate spiritual and existential transformation as well as structural and systemic change if this hegemony is to be undermined and overcome. Only by fostering such cultural and spiritual change can we rip out the cancer of austerity by its roots and build a society in which poverty becomes morally unacceptable (Shannahan, 2018).

Unlikely as it might sound, a re-imagining of apocalypse can help us to move along from austerity-age lament to the emergence of a new expression of liberation theology (Shannahan, 2022). In the popular imagination, within much Christian spirituality and apocalyptic theology apocalypse is a term that is used to refer to the end of time and the Day of Judgement. We need to rid our minds of this image and focus instead on the deeper existential meaning of 'apocalypse' as 'uncovering', 'unmasking' or making clear that which is hidden or masked in order to foster a form of false consciousness that accepts the justification of injustice by the powerful as normative. Within our Life on the Breadline research, the Asset-Based Community Development-oriented work of Hodge Hill Church, which sought to subvert shame-inducing stigma (Chapter 6), the Therapeutic Interventions of Power the Fight alongside young adults and socially excluded communities damaged by knife crime (Chapter 5) and Church Action on Poverty's Church at the Margins and Self-Reliant group initiatives (Chapter 4) all exemplify such apocalyptic conscientization. In Chapter 1 I argued that the unmasking of the hidden causes of the structural injustice that gives rise to systemic poverty is an essential first step on the road to conscientization (Freire, 1970), liberative praxis and, ultimately an inclusive and egalitarian vision of the common good. Only then will it be possible, as Gutiérrez puts it, for us to reimagine theology as a liberative task that is shaped by those who are left out and left behind (1983, p. 204). The unmasking of the hegemonic cultural violence that justifies austerity and an awakening to the possibility of the transformation of structural injustice in breadline Britain can only resource the development of an empathetic and pastorally centred theology of holistic liberation if they are shaped by what Martin Luther King Jr called an 'act of love' in his 1962 'Levels of Love' sermon. King suggested to the congregation of Ebenezer Baptist Church in Atlanta, Georgia, that countercultural, counter-hegemonic, all-inclusive, Kingdom-oriented love represents the ultimate form of liberative praxis.[2] It alone, he argued, has the capacity to generate existential emancipation and a holistic model of liberation capable of defeating structural injustice and fostering an inclusive vision of the common good that is rooted in God's peferential option for the poor. An austerity-age theology of liberation will need to draw on such love-focused egalitarianism to dub dominant ideologies based on an emancipatory liberative ethic, as shown in Figure 9.

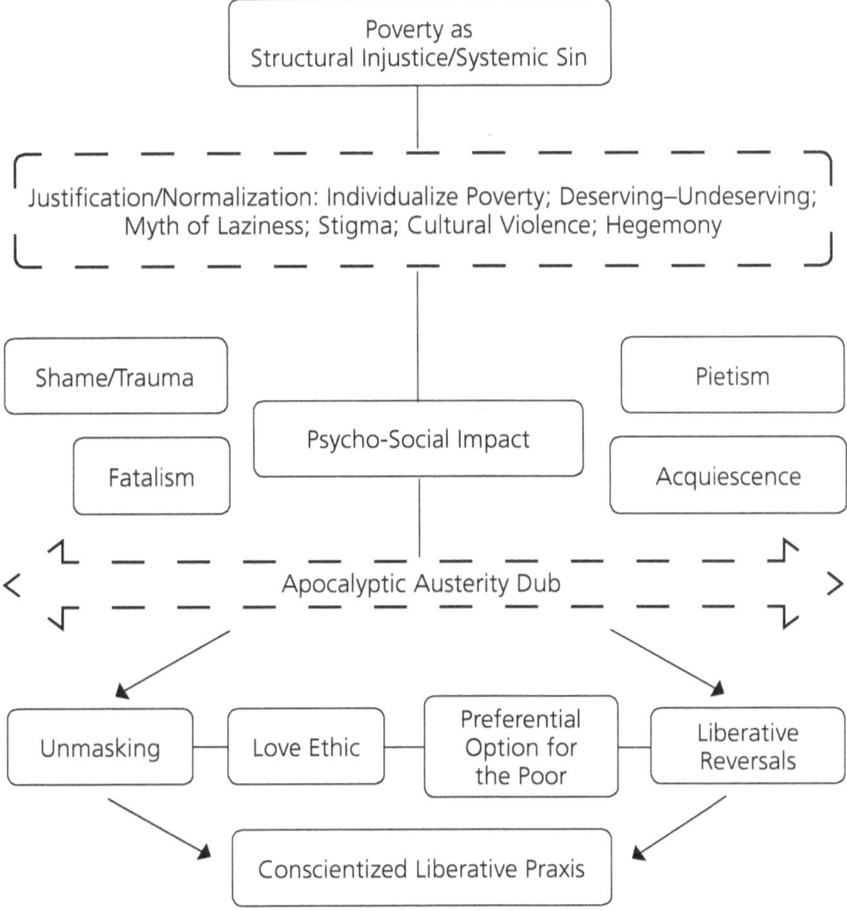

Figure 9. Apocalypse and Austerity Dub

Shalom spiritualities – human security meets the common good

Our Life on the Breadline research has illustrated the central role that Catholic Social Teaching about the common good, the biblical vision of *Shalom* and the multidimensional interdisciplinary concept of human security need to play in an austerity-age theology of liberation. The rooting of a dialogue between these interrelated concepts in a transformational love-oriented liberative ethic that reflects the messy complexity of contemporary poverty will be essential in the forging of a culturally credible theology of liberation.

In Chapter 3 I discussed the ways in which the 'Caring' Christian approach to contemporary poverty that we identified during Life on the Breadline is rooted – explicitly and implicitly – in Catholic Social Teaching and social gospel understandings of the theological, pastoral and political significance of the concept of the common good. Rooted implicitly in the virtue ethics of Aristotle and the theology of Thomas Aquinas and Ignatius Loyola, common-good thinking, whilst not exclusively Christian, is largely identified with the contemporary Catholic Social Teaching tradition that traces its roots to Pope Leo XIII's *Rerum Novarum*. As I noted in Chapter 3, the common-good teaching that shapes most of the Christian engagement with austerity-age poverty that we studied during the Life on the Breadline project is characterized by a core belief that God has a preferential option for the poor; the linking of individual and communal well-being; a commitment to the welfare of the communities in which we live; a vision of solidarity with socially excluded communities as an ethical priority; a belief that all people are endowed with an inherent dignity that must be respected and nurtured and a fundamental commitment to human mutuality.

As we explore the shape that a contextualized austerity-age theology of liberation might take, an engagement with the concept of human security can inform, critique and enrich theological analyses of structural injustice and egalitarian visions of the common good. To date, this is a theoretical framework that has barely even been acknowledged within political theology. The concept is rooted in the work of the United Nations Development Programme, beginning with its *Human Development* report in 1994, which sought to frame individual and communal vulnerabilities in holistic terms. The UNDP framework referred to seven dimensions of human security – economic security, food security, health security, environmental security, political security, personal security and community security, which have been summarized as freedom from fear, freedom from want/vulnerability and freedom from shame (United Nations Development Programme, 1994). Mary Martin and Taylor Owen point to the policy-related impact of the concept of human security but recognize that, to date, its use in interdisciplinary research has been limited (2014, pp. 2–3). For Martin and Taylor, an ongoing discussion about human security can enable more multidimensional understandings of collective and individual insecurity and holistic understandings of security and well-being (2014, p. 3). At the International Symposium on Human Security, Amartya Sen (2000) suggested that a multifaceted understanding of the nature of insecurity can help us to reflect on the ways in which differing forms of vulnerability intersect with and compound each other.

Des Gasper (2005) recognizes the ambivalence of the language of 'security' as a way of conceiving of individual and communal well-being, given the common linkage of the term with national security and its use in relation to the social cohesion agendas of successive governments. It is vital that this ambivalence is recognized if the concept of human security is to play a role in the forging of a contemporary theology of liberation. However, as Gasper also points out, the concept can be helpfully aligned with the 'securing of humanity', 'cultivating humanity' and visions of human flourishing which, from a theological perspective, echo similar commitments within theologies of the common good (2005, p. 225). Gasper points to the ways in which human security thinking interweaves a concern for human needs, human development and human rights (2005, p. 230). Such a conceptual triumvirate was hinted at in a number of our Life on the Breadline case studies and interviews with Church leaders and has the potential to enhance the reframing of the multidimensional biblical concept of *Shalom* as a key component in the development of a liberative spirituality and emancipatory vision of human security.

Human security analysis is usually aligned with development studies and international relations (Hanlon and Christie, 2016). However, I suggest that this way of discussing individual and communal vulnerability and insecurity and the preconditions for human flourishing can provide a creative new tool for all who are engaged in holistic liberative theological analyses of multidimensional contemporary poverty in the UK and other comparable societies in the global North. Currently the potential use of the concept of human security as a lens through which to view the jigsaw of austerity-age poverty is a completely untapped resource within political theology. I hope, therefore, that my own engagement with the concept as it relates to our Life on the Breadline research, can serve as a model for the use of human security within contemporary theologies of liberation in the future. Human security complements a use of the concept of intersectionality to capture the complexity of poverty and the very different ways in which we experience it in the face of structural inequality (Shannahan, 2022; Shannahan and Denning, 2022). As I noted in Chapters 1 and 6, the Church Urban Fund's discussion of the interlocking poverty of resources, poverty of relationships and poverty of identity in a 'web of poverty' (Church

Urban Fund, 2014) captures the complex and interwoven nature of poverty and, importantly, challenges us to move beyond a narrow focus on economic factors alone. The nuanced analysis made possible through CUF's 'web of poverty' can be further enhanced through a use of the multidimensional exploration of individual and communal vulnerabilities and sources of security exemplified by human security thinking. Furthermore, the use of a human security approach, when set alongside theological understandings of the common good can enhance the development of an intellectually rigorous theology of liberation that relates both to a multidimensional understanding of individual and communal vulnerability and to interdependent human flourishing.

Whilst the concept was rarely even hinted at during Life on the Breadline, our research can illuminate the conceptual value of human security as a reference point in contemporary theologies of liberation. The seven dimensions of individual and communal vulnerability identified within the UNDP's human security framework were evident in four of our Life on the Breadline case studies, as was its identification of three fundamental freedoms – freedom from fear, freedom from want and freedom from shame.

As I demonstrated in Chapter 6, our case study of Hodge Hill Church in Birmingham showed how their work engages on a long-term basis with economic, environmental and political vulnerabilities that are fed by a public discourse that elicits political and psycho-social vulnerability, the internalization of stigma and prevalence of shame and low self-esteem. The 'Community Building' approach of Hodge Hill Church revolves around a commitment to fostering an inclusive shared sense of human security on the Firs and Bromford estate that is rooted in an Incarnational spirituality of solidarity and presence and a vision of an egalitarian model of the common good that is forged through an Asset-Based Community Development model of relationship building and social action. The multifaceted framework provided by human security thinking can inform and enhance Hodge Hill's vision of the common good and an implicit theology of human flourishing that asserts the inherent dignity of all people, especially those who feel marginalized and devalued or diminished by the slow violence of poverty. Our case study of B30 food bank in Birmingham, which I discussed in Chapter 3, provided a clear snapshot of multiple forms of individual and communal vulnerability. The growth of poverty during the Age of Austerity led to a rapid rise in the numbers of people served by B30 and exemplified a perfect storm of human insecurity – food vulnerability, economic vulnerability, personal vulnerability, and physical and mental health vulnerabilities converged and compounded experiences of exclusion.

There was also a recognition that freedom from want, fear and shame demanded more than a three-day food parcel.

Genuine human security rests on the transformation of the structural injustice that leads a person to a food bank in the first place. Our study of Power the Fight's engagement with the confluence between knife crime and austerity in South London and its advocacy and therapeutic approach, which I reflected on in Chapter 5, exemplified the systemic violence of poverty and the intersection between economic, political, personal and communal security. In a similar manner our exploration of Notting Hill Methodist Church's response to homelessness and housing injustice in North Kensington in the aftermath of the 2017 Grenfell Tower fire, which I considered in Chapter 4, shows how the slow traumatizing violence of austerity-age poverty and inequality (Shannahan, 2022) can be viewed through a human security lens, embodying, as it does, the perfect storm of economic, political, personal, health, environmental and communal vulnerability.

The use of the concept of human security as a lens through which we can view the Christian responses to multidimensional austerity-age poverty that we explored during Life on the Breadline can sharpen and add clarity to reflections on the implications of God's preferential option for the poor, and appeals to the common good in a structurally unjust age for the development of a counter-hegemonic pattern of liberative praxis as the basis for a holistic theology of liberation. Such reflections invite us to reach back to the ancient biblical concept of *Shalom* in the search for such a theology, as I have noted in previous chapters. Often translated as 'peace', the Hebrew term *Shalom* relates to a richer and more complex set of ideas about holistic human flourishing. More than mere peace, *Shalom* speaks to us of justice, interconnectedness, liberation, integrated well-being, holistic human security and an inclusive vision of an egalitarian common good. This vision of a just, inclusive and egalitarian society within which the voices of those have been marginalized, silenced or ignored are foregrounded provides an invaluable but under-used resource for the development of a holistic austerity-age theology of liberation that is characterized by existential, as well as economic emancipation and human security. However, a *Shalom*-infused vision of human security is not inevitably always a force for liberative systemic change and the transformation of structural injustice, any more than an apolitical vision of the common good. Such an orientation, therefore, relies on the deployment of a counter hegemonic hermeneutics of suspicion and dub hermeneutics that is animated by a conscious liberative ethic, as I show in Figure 10.

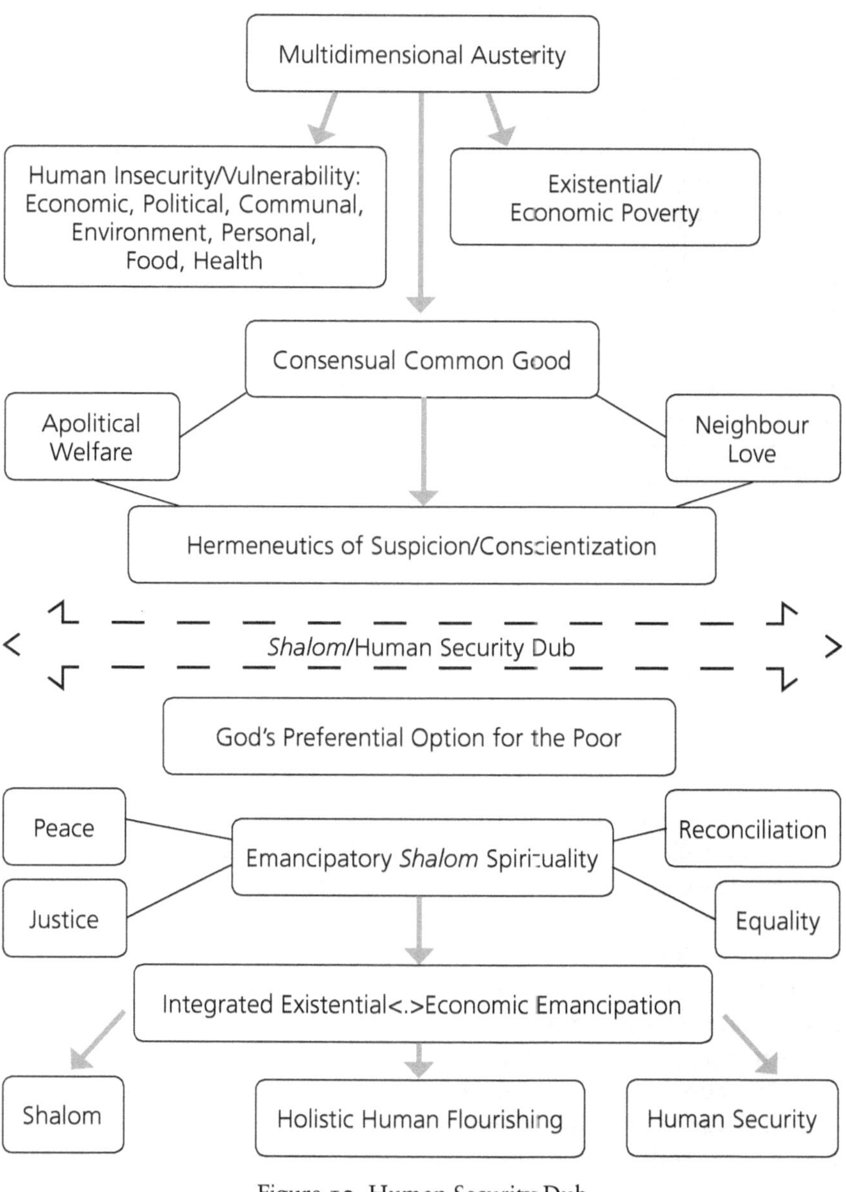

Figure 10. Human Security Dub

God's preferential option for the poor in an Age of Austerity

Liberation theology emerged out of the systemic inequality of 1960s Latin America and the forging of a model of the Church as a conscientized liberative social movement in emancipatory solidarity with people trapped by debilitating poverty. Leonardo and Clodovis Boff suggested that 'Liberation theology was born when faith confronted the injustice done to the poor' (1987, p. 3). An Incarnational vision of God in solidarity with oppressed peoples everywhere and a rediscovery of the liberative preaching of the Hebrew prophets, combined with a critical appropriation of aspects of Marxist analyses of class and hegemonic ideology and an embrace of Freire's (1970) call for liberative conscientization gave rise to a simple but revolutionary statement of faith – in a structurally unjust society the God of Creation who shapes all people in the divine image and becomes our brother in Jesus necessarily has a preferential option for the poor, not because the rich are sinners and the poor are saints but because structural injustice contradicts the nature and the will of God. This conviction formed the basis of the pioneering reflections of the first generation of Latin American liberation theologians and is the foundation upon which Gutiérrez's seminal *A Theology of Liberation* is built. For Gutiérrez's poverty robs us of our dignity and strips away our sense of personhood (1974, p. 289). We become non-people. Such poverty, he concludes, can be seen as a form of interwoven and multidimensional violence – a kind of slow death (1988, p. xxi).

Latin American liberation theology has been accused (particularly during the 1980s by Cardinal Joseph Ratzinger, the head of the Vatican's Congregation of the Faith who later became Pope Benedict XVI) of owing more to secularism and Marxist theory than Christian teaching (Ratzinger, 1984). It is true that early liberation theologians drew on the social critique of Marx and on Gramsci's reflections on the nature and impact of hegemony. However, the implied accusation that liberation theology did not engage with the Bible is misleading and untrue as even a cursory reading, for example, of the work of Gutiérrez (1974; 1983), Segundo (1976), Sobrino (1978), Boff and Boff (1987) and Jorge Pixley and Clodovis Boff (1989) demonstrates. Poverty and the experience of the poor is a central theme within the Bible (referred to more than 2,000 times) and God's solidarity with the oppressed represents a golden thread within the Jewish and Christian Scriptures. Examples of this biblical witness that impacted on the emergence of Latin American liberation theology include Exodus 3.7–10; Leviticus 25.1–55; Deuteronomy 15.1–11; Psalms 34.4–7, 37.9–15, 74.19–21, 82.2–4, 146.7–9; Isaiah 1.15–17, 58.6–12, 61.1–4; Jeremiah 5.27–28, 22.13–17; Amos

2.6–7, 5.10–12; Micah 6.11–16; Matthew 5.3–12, 19.16–24, 25.31–45; Luke 1.46–55, 4.16–21, 6.20–26, 12.13–21, 16.19–31, 22.24–27; 2 Corinthians 8.9; James 2.1–6, 5.1–6; and 1 John 3.17, 4.19–21.

God's unconditional identification with people experiencing poverty represents a profound challenge to people of faith. The adoption of such an unconditional preferential option for the poor, therefore, has profound existential, as well as economic implications for the forging of a spirituality of liberation, not just social action intended to transform structural injustice (Gutiérrez, 1974, p. 205). Liberation theology bears witness to the integral interconnection between existential emancipation and liberative social change and, 'a commitment to solidarity with the poor, with those who suffer misery and injustice ... to witness to the evil which has resulted from sin and is a breach of communion' (Gutiérrez, 1974, p. 299). The embodiment of God's preferential option for the poor and the transformation of structural injustice, therefore, are expressions of spiritual resistance as well as political interventions in the public sphere, what Gutiérrez calls 'an act of love and liberation' (1974, pp. 300–1).

Christopher Rowland suggests that 'Liberation theology is not a body of knowledge which can be learnt but a way of understanding God in the midst of history' (cited in Bennett and Gowler, 2012, pp. 2–3). Consequently, whilst liberation theology first emerged from the specific struggles and cultural particularities of Latin America in the 1960s and 1970s, it is not limited by geography. Rather, liberation theology exemplifies a mindset, a commitment and a way of thinking about God and the nature of faith in structurally unjust societies. Therefore, it is possible to identify liberative readings of Christian faith in times and places far removed from the *favelas* of Latin America. From the early communism of the first Christian communities in Jerusalem (Acts 2.42–47) to the Christian Socialists and the Catholic Workers Movement and the Worker Priests of the early decades of the twentieth century, the theological essence of liberation theology has woven its way, often marginalized or repressed, through Christian history. It is important to recognize, however, that the earliest forms of Latin American liberation theology have reasonably been criticized for their neglect of the multidimensional nature of oppression and the intersectionality of our experience. Gender, ethnicity and sexuality are of equal importance in our understanding of structural injustice but were often absent from the earliest expressions of liberation theology. These significant flaws notwithstanding, the vision of God's preferential option for the poor and the central importance of liberative grassroots praxis that gave rise to Latin American liberation theology has stimulated similar movements in many different contexts across the globe. The last half-century has seen the emergence, for example, of Dalit theology in South India (Rajikumar, 2010); Black liberation theology forged during the US Civil Rights and Black Power Struggle (Cone, 1975) and in the fires of Apartheid South Africa (Boesak, 1976); Womanist (Grant, 1989) and Feminist (Radford-Ruether, 1983) theologies of liberation; Queer theologies (Althaus-Reid, 2002) and the urban liberation theology (Vincent, 1982) that emerged in the UK in the 1980s.

Ivan Petrella is right, however, to remind us that the configuration and complexity of structural injustice in the twenty-first century is dramatically different from the culture and the context within which the movement first emerged (2006, p. 11ff). The bipolar geopolitics of the Cold War has been largely displaced by an increasingly fluid multipolar world and multidimensional intersectional expressions of structural injustice. I have noted the critiques of the early generation of Latin American liberation theologians above. However, Petrella's challenge to contemporary theology is still timely almost 20 years after he wrote (2006, p. 11ff). Liberation theology needs to identify and analyse a new arena of struggle if it is to address contemporary structural injustice with credibility and rigour. In light of our research during Life on the Breadline it is clear that, whilst liberation theologians' assertion of God's preferential option for the poor was a response to the poverty and inequality of Latin America more than half a century ago, its depiction of a God, a gospel and a Church in solidarity with those most left out and left behind resonates deeply in austerity-age Britain.

Austerity represents a new site of liberative struggle. It is the crucible within which a new vision of God's preferential option for the poor needs to be forged and a new, multidimensional and intersectional liberation theology brough to birth. However, if such a re-imagining is to arise authentically from the economic, political and cultural landscape of austerity, lessons need to be learned from previous attempts to 'import' a commitment to God's preferential option for the poor in uncritical and decontextualized ways that did not fashion a sufficiently interdisciplinary analysis or take sufficient account of the particularities of the UK context (Shannahan, 2010). In previous chapters I have discussed the widespread emphasis on God's preferential option for the poor amongst the Church leaders from across the UK with whom we spoke during Life on the Breadline. I have affirmed the value of such commitments but also noted the need to point to their limitations in moving the Church beyond a welfare-based commitment to an egalitarian vision of the common good to a prophetic and sustained political engagement in the public sphere intended to transform the structural injustice of systemic poverty. As I have argued elsewhere (Shannahan, 2010) and shown in this book, an academically rigorous, culturally resonant and politically transformative austerity-age theology of liberation needs to be rooted in a deep engagement with social science analyses of poverty, power and politics. It must be thoroughly informed by a witness to God's preferential option for the poor that is shaped by extensive fieldwork. This was the approach we modelled during Life on the Breadline. Consequently, a contemporary re-imagining of the option for the poor will be enriched by grasping six key lessons that we learned during our research.

First, austerity-age poverty is not neutral. It arose from ideologically motivated neoliberal free-market capitalist policymaking and the conscious withdrawal of the State from socially excluded communities. Power is attributed not to the State but to a globally dispersed market. Individualism and entrepreneurialism are valorized and collectivism and solidarity devalued. Regulation, social cohesion and the common good take second place to ever increasing profit-margins as we saw in our case study of Christian responses to the tragic Grenfell Tower fire. Neither neutral, nor inevitable, Grenfell was the price people in poverty paid for being poor. Life on the Breadline invites theologians to re-imagine God's preferential option for the poor as a challenge to the everywhere-but-nowhere dispersed power of a globalized neoliberal capitalism within which community is devalued, and entrepreneurial individuals are presented as the answer to all our prayers.

Second, austerity-age poverty was not the inevitable consequence of the 2008 global financial crash, but the result of political decisions taken by Prime Minister David Cameron and his Chancellor, George Osborne in the aftermath of the 2010 UK General Election and in particular following the 2012 Welfare Reform Act, which I discussed in Chapter 1. At the time of writing, it is possibly too early to make a definitive judgement on the social policies of the Labour government led by Keir Starmer following their 2024 General Election victory. However, soon after coming to power the Starmer government suspended seven back-bench MPs for opposing the decision to retain the two-child benefit cap introduced by the Conservatives in 2017 (Francis and Eardley, 2024). Several months later in November 2024 the Starmer government restricted the Winter Fuel Allowance of £300 to those elderly people claiming Pension Credit benefits and in March 2025 the Labour Chancellor Rachel Reeves announced welfare spending cuts of £4.8 billion which, it was projected, would leave three million households £1,720 a year worse off. Reeves claimed this was a move intended to balance the nation's books, language not so very different from that used by Conservative Chancellor George Osborne in 2010. Life on the Breadline challenges theologians to re-imagine God's preferential option for the poor in a manner that enables the Church to meet the demands of this *Kairos* moment and fashion a proactive presence in the public sphere that moves beyond 'Caring' to agitate for transformative systemic change – unafraid of taking sides in the struggle to overcome structural injustice.

Third, it is important for a contemporary re-imagining of God's preferential option for the poor to identify and subvert the cultural violence of hegemonic public discourse that claims that poverty is accidental, or the result of laziness or a poor work-ethic. As Life on the Breadline illustrated and as I have shown in this book, poverty is systemic – an inevitable by-product of neoliberal capitalism, rather than an unexpected aberration. Christian responses to austerity poverty must recognize this and move beyond a welfare-based commitment to the common good if the theology of liberation they seek is to generate the liberative praxis needed to transform structural injustice.

Fourth, the fashioning of an austerity-age vision of God's preferential option for the poor needs to move beyond an understandable but reductionist focus on food poverty, which narrows our understanding, blunts our analysis and limits the impact of our action. As we demonstrated during Life on the Breadline fieldwork (Shannahan and Denning, 2022) and as I have argued in previous chapters, only a fieldwork-informed analysis of our intersectional experience of the multidimensional nature of the jigsaw of contemporary poverty can provide an austerity-age theology of liberation with broad-based academic credibility and cultural traction. The Jigsaw of Poverty image created by Beth Waters for us during Life on the Breadline (Figure 3 above) highlights the multidimensional nature of contemporary poverty and the interconnectedness of differing aspects of such social exclusion. Our case study of B30 food bank in Birmingham showed that we cannot respond adequately to austerity-age structural injustice if we fail to grasp the ways in which food insecurity, fuel poverty, insecure employment, low pay and housing injustice collide with and compound one another. Too often, however, policymakers, preachers and researchers reduce austerity to food poverty.

Fifth, an austerity-age vision of God's preferential option for the poor needs to engage with existential as well as economic oppression. As I showed in earlier chapters, Hodge Hill Church in Birmingham roots its Asset-Based Community Development (ABCD) oriented ecclesiology in a long-term commitment to challenging a 'poverty of relationships' and a 'poverty of identity' (Revd Al Barrett, Hodge Hill Vicar, Interview 2020) and the internalization of low self-esteem and shame that results from a persistent stigmatizing of the estate. Consequently, a renewed framing of God's preferential option for the poor needs to be character-ized by a long-term commitment to solidarity, an affirming spirituality that emphasizes inherent human dignity and agency, challenges stigma-tizing cultural violence and a recognition of the need for existential as well as economic liberation if it is to stand a chance of sustaining a dynamic movement-oriented ecclesiology capable of transforming structural injustice.

Sixth, if it is to gain traction, a contemporary reimagining of God's preferential option for the poor needs to recognize the unequal and violent nature of austerity. As I noted in earlier chapters, a detailed engagement with the concept of intersectionality first articulated by Crenshaw (1989; 1991) and the framing of poverty as a form of trauma-tizing slow structural and direct violence (Galtung, 1990; Nixon, 2011; Shannahan, 2022) is essential if political theologians want to fashion analyses capable of generating liberative social change. Our Grenfell Tower and Power the Fight case studies illustrate the importance of such an analysis. In spite of assertions to the contrary by former Con-servative Chancellor George Osborne, we have never 'all been in this together'. Class and ethnicity; geography and housing injustice; gentri-fication and housing deregulation; and social exclusion exacerbated by dramatic reductions in the funding of youth and children's services have compounded one another in a traumatizing perfect storm of violent and unequal austerity-age poverty. A new vision of God's preferential option for the poor needs to recognize, understand and respond to such complexity because well-intentioned apolitical 'Caring' commitments to the common good will not generate the systemic change needed to trans-form structural injustice.

Human security and the common good in an Age of Austerity

At this *Kairos* moment it is time for theologians to step out of their comfort zone as we strive to fashion a theology of liberation that is fit for the present age and capable of meeting the challenges of a seemingly unending Age of Austerity. Life on the Breadline has shown that we need to re-imagine old ideas and engage in critical dialogue with new concepts and disciplines. Our research shone a light on the challenges facing the Church in the UK as it seeks to fashion a progressive space in the public sphere that can enable it to live up to its calling to transform structural injustice.

Most Christian responses to contemporary poverty are, at the very least, implicitly shaped by teaching about the common good as was evidenced during Life on the Breadline in an overwhelming majority of the interviews we held with regional and national Church leaders. Whilst common-good thought is not specifically Christian it has become synonymous with the Church's response to poverty and inequality and with Catholic Social Teaching and the social gospel tradition in particular. Most of the 'Caring' responses to austerity-age poverty that we encountered during Life on the Breadline were informed by biblical teaching about the common good, for example Jeremiah 29.7, Matthew 25.31–45 and Acts 2.42–47. As I have noted, Rowlands (2015) argues that Catholic Social Teaching (CST) on the common good is directly relevant to discussions about austerity-age structural injustice. In particular, where it is informed by a hermeneutics of suspicion and an *a priori* emancipatory standpoint, CST's emphasis on inherent human dignity, solidarity, human equality, the dignity of work and God's preferential option for the poor can help to sharpen re-imagined understandings of the common good as the Church fashions a truly liberative role in the public sphere that can help it to avoid any kind of collusion with structural injustice. Discussions about multidimensional human security can also offer creative resources to interdisciplinary political theologians engaged in this task. The search for a holistic liberative vision of an egalitarian common-good ethic to guide the Church's role in the public sphere can be enhanced by drawing common-good teaching and analyses of our intersectional experience of multidimensional poverty into a dialogue with thinking about the seven dimensions of human security – economic security, food security, health security, environmental security, political security, personal security and community security, as I noted earlier in this chapter. Our experience during Life on the Breadline suggests that such a perspective can enable the fashioning of an authentically liberative *Shalom*, as I suggested in Chapter 6.

The search for a model of the common good that is shaped by a holistic vision of liberative *Shalom* needs to draw on intersectional insights about social location and systemic inequality if it is to foster greater human security for people experiencing poverty. Our Life on the Breadline research challenges theology to pay far greater attention to our intersectional experience of the multidimensional jigsaw of poverty. In previous chapters I have highlighted the need for theological responses to contemporary poverty to root their analyses much more deeply in extensive primary research. Our case studies of Christian responses to the Grenfell Tower fire and the therapeutic advocacy of Power the Fight's engagement with austerity-induced knife crime, which I discussed in Chapters 4 and 5, show that an attention to intersectional thinking can highlight the ways in which housing injustice, racialized poverty, gentrification, huge cuts to youth and children's services, welfare spending cuts and localized inequalities converge, collide and compound the traumatizing violence of austerity. It is important for theological engagements with contemporary poverty and the fashioning of a new theology of liberation to grasp the insights that an intersectional framework offers us. Who we are, where we live, what we look like, where we pray and how we talk shapes our experience of austerity. As our engagement with the work of Hodge Hill Church in Birmingham demonstrates, if they are to foster holistic liberation and an integrated vision of a *Shalom*-oriented common good, political theologians need to fully understand the psychosocial and spiritual damage caused by relational poverty and poverty of identity and the shame induced by the internalization of stigmatizing narratives about working-class communities. A liberative, holistic and egalitarian theology of the common good that has the capacity to foster the multidimensional human security of people worn down by their experience of poverty in the structurally unjust Age of Austerity rests on the emancipatory potential of the dub hermeneutics I have developed in this book, as depicted in Figure 7.

As Figure 11 shows, the use of a dub hermeneutics makes it possible to deconstruct existing Christian approaches to contemporary poverty and to reconstruct an engagement with austerity that can generate the liberative praxis needed to enable the development of an egalitarian vision of the common good that addresses our intersectional experience of multidimensional social exclusion. Such an approach can facilitate the fashioning of a form of human security that addresses the multifaceted vulnerabilities of people with direct experience of poverty. This will need to address existential oppression as well as economic marginalization if it is to resource a *Shalom*-informed vision of the common good. However, as we discovered during Life on the Breadline and as I indicate in Figure 11, in the context of the structural injustice that characterizes austerity-age Britain, a faith-based fashioning of an egalitarian common good relies on three things. First, the Church needs to be ready to translate its network-building bridging social capital into the more politicized linking capital that I discuss above if it is to use its presence and its resource to challenge asymmetric power and structural injustice. Second, the use of such linking capital is only likely to be effective if it is based on a clear vision of God's preferential option for the poor. Third, the practical outworking of the embodiment of the option for the poor through the use of linking capital needs to be characterized by a series of what I have previously called 'liberative reversals' (Shannahan, 2010, p. 240). These transformative acts can be compared to the emancipatory inversions of systemically unjust power relations to which Jesus refers in

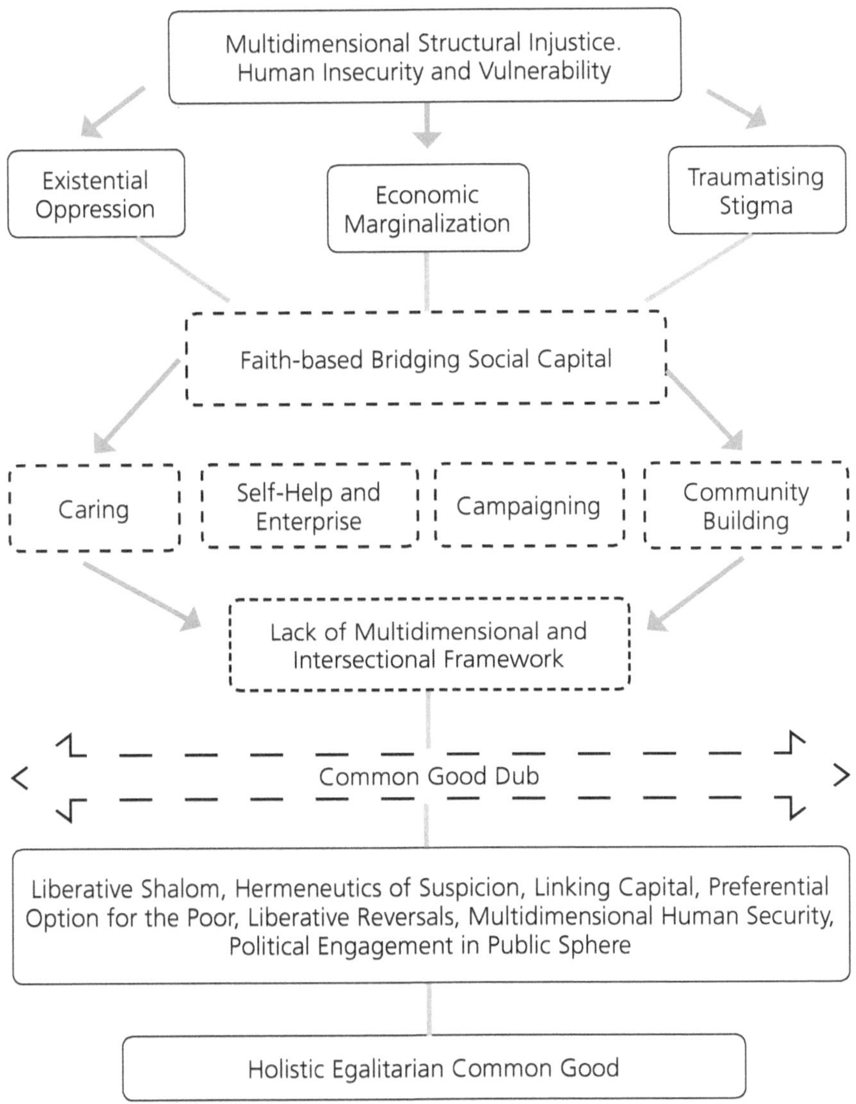

Figure 11. Common Good Dub

the Beatitudes in Matthew 5 and the Blessings and Woes in Luke 6. If the vision of an egalitarian common good within an austerity-age theology of liberation is to generate the liberative praxis capable of transforming structural injustice such liberative reversals, or inversions of injustice, calling the Church to step from 'Caring' loving service to proactive and prophetic political engagement, are absolutely vital. Examples of such liberative praxis from our Life on the Breadline research illustrate the point with graphic clarity. Such Breadline beatitudes were particularly evident in three of our case studies.

First, as I discussed in Chapter 5, Power the Fight's use of its liberative therapeutic intervention programme in relation to the experience of social exclusion, marginalization, traumatization and disempowerment caused by austerity-induced knife crime has transformed the experience and social location of teenagers and young adults. A liberative reversal has empowered excluded teenagers and young adults to reclaim their dignity, value and agency through their involvement in the Mayor of London's Violence Reduction Unit. Second, as I explained in Chapter 5, the use of Asset-Based Community Development has helped Hodge Hill Church to enable a series of liberative reversals amongst young people on the Bromford housing estate in Birmingham. The Gear Up bicycle repairs initiative illustrates the way in which social enterprise can be harnessed to foster liberative reversals that enhance economic empowerment and agency in the face of endemic unemployment and insecure work. Third, as I demonstrated in Chapter 4, the 'Campaigning' and 'Advocacy' of Church Action on Poverty stimulates a variety of liberative reversals. Church Action's development and facilitation of Living Wage campaigns has persuaded local churches across the UK to become Living Wage employers, exemplifying liberative reversal as a form of vitally important economic empowerment. Furthermore, as I discussed in Chapter 6, the liberative reversal embodied by Church Action's fashioning of small Communities of Self Reliance has enhanced the agency, sense of dignity and economic self-reliance of marginalized women, particularly in the North of England.

Dubbing the Church – a new ecclesiology for a postsecular age

Life on the Breadline demonstrated how the Church has been in the forefront of responses to austerity-age poverty since the 2008 global financial crash. Our research shone a light on the breadth, value and impact of such engagements with poverty, as I have shown in previous chapters. I have stressed the provisional, fluid and evolving nature of the four Christian approaches to austerity-age poverty that we identified within our ethnographic case studies during Life on the Breadline and cautioned against viewing them as a fixed typology. That said, I have argued that the 'Caring', 'Campaigning and Advocacy', 'Self-Help and Enterprise' and 'Community Building' approaches to austerity-age poverty that we identified during our research exemplify distinct and discernible traditions of Christian social ethics, missiology and ecclesiology. Each approach sketches out a vision of the nature and calling of the Church in a structurally unjust society as I demonstrated in previous chapters. The 'Caring' approach, which I discussed in Chapter 3, frames the Church as a servant community, 'bandaging' the wounds of those broken by austerity. The 'Campaigning and Advocacy' approach, which I explored in Chapter 4, argues that the Church needs to become a liberative movement agitating for systemic change and the transformation of structural injustice. The 'Self-help and Enterprise' approach, which I described in Chapter 5, sees the Church as an empowering enabler, providing individuals in poverty with opportunities to transform their own situation without, our research suggests, dismantling the structures and systems that give poverty life in the first place. Finally, the 'Community Building' approach that I discussed in Chapter 6, which draws on Asset-Based Community Development, views the Church as a listening, receptive and empathetic 'Companion', standing in long-term solidarity with people experiencing poverty and building a model of community that challenges stigma and relational poverty by drawing on what is 'strong' in local neighbourhoods, rather than focusing only on what is 'wrong'.

Our conversations with national and regional Church leaders during Life on the Breadline, which I discussed in earlier chapters, reflect five broad themes that are directly relevant in a discussion about the forging of a new liberative ecclesiology capable of resourcing a Church that can live up to its calling to 'transform structural injustice'. First, Church leaders across the denominational spectrum articulated a clear but very generalized, and largely apolitical, commitment to God's preferential option for the poor. Second, most Church leaders expressed strong support for what might be called a 'Caring' plus approach to poverty that combined pastoral and physical support for people experiencing poverty with 'Advocacy' – speaking truth to power via email, petition and letter, but usually from a safe distance and not often on the frontline. Third, most Church leaders spoke eloquently about the Christian tradition of loving service, neighbour love and a welfare-oriented commitment to human flourishing and the common good. Fourth, whilst a significant minority of Church leaders were critical of Government policy and expressed a commitment to God's preferential option for the poor, most expressed a nervousness about moving beyond welfare to translate this commitment in a proactive and prophetic political engagement in the public sphere. Fifth, a smaller, but still significant number of Church leaders reflected on factors that inhibited the Church's engagement with contemporary poverty. Some argued that, in their experience, most congregations, whilst 'Caring', are relatively affluent and cushioned from the raw realities of austerity and other Church leaders suggested that their own denominations were too small, too fragile and too powerless to have any significant impact on systemic poverty.

During our Life on the Breadline research, we encountered Christian activists who argued that David Cameron had sought to 'co-opt' faith-based organizations into his 'Big Society' agenda as the austerity State began to withdraw after the 2010 UK General Election. Bretherton suggested that when faith groups become 'co-opted' by the State they can find themselves 'instrumentalised' as unwitting vehicles for the delivery of social policy agendas (2011, p. 355ff). As I noted in earlier chapters, Robert Beckford (2004) makes a comparable argument, suggesting that Black Pentecostal churches can 'sell out' (to a materialistic gospel), be 'bought out' (in exchange for community work grants) or 'scared out' of marginalized communities, to avoid liberative engagement with structural injustice. Reading such reflections from the perspective of our Life on the Breadline findings and through the lens of a hermeneutics of suspicion has shown how such examples of avoidance and co-option can become forms of implicit collusion. At this *Kairos* moment we need a new vision of a Church that is bold enough to engage proactively and prophetically in the public sphere and embody an unafraid austerity-age preferential option for the poor.

The emergence of a liberative post-Christendom Church that is ready and willing to become unseen but energizing yeast in the struggle for holistic liberation and an egalitarian common good demands a spiritual revolution. Reform and re-orientation are not enough. Valuable as the top-down 'Caring' and 'Campaigning' social action we encountered during Life on the Breadline undoubtedly is, arms-length activism undertaken a safe distance from the traumatizing slow violence of austerity cannot unmask the hegemonic nature of systemic poverty unless such painful exclusion is fully known and felt. Conversion rests on conscientization, the deployment of a hermeneutics of suspicion and a consequent waking up to the brutal realities of neoliberal capitalism and the structural injustice of austerity. In what Gramsci (2007) calls the 'cultural war of position', the hegemonic hold of the cultural violence that Galtung (1990) describes can only be broken through engagement in the battle of ideas to which Castells refers (2010, p. 360). Our work during Life on the Breadline makes it clear that a new ecclesiology characterized by a holistic vision of existential-economic emancipation and a commitment to fashioning a pattern of liberative praxis capable of transforming structural injustice and building a truly egalitarian common good can only emerge when the vision of a new society has displaced the hegemonic justification of injustice in the public imagination. Within Christian communities the existential power of hymns, prayers and sermons can be deployed, as they have been in the face of injustice before, to defeat the cultural violence that underpins hegemonic narratives that individualize, normalize, moralise or even bless systemic poverty. There is power in an idea and, in the context of Christian community, power in the spiritual stories shared in worship. Change begins with ideas, the imagination and a new liberative vision of a society within which everyone can flourish and none are left behind. Sometimes such new visions hang in art galleries, but they can be found on walls in places like the People's Gallery beneath the Westway, just a stone's throw from Notting Hill Methodist Church and the broken shell of what remains of Grenfell Tower as my photograph of a child's anguished lament in Figure 12 reminds us.

Figure 12. Photograph of a child's painting from the Grenfell Tower People's Art Gallery

If it is to meet the challenge of this *Kairos* moment and resource the development of a *Shalom*-oriented austerity-age theology of liberation the Church needs to be fed by an ecclesiology of solidarity. Only an embedded dynamic Church that is rooted in the everyday experience of austerity 'Caring', 'Campaigning', speaking truth to power, fostering emancipatory 'Enterprise' and building inclusive community can 'transform the structures of injustice' that scar, damage and wound so many. It is time for the Church to move unafraid beyond servanthood and welfare-based neighbour love to embrace a prophetic political presence in the public sphere. Only then will it become possible to 'transform the structures of injustice' that have wounded so many for so long.

Conclusion

In this final chapter, I have drawn on the arguments I have developed in previous chapters, which arise from our Life on the Breadline research to begin sowing the seeds of an interdisciplinary fieldwork-led austerity-age theology of liberation. I have argued that such a theology rests on the willingness of theologians to turn our backs on the myth of neutrality.

Objectivity in the face of structural injustice amounts to acquiescence and unconscious collusion. I have argued that the time has come for theologians to commit ourselves to give voice to the struggle for holistic liberation as engaged organic intellectuals shining a light on the traumatizing oppressive damage wrought by the slow violence of systemic poverty and fashioning a new narrative founded on liberative praxis.

Whilst it needs further development in future research, I have shown that the dub hermeneutics I have developed in this book can make an original contribution to hermeneutics, contextual theological methodology, political theology, liberation theology and interdisciplinary studies of Christian engagement with structural injustice. I have argued that such praxis-led theology demands radical, long-term embeddedness – engaged theology and an engaged Church. Only then can a truly Incarnational theological analysis emerge that sits with people in the pain and lament of austerity-age poverty, rather than rushing past the mess and anguish to liberation. I have shown that by developing such a holistic way of doing theology and being imaginative enough to engage with theoretical discussions about multidimensional human security it becomes possible to re-imagine a *Shalom*-oriented egalitarian vision of the common good. Finally, I have shown how a creative dubbing of thinking about apocalypse as a process of unmasking the hegemonic cultural violence that underpins and justifies the structural injustice of austerity can awaken us to the urgent task of liberation and the need for the Church to fashion a new future as a network of grassroots communities of liberative resistance and hope. In so doing, we prepare the ground and make it possible to nurture the seeds of the austerity-age theology of liberation that I have sown in this book.

Notes

1 See VoiceOver, 2017, 'LOWKEY ft. MAI KHALIL – GHOSTS OF GRENFELL (OFFICIAL MUSIC VIDEO)', *YouTube*, 8 August, https://www.youtube.com/watch?v=ztUamrChczQ, accessed 25.02.2025.

2 See Martin Luther King, 'Levels of Love', Ebeneezer Baptist Church, Atlanta, Georgia, 16 September 1962, https://kinginstitute.stanford.edu/king-papers/documents/levels-love-sermon-delivered-ebenezer-baptist-church, accessed 3.03.2025.

Conclusion

This book is a wake-up call. Weaving through every chapter is a plea to theologians, to the Church, to activists and to policymakers to open our eyes and ears to the searing witness of women and men damaged by debilitating austerity-age poverty. This book is not the last word on theology and contemporary poverty, but it does represent a theological first step on the journey towards a re-imagined theology of liberation for an Age of Austerity in two important ways. First, this book represents the first sustained interdisciplinary exploration of the spectrum of Christian responses to multidimensional austerity-age poverty within academic theology in the UK. Second, this book represents the first theological analysis of Christian responses to austerity-age poverty to have been so deeply rooted in and shaped by an extensive, in-depth and varied body of UK-wide qualitative primary research. My hope is that it can serve as a stimulus and a resource for future liberative theological engagements with austerity-age poverty and a gentle nudge to my colleagues within academic theology to step up to the plate.

Drawing on the detailed ethnographic fieldwork that we developed during Life on the Breadline, I have identified, described and analysed an ecosystem of four broad Christian approaches to austerity-age poverty and engagement in the public sphere that we uncovered and explored during our research. I have shown that, whilst 'Caring', 'Campaigning and Advocacy', 'Self-help and Enterprise' and 'Community Building' arise from and reflect differing Christian traditions of social ethics, theology, ecclesiology and missiology, they often converge and intersect with each other over time. These are not fixed ideal types but detailed provisional analyses of evolving approaches to poverty, social action and engagement in the public sphere. They do, however, reflect a spectrum of distinct Christian traditions that have not been analysed alongside one another in relation to austerity-age poverty within academic theology, until now. I have assessed the key features of each approach, drawing extensively on insights from our fieldwork, as well as an interdisciplinary body of literature, and analysed their strengths, weaknesses and extent to which each response can play a key role in the forging of a new austerity-age theology of liberation. I have concluded that none of the approaches has the capacity to resource a *Shalom*-oriented austerity-age theology of liberation in their own strength. Each approach has its limitations, as well as its strengths. However, I have shown that through a creative use of the dub hermeneutics that I have developed in this book, and a careful deployment of a nitty-gritty hermeneutics of suspicion, all of these approaches have the potential to inform and contribute to a new austerity-age theology of liberation that is capable of supporting the development of the liberative praxis needed to 'transform structural injustice'.

Implications for theology and challenges for the Church

This book and the Life on the Breadline project from which it arises are examples of contextualized political theology. Both have emerged from a commitment to rigorous interdisciplinary fieldwork-led theology, but neither project nor book make any claims to political neutrality. Indeed, as I have argued, neutrality in the face of structural injustice amounts to acquiescence, at best, and quiet collusion at worst. Life on the Breadline and the reflections, analyses and arguments in this book emerge from the assertion that theological research can, indeed must, be a force for liberative social change. Consequently, the acid test for this book lies not only in a judgement about its intellectual rigour but, perhaps more importantly, in its potential to lay the foundations for the building of a new interdisciplinary fieldwork-led austerity-age theology of liberation that can help people of faith to forge the liberative praxis needed to embody God's preferential option for the poor and enable the Church to fulfil its calling to 'transform structural injustice'. Therefore, it is appropriate to close by identifying ten challenges that Life on the Breadline poses for theologians and for the Church. Only by responding to these challenges can we begin the work of fashioning a credible austerity-age theology of liberation.

Challenge 1 – The work of the theologian

Two steps need to be taken to develop and sustain a rigorous and contextually authentic austerity-age theology of liberation and ensure its traction within and beyond the academy. First, theologians need to deepen and broaden our critical engagement with other disciplines. More than just a fleeting reference to political philosophy, or social theory, or postcolonial criticism is needed. Sustained in-depth dialogue with the theoretical and fieldwork-informed insights of human geographers, sociologists of religion, trauma studies specialists, peace studies researchers and theorists of intersectionality will give energy, clarity, breadth and nuance to our theological analyses. Second, as I have indicated in previous chapters, Life on the Breadline demonstrates the need for theology to get out of the library and onto the street. It is essential for theologians to follow the lead of our social science compatriots and engage extensively and proactively in qualitative primary research. Such fieldwork-led interdisciplinary theological exploration will provide theology with the contextual authenticity and theoretical depth that can enable and sustain the arguments needed to develop an effective austerity-age theology of liberation.

Challenge 2 – Ecclesiology and liberation

Based on our Life on the Breadline ethnographic fieldwork, I have argued in this book that an austerity-age ecclesiology needs to be premised on a bold liberative ethic that prioritizes faithfulness to the Church's calling to 'transform structural injustice' over institutional growth or organizational survival. We caught glimpses of this perspective during Life on the Breadline in aspects of 'Caring', 'Campaigning', 'Self-help and Enterprise' and 'Community Building'; particularly as these approaches fed into each other. However, these expressions of a multidimensional liberative ethic were too fleeting and sporadic to sustain the kind of long-term proactive presence in the public sphere that is needed to challenge systemic poverty. Even initiatives as pastorally sensitive and progressive as Pope Francis' consistent emphasis since the beginning of his papacy in 2013 on the urgent need for a Church *of* the poor to displace a concerned but distant Church *for* the poor are insufficiently nuanced, inclusive, embedded and grassroots-led to de-centre the institutional Church and foreground the insights and wisdom of people with direct experience of poverty. Equally the public commitments to 'transforming structural injustice' and to God's preferential option for the poor by the Church leaders with whom we spoke during Life on the Breadline, and by Christian denominations across the UK, reflect a largely institutionally bound welfare-based common good ethic, rather than a 'spoke' rammed into the 'wheel of injustice'. It is time for Christian communities to move beyond the institutional Church to fashion a networked movement of liberative communities of resistance and hope that are animated by the gospel mandate to reflect God's preferential option for the poor.

Challenge 3 – *Spirituality and existential oppression*

A liberative austerity-age ecclesiology needs to be characterized by a *Shalom*-shaped spirituality and a holistic vision of God's preferential option for the poor that recognizes the debilitating ways in which economic and existential marginalization have combined and compounded one another during the Age of Austerity. 'Campaigning' for a living wage, 'Caring' for people caught in the trap of food insecurity, enabling people to become empowered through their 'Enterprise' or supporting people to use ABCD to build community are all vital but only represent half of the job. As I have indicated in this book, it is essential to recognize that the violence of poverty cannot be reduced to economic marginalization alone, however important this might be. Too often we forget that the normalizing of poverty is achieved through the hegemonic force of cultural violence and shame-inducing stigma. Theologians, policymakers and preachers need to grasp the pivotal importance of engaging with the existential oppression that scars the spirit, saps our energy to resist and persuades us to believe the lie that we are poor because we're not good enough or hardworking enough. Unless the psychosocial trauma and existential damage of stigmatizing and debilitating narratives about the 'skiver' and the 'striver', the 'deserving' and the 'undeserving' poor are recognized, understood and overcome, an austerity-age holistic theology of liberation will not get off the starting blocks.

Challenge 4 – *Engaging in the public sphere*

The renewed visibility of the Church in the public sphere has been widely documented as I have noted in previous chapters. Life on the Breadline shone a light on the key role the Church has played in responding to austerity-age poverty. Our case studies and interviews with Church leaders have illustrated the ways in which the Church has used its deep reservoirs of social capital in its 'Caring', 'Campaigning', 'Self-help and Enterprise' and 'Community Building'. In fashioning a liminal liberative space in the public sphere it will be increasingly important for the Church to use such social capital to address the multidimensional nature of contemporary poverty and translate its bridging capital into a more politicized linking capital if it is to engage with our intersectional experience of austerity. Whilst political theologians in the UK have increasingly considered the role the Church plays in the public sphere and its political significance in an evolving postsecular cultural context, there is still far too little interdisciplinary fieldwork-led theological engagement with the Church's role in a civil society that has been wracked by more than a decade of austerity.

Challenge 5 – Charity versus politics

Our Life on the Breadline project demonstrated the breadth, depth and impact of 'Caring' Christian engagements with poverty and the increasing visibility of the Church in the public sphere during the Age of Austerity. It is not melodramatic to suggest that the food bank, the soup run and the breakfast club have saved hundreds of thousands of lives during the Age of Austerity. Christian engagements in the public sphere that bandage up the broken have immense pastoral value and embody the core values of servanthood and neighbour-love. Their impact should not be minimized or dismissed. However, as I have argued in this book, such an approach does not challenge systemic poverty and, therefore, it cannot dismantle the structural injustice that gives it life. Whilst a clear commitment to the common good and God's preferential option for the poor characterized the responses of most of the Church leaders with whom we spoke during Life on the Breadline, and the practice of most of our case study partners in Birmingham, London and Manchester, our research revealed an ongoing and widespread nervousness about moving beyond welfare to engage in civil society politics. In the work of Church Action on Poverty, in Christian responses to the housing injustice exemplified by the Grenfell Tower fire and Power the Fight's advocacy for teenagers and young adults impacted by austerity-age knife crime we glimpsed the kind of movement beyond welfare-based neighbour love that needs to characterize the Church's engagement with systemic austerity-age poverty. Only when the Church overcomes its institutional hesitation and embraces its calling to fashion a sustained prophetic political engagement in the public sphere can it deliver on its commitment to transforming structural injustice and reflecting God's preferential option for the poor. Is the Church ready to step out of its comfort zone and exchange charity for such political activism?

Challenge 6 – From caring but disengaged to a movement of solidarity

The ambivalent heritage of the Church in relation to poverty became evident during Life on the Breadline. We encountered examples of a politically engaged Christian community in solidarity with people with direct experience of poverty in our ethnographic case studies but also widespread reference to a caring but disengaged Church that has strong historic and contemporary ties to those with power – a relatively affluent Church most of whose members are cushioned from the raw realities of austerity or are interwoven with the political establishment and challenging government policy from a safe distance. It is 40 years ago that the authors of *Faith in the City* claimed, somewhat selectively, that, 'throughout its history [the Church] has acknowledged its obligation to remember the poor …' and has 'consistently followed [Jesus] in stressing the inalienable dignity and worth of every individual and the absolute equality of all before God' (Archbishop of Canterbury's Commission on Urban Priority Areas, 1985, pp. 47–8). The Church has cared for people in poverty for centuries and has been at the forefront of pastoral and direct support for people experiencing poverty during the Age of Austerity. However, it is not credible to claim that this is the whole story, to quietly forget the Church's intertwined relationship with those with power and money, the way it has benefited from this and, on occasions, blessed the structural injustice of systemic poverty and inequality. It is important to recognize that the institutional Church's relationship with poverty is ambivalent and contested. If this lesson is not learned the Church cannot fulfil its calling. However valuable Christian 'Caring', 'Campaigning and Advocacy' and 'Enterprise' approaches to people with direct experience of poverty are, our experience during Life on the Breadline has shown that they can never fully embody the spirituality of liberation needed to sustain a *Shalom*-oriented preferential option for the poor because such responses often remain arms-length and continue, however unintentionally, to objectify those left out or left behind by austerity. Only a re-imagining of the Church as a dynamic movement-oriented network of grassroots communities of resistance and hope, much like the early Christian movements described in Acts 2 or the Base Ecclesial Communities of Latin American liberation theology, can interconnect the deep reservoir of liberative spirituality and God's preferential option for the poor with an experiential understanding of austerity-age poverty. As our Life on the Breadline partner Church Action on Poverty and the Poverty Truth Network remind us – 'Nothing about us without us is for us.'

Challenge 7 – Becoming a network of Christian communities of faith and resistance

The suggestion that the future of the Church lies in small grassroots communities of faith is not new as just a skim through Christian history demonstrates. However, the potential of a network of interconnected conscientized communities of faith and resistance to model a holistic *Shalom*-oriented liberative praxis on the plural, contested and increasingly postsecular cultural landscape of breadline Britian represents a timely challenge to the institutional Church. What might such grassroots communities look like? An initiative that we explored during Life on the Breadline offers an interesting, if incomplete, response to this question. As I discussed in Chapter 6, beginning with its 2016 *Church of the Poor?* report, Church Action on Poverty began to develop its Church on the Margins initiative to counter the institutional Church's withdrawal from many poor urban communities. The initiative began to emerge during the Covid-19 lockdown of 2020. These emergent 'communities of praxis' bear some tentative similarities with the Base Ecclesial Communities that provided the foundation-stone for Latin American liberation theology in the 1960s and 1970s. Church Action's intention was to facilitate the grassroots development and leadership of such small 'communities of praxis', solidarity, empowerment, reflection and worship as Niall Cooper intimated to us (Interview 2020) and as Deirdre Brower Latz, Carmel Murphy Elliott and Sarah Purcell noted in their February 2023 *Church on the Margins* report. To date, however, the initiative has been largely limited to Greater Manchester and focused mostly on White-majority neighbourhoods and congregations and was partially curtailed by the Covid pandemic (Brower Latz et al., 2023). In spite of these limitations, Church Action's Niall Cooper (2021) suggests that the Church on the Margins initiative has begun to hint at the shape that a postsecular, networked liberative movement-based ecclesiology might take. Such a radically inclusive model of liberative Christian community, if tended and nurtured, can support the Church to recover its theological radicalism and fulfil its calling to 'transform structural injustice'.

Challenge 8 – Developing dub practice

Building on Beckford's (2006) groundbreaking work on dub practice, I have developed a new approach to hermeneutics that has the capacity to enable the transformation of the Christian engagement with poverty and wider structural injustice (Shannahan, 2010). I have deployed this dub hermeneutics in this book and shown how, when allied with a hermeneutics of suspicion, it can enable the process of deconstructing dominant Christian social ethics, ideas about the common good, ecclesiology and the Church's engagement in the public sphere and reconstructing these themes on the basis of a *Shalom*-oriented liberative ethic. Such hermeneutical practice raises further challenges for the ways in which we think about theology, austerity and structural injustice that need exploring further in future work if the full potential of dub hermeneutics is to be realized.

Challenge 9 – Lament and existential liberation

I have drawn on the raw expressions of loss, anger and confusion that we encountered during Life on the Breadline to re-imagine the ways in which the biblical concept of lament can deepen the relationship between theological reflection and the visceral experience of systemic poverty and multidimensional structural injustice. I have also shown how we need to foreground the interconnectedness of economic and existential oppression and alienation. Too often theologians and practitioners are keen to move quickly beyond the traumatizing pain of debilitating poverty and the desperation of abandonment to fashion a hope-filled vision of overcoming, emancipation and liberation. As Life on the Breadline taught us, and as I have shown in this book, such rushed reconstruction can leave the corrosive power of cultural violence untouched and existential oppression still holding us in its grip. By drawing in greater depth on biblical and contemporary thinking about lament we can begin to fashion a theology of liberation that sits and stays with people who have direct experience of poverty as a first step to existential emancipation.

Challenge 10 – Linking capital and liberative reversals

In this book I have suggested that there is an urgent need for the Church to translate its bridging social capital into the more politicised and transformative linking capital as a means of resourcing prophetic engagement in a structurally unjust public sphere that is characterized by oppressive power relations. Our research during Life on the Breadline showed how such a step can enable a more proactive and sustained commitment to liberative reversals as a means of subverting injustice and inverting oppressive social hierarchies (Shannahan, 2010). Further reflection on the ways in which a more effective use of linking capital can enable the Church to fashion more breadline beatitudes can help to pave the way for the development of such liberative praxis as a core element of an austerity-age theology of liberation.

Standing at a *Kairos* moment

We stand at a *Kairos* moment – a time of judgement, opportunity and possibility for theology and for the Church. As the Conservative-created austerity that has characterized life in breadline Britain since the 2008 global financial crash rumbles on under a Labour government and the slow violence of systemic poverty continues to traumatize whole communities, the Church stands at a crossroads. Is the commitment to 'transforming structural injustice' serious? Is the affirmation of God's preferential option for the poor more than a righteous soundbite? The time has come to translate such words into action, to move beyond the common good and ram a spoke into the wheel of injustice. During Life on the Breadline, we caught glimpses of the politically engaged, imaginative, inclusive, holistic, bold and bottom-up Church that must arise if an austerity-age theology of liberation is to emerge and gain traction. Only such a movement-based Church that values every person's dignity and agency and stands in solidarity with all who are left out or left behind as it engages unafraid in the prophetic politics of *Shalom*-oriented liberation can transform the structures of injustice that have limited so many lives for so long. It is time to act. For the sake of all whose lives have been lost to the slow systemic violence of austerity-age poverty there can be no more delay. The *Kairos* moment has arrived.

Bibliography

Aitchison, Gav, Brown, Rachel and Perry, Jane, 2024, *Places of Hope 2024: How Local Pantries Help Build Thriving Communities*, Greater Manchester: Church Action on Poverty and the Co-op.

Allen, Chris, 2016, 'Food Poverty and Christianity in Britain: A Theological Re-assessment', *Political Theology* 17, pp. 361–77.

Althaus-Reid, Marcella, 2002, *Indecent Theology: Theological Perversions in Sex, Gender and Politics*, New York: Routledge.

Anglican Consultative Council, 1984, *Bonds of Affection: Proceedings of ACC 6*, London: Anglican Consultative Council.

Archbishop of Canterbury's Commission on Urban Priority Areas, 1985, *Faith in the City: A Call for Action by Church and Nation*, London: Church House Publishing.

Aristotle, 1962, *Nicomachean Ethics*, translated by Martin Ostwald, London: Macmillan.

Baker, Chris and Skinner, Hannah, 2006/2014, *Faith in Action: The dynamic connection between spiritual and religious capital*, Manchester: William Temple Foundation.

Baker, Christopher, 2009, *The Hybrid Church in the City: Third Space Thinking*, London: SCM Press.

Baker, Christopher R., and Elaine Graham (eds), 2018, *Theology for Changing Times: John Atherton and the Future of Public Theology*, London: SCM Press.

Barrett, Al, 2018, 'Interrupting the church's flow: hearing "other" voices on an outer urban estate', *Practical Theology*, 11, 1, pp. 79–92, DOI: 10.1080/1756073X.2017.1416221.

———, 2020, *Interrupting the Church's Flow: Developing a radically receptive political theology in the urban margins*, London: SCM Press.

Barrett, Al and Harley, Ruth, 2020, *Being Interrupted: Reimagining the Church's Mission from the Outside In*, London: SCM Press.

Baum, Gregory, 1994, *Essays in Critical Theology*, Kansas City, KS: Sheed and Ward.

Beattie, Jason, 2014, '27 bishops slam David Cameron's welfare reforms as creating a national crisis in unprecedented attack in letter to the Daily Mirror', *Daily Mirror*, 19 February, https://www.mirror.co.uk/news/uk-news/27-bishops-slam-david-camerons-3164033, accessed 7.06.2024.

Beaumont, Justin and Paul Cloke (eds), 2012, *Faith-Based Organisation and Exclusion in European Cities*, Bristol: Policy Press.

Beckford, Robert, 1998, *Jesus is Dread: Black Theology and Black Culture in Britain*, London: Darton, Longman & Todd.

———, 2000, *Dread and Pentecostal: A Political Theology for the Black Church in Britain*, London: SPCK.

———, 2004, *God and Gangs: An Urban Toolkit for Those who won't be Sold Out, Bought Out or Scared Out*, London: SPCK.

———, 2006, *Jesus Dub: Music, Theology and Social Change*, London: Routledge.

———, 2021,talk from National Poverty Consultation, https://www.youtube.com/watch?v=WxaZLtsc8gE, accessed 24.07.2025.

Beckford, Robert, Shannahan, Chris, Denning, Stephanie and Scott, Peter, 2022, *Life on the Breadline: Christianity, Poverty and Politics in the 21st Century City: A Report for Church Leaders*, Coventry: Centre for Trust, Peace and Social Relations.

Beddoe, Liz and Emily Keddell, 2016, 'Informed outrage: tackling shame and stigma in poverty education in social work', *Ethics and Social Welfare*, 10, 2, pp. 149–62, DOI: 10.1080/17496535.2016.1159775.

Bennett, Zoe, and Gowler, David B. (eds), 2012, *Radical Christian Voices and Practice: Essays in Honour of Christopher Rowland*, Oxford: Oxford University Press.

Berger, Peter, 1967, *The Sacred Canopy: Elements of a Sociological Theory of Religion*, Barden City: Doubleday.

———, 1997, 'Epistemological modesty: An interview with Peter Berger', *The Christian Century*, 29 October, pp. 972–78.

Berger, Peter and Thomas Luckmann, 1966, *The Social Construction of Knowledge: A Treatise in the Sociology of Knowledge*, London: Penguin Books.

Bethge, Eberhard (ed.), 1995, *Dietrich Bonhoeffer's Ethics*, New York: Simon & Schuster.

Bevans, Stephen, 1992/2002, *Models of Contextual Theology*, Maryknoll, NY: Orbis Books.

Bhabha, Homi, 1994, *The Location of Culture*, London/New York: Routledge.

Boesak, Allan, 1976, *Farewell to Innocence: A Socio-Ethical Study on Black Theology and Power*, Eugene, OR: Wipf & Stock.

———, 2016, *Kairos, Crisis, and Global Apartheid*, Basingstoke: Palgrave Macmillan.

Boff, Leonardo and Boff, Clodovis, 1987, *Introducing Liberation Theology*, Tunbridge Wells: Burns & Oates.

Bottici, Chiara, 2011, 'Towards a Philosophy of Political Myth', *Iris – European Journal of Philosophy and Public Debate* III, pp. 31–52.

Bottici, Chiara and Challand, Benoît, 2006, 'Rethinking Political Myth: The Clash of Civilizations as a Self-fulfilling Prophecy', *European Journal of Social Theory*, 9, 3, pp. 315–36.

Bourdieu, Pierre, 1979, 'Symbolic Power', *Critique of Anthropology*, 4 (13–14), pp. 77–85, https://doi.org/10.1177/0308275X7900401307.

———, 1986, 'The Forms of Capital' in J. G. Richardson (ed.), *Handbook of Theory and Research for the Sociology of Education*, New York: Greenwood Press, pp. 241–58.

Bowler, Kate, 2013, *Blessed: A History of the American Prosperity Gospel*, New York: Oxford University Press.

Bradstock, Andrew, 2010, 'Profits Without Honour? Economics, Theology and the Current Global Recession', *International Journal of Public Theology* 4, pp. 135–57.

Bradstock, Andrew and Rowland, Christopher (eds), 2002, *Radical Christian Writings: A Reader*, Oxford: Blackwell.

Bramhall, Rebecca, 2013, *The Cultural Politics of Austerity: Past and Present in Austere Times*, Basingstoke: Palgrave Macmillan.

Bretherton, Luke, 2010, *Christianity and Contemporary Politics: The Conditions and Possibilities of Faithful Witness*, Oxford: Wiley-Blackwell.

———, 2011, 'A Postsecular Politics? Inter-faith Relations as a Civic Practice', *Journal of the American Academy of Religion*, 79 (2), pp. 346–77, http://www.jstor.org/stable/23020430.

———, 2015, *Resurrecting Democracy: Faith, Citizenship and the Politics of a Common Life*, Cambridge: Cambridge University Press.

Brower Latz, Deirdre, Murphy Elliott, Carmel and Purcell, Sarah, 2023, *Church on the Margins*, Greater Manchester: Church Action on Poverty.

Brueggemann, Walter, 1978, *The Prophetic Imagination*, Minneapolis, MN: Fortress Press.

Bufacchi, Vittorio, 2005, 'Two Concepts of Violence', *Political Studies Review*, 3 (2), pp. 193–204, https://doi.org/10.1111/j.1478-9299.2005.00023.x.

Burgess, Richard, 2009, 'Nigerian Pentecostal Theology in Global Perspective', *PentecoStudies*, 7 (2), pp. 29–63, DOI: 10.1558/ptcs.v7i2.29.

Burgess, Richard, 2020, 'Megachurches and "Reverse Mission"' in Stephen J. Hunt (ed.), *Handbook of Megachurches*, Leiden: Brill, https://doi.org/10.1163/9789004412927_013.

Cameron, Helen, 2014, 'The Morality of the Food Parcel: Emergency Food as a Response to Austerity', *Practical Theology* 7, pp. 194–204.

Cameron, Helen, Bhatti, Deborah, Duce, Catherine, Sweeney, James and Watkins, Clare, 2010, *Talking About God In Practice: Theological Action Research and Practical Theology*, London: SCM Press.

Campbell, Joseph, 1988, *The Power of Myth*, London: Bantam Doubleday Dell Publishing Group.

Campbell, Sarah and Tyler, Imogen, 2024, *Poverty Stigma: A glue that holds poverty in place*, Joseph Rowntree Foundation, https://www.jrf.org.uk/stigma-power-and-poverty/poverty-stigma-a-glue-that-holds-poverty-in-place, accessed 26.06.2025.

Caruth, Cathy, 1996, *Unclaimed Experience: Trauma, Narrative and History*, Baltimore, MD: Johns Hopkins University Press.

Casanova, José, 2012, 'Are We Still Secular? Explorations on the Secular and the Post-Secular' in Peter Nynas, Mi Lassander and Terhi Utriainan (eds), *Post-Secular Society*, New Brunswick, NJ: Transaction Books.

Castells, Manuel, 1996, *The Rise of the Network Society: The Information Age … Economy, Society and Culture*, Oxford: Blackwell.

———, 1998, *The End of the Millennium: The Information Age … Economy, Society and Culture*, Oxford: Blackwell.

———, 2010, *The Power of Identity: The Information Age … Economy, Society and Culture*, Oxford: Blackwell.

Catholic Bishops' Conference of England and Wales, 1996, *The Common Good and Catholic Social Teaching*, https://cbcew.org.uk/plain/wp-content/uploads/sites/3/2018/11/common-good-1996.pdf, accessed 26.06.2025.

Charity Commission, 2016, *Inquiry Report: Kingsway International Christian Centre*, available at https://assets.publishing.service.gov.uk/government/up

loads/system/uploads/attachment_data/file/577308/kingsway_international_ christian_centre.pdf, accessed 27.01.2023.

Chase, E. and Walker, R., 2012, 'The Co-construction of Shame in the Context of Poverty: Beyond a Threat to the Social Bond', *Sociology*, 47 (4), pp. 739–54, https://doi.org/10.1177/0038038512453796.

Church Action on Poverty, 2021, 'Robert Beckford talk from National Poverty Consultation 2021', *YouTube*, 22 January, https://www.youtube.com/watch?v=WxaZLtsc8gE, accessed 25.06.2025.

Church Urban Fund, 2014, 'The Web Of Poverty', https://cuf.org.uk/uploads/ resources/Web-of-Poverty_2014.pdf, accessed 18.06.2023

Clarke, J. and Newman, J., 2012, 'The alchemy of austerity', *Critical Social Policy*, 32 (3), pp. 299–319, https://doi.org/10.1177/0261018312444405.

Cloke, Paul, Williams, Andrew and Thomas, Sam, 2009, 'Faith-based Organisations and Social Exclusion in the United Kingdom' in Danielle Dierckx, Jan Vranken and Wendy Kerstens (eds), *Faith-based Organisations and Social Exclusion in European Cities*, National Context Reports, Leuven: Acco, pp. 283–342.

Cloke, Paul, Baker, Christopher, Sutherland, Callum and Williams, Andrew, 2019, *Geographies of Postsecularity. Re-Envisioning Politics, Subjectivity and Ethics*. London: Routledge.

Collier, David, LaPorte, Jody and Seawright, Jason, 2012, 'Putting Typologies to Work: Concept Formation, Measurement and Analytic Rigor', *Political Research Quarterly* 65, 1, pp. 217–32, http://www.jstor.org/stable/23209571.

Commission on Urban Life and Faith, 2006, *Faithful Cities: A Call for Celebration, Vision and Justice*, London: Methodist Publishing House and Church House Publishing.

Cone, James H., 1975, *God of the Oppressed*, San Francisco, CA: Harper Collins.

Cooper, Niall, 2021, *Building Dignity, Agency and Power Together: Practical Steps to building a grassroots social movement to challenge poverty*, Greater Manchester: Church Action on Poverty.

Cooper, Niall and Dumpleton, Sarah, May 2013, *Walking the Breadline: The scandal of food poverty in the 21st century*, Greater Manchester: Church Action on Poverty/Oxfam.

Cooper, Vickie and Whyte, David (ed.), 2017, *The Violence of Austerity*, London: Pluto Press.

Crenshaw, Kimberlé, 1989, 'Demarginalizing the intersection of race and sex: A black feminist critique of anti-discrimination doctrine, feminist theory and anti-racist politics', *University of Chicago Legal Forum*, pp. 139–67.

——, 1991, 'Mapping the Margins: Intersectionality, Identity Politics and Violence against Women of Color', *Stanford Law Review* 43, 6, pp. 1241–99.

——, 2017, 'What is Intersectional Feminism?' Omega Institute for Holistic Studies, *YouTube*, 19 February, https://www.youtube.com/watch?v=oTFy4zR sItY, accessed 27.06.2025.

Davey, Andrew, 2001, *Urban Christianity and Global Order*, London: SPCK.

Davie, Grace, 1994, *Religion in Britain since 1945: Believing without belonging*, Oxford: Blackwell.

Davies, Nick, 1998, *Dark Heart: The Shocking Truth About Hidden Britain*, London: Vintage.

Davis, Kortwright, 1990, *Emancipation Still Comin': Explorations in Caribbean Emancipatory Theology*, Eugene, OR: Wipf & Stock.

De Gruchy, John, 2016, 'Kairos moments and prophetic witness: Towards a prophetic ecclesiology', *HTS Teologiese Studies/Theological Studies* 72 (4), a3414, http://dx.doi.org/10.4102/hts.v72i4.3414.

Denning, Stephanie, Shannahan, Chris, Beckford, Robert and Scott, Peter, 2021, *Life on the Breadline: Christianity, Poverty and Politics in the 21st century City: A Report for Policymakers in the UK*, Coventry: Centre for Trust, Peace and Social Relations.

Dinham, Adam, 2008, 'Commentary: From Faith in the City to Faithful Cities: The "Third Way", the Church of England and Urban Regeneration', *Urban Studies*, 45 (10), pp. 2163–74.

Dinham, Adam, Furbey, Robert and Lowndes, Vivien (eds), 2009, *Faith in the Public Realm: Controversies, Policies and Practices*, Bristol: The Policy Press.

Dorrien, Gary J., 1990, *Reconstructing the Common Good: Theology and the Social Order*, Maryknoll, NY: Orbis Books.

Edmiston, Daniel, Patrick, Ruth and Garthwaite, Kayleigh, 2017, 'Introduction. Austerity, Welfare and Social Citizenship', *Social Policy & Society*, 16, pp. 253–9.

Espiet-Kilty, Raphaële, 2016, 'David Cameron, Citizenship and the Big Society: a New Social Model?', *Revue Française de Civilisation Britannique* [Online], XXI-1, http://journals.openedition.org/rfcb/796; DOI: https://doi.org/10.4000/rfcb.796.

Evans, Matthew and Walker, Brian, 2020, 'The Beginning of the Age of Austerity: A Critical Stylistic Analysis of David Cameron's 2009 Spring Conference Speech', *CADAAD Journal*, 11, pp. 169–86.

Farnsworth, Kevin and Irving, Zoe, 2018, 'Austerity: Neoliberal dreams come true?', *Critical Social Policy*, 38 (3), pp. 461–81, https://doi.org/10.1177/0261018318762451.

Fairclough, Norman, 1992, *Discourse and Social Change*, Cambridge: Polity Press.

Farrell, Kirby, 1998, *Post-traumatic Culture: Injury and Interpretation in the Nineties*, Baltimore, MD: Johns Hopkins University Press.

Feldman, Guy, 2019, 'Neoliberalism and Poverty: An unbreakable relationship' in Greve, Bent (ed.), *Routledge International Handbook of Poverty*, London: Routledge, pp. 340–51.

Flood, Christopher, G., 2002, *Political Myth: A Theoretical Introduction*, London: Routledge.

Foucault, Michel, 2019, *Power: The Essential Works of Michel Foucault 1954–1984*, London: Penguin.

Francis (Pope), 2015, *Laudato Si'*, 24 May, Vatican City: The Holy See.

Francis, Sam and Eardley, Nick, 2024, 'Labour suspends seven rebel MPs over two-child benefit cap', https://www.bbc.co.uk/news/articles/c978m6z3egno, accessed 25.07.2025.

Freire, Paulo, 1970, *Pedagogy of the Oppressed*, New York: Seabury Press.

———, 2004, *Pedagogy of Indignation*, Boulder, CO: Paradigm Publishers.

Frey, Donald E., 1998, 'Individualist Economic Values and Self-Interest: The Problem in the Puritan Ethic', *Journal of Business Ethics*, 17, 14, pp. 1573–80, http://www.jstor.org/stable/25073991.

Galtung, Johann, 1969, 'Violence, Peace and Peace Research', *Journal of Peace Research*, 6, 3, pp. 167–91.

———, 1990, 'Cultural Violence', *Journal of Peace Research*, 27, 3, pp. 291–305.

Gardiner, Mark Quentin and Engler, Steven, 2010, 'Charting the map metaphor in theories of religion', *Religion*, 40, 1, pp. 1–13, DOI: 10.1016/j.religion.2009.08.010.

Garland, Caroline (ed.), 2019, *Understanding Trauma: A Psychoanalytical Approach*, Abingdon: Routledge.

Garthwaite, Kayleigh, 2016, 'Stigma, shame and "people like us": an ethnographic study of food banks in the UK', *Journal of Poverty and Social Justice*, 24, 3, pp. 277–89, DOI: 10.1332/175982716X14721954314922.

Gasper, Des, 2005, 'Securing Humanity: Situating "Human Security" as Concept and Discourse', *Journal of Human Development*, 6, 2, pp. 221–45, DOI: 10.1080/14649880500120558.

Gaston, Ray and Shakespeare, Steven, 2010, 'Common Wealth: Christians for Economic and Social Justice', *Political Theology*, 11, 6, pp. 793–801, https://doi.org/10.1558/poth.v11i6.793.

Geertz, Clifford, 1973, *The Interpretation of Cultures*, New York: Basic Books.

Gilroy, Paul, 2000, *Against Race: Imagining Political Culture Beyond The Color Line*, Cambridge, MA: Harvard University Press.

Gladden, Washington, 1877, *The Christian Way: Whither it leads and how to go on*, New York: Dodd, Mead & Company.

Gledhill, Ruth, 2015, 'How black majority churches could swing the election', *Christian Today*, https://www.christiantoday.com/news/how-black-majority-churches-could-swing-the-election, accessed 25.07.2025.

Graham, E. L., 2002, *Representations of the Post/Human: Monsters, Aliens, and Others in Popular Culture*, Brunswick, NJ: Rutgers University Press.

———, 2013, 'Is practical theology a form of "action research"?', *International Journal of Practical Theology*, 17 (1), pp. 148–78.

———, 2013, *Between a Rock and a Hard Place: Public Theology in a Post-Secular Age*, London: SCM Press.

———, 2016, 'A New Apologetics: Speaking of God in a world troubled by Religion', Chester Cathedral lecture.

Graham, Elaine L., Walton, Heather and Ward, Frances, 2005, *Theological Reflection: Methods*, London: SCM Press.

Gramsci, Antonio, 1971, *Selections from the Prison Notebooks*, London: Lawrence & Wishart.

———, 2007, *Prison Notebooks Volume III*, edited and translated by J. A. Buttigieg, New York: Columbia University Press.

Grant, Jacquelyn, 1989, *White Women's Christ and Black Women's Jesus: Feminist Christology and Womanist Response*, Oxford: American Academy of Religion Scholars' Press.

Green, Laurie, 1990, *Let's Do Theology: A Pastoral Cycle Resource Book*, London: Mowbray.

———, 2013, *Urban Ministry and the Kingdom of God*, London: SPCK.

Grootaert, Christiaan, Narayan, Deepa, Nyham Jones, Veronica and Woolcock, Michael, 2004, *Measuring Social Capital: An Integrated Questionnaire*, Washington D.C.: The World Bank.

Gutiérrez, Gustavo, 1974, *A Theology of Liberation*, London: SCM Press.

———, 1983, *The Power of the Poor in History*, London: SCM Press.

———, 1988, *A Theology of Liberation – 15th Anniversary Edition*, Maryknoll, NY: Orbis Books.

Habermas, Jürgen, 2006, 'Religion in the Public Sphere', *European Journal of Philosophy*, 14, pp. 1–25.

———, 2008, 'Notes on Post-Secular Society', *New Political Quarterly*, 25, pp. 17–29.

Hall, Sarah-Marie, 2018, 'Everyday austerity: Towards relational geographies of family, friendship and intimacy', *Progress in Human Geography*, 43, pp. 1–21.

———, 2019, *Everyday Life in Austerity: Family, Friends and Intimate Relations*, Basingstoke: Palgrave Macmillan.

———, 2020, 'The personal is political: Feminist geographies of/in austerity', *Geoform*, 110, pp. 242–51.

Hall, Stuart, Gilroy, Paul and Wilson-Gilmore, Ruth (eds), 2021, *Selected Writings on Race and Difference*, Durham, NC: Duke University Press.

Halliday, Michael A. K., 1978, *Language as a Social Semiotic: Social Interpretation of Language and Meaning*, London: Hodder Arnold.

Hanlon, Robert J. and Christie, Kenneth, 2016, *Freedom from Fear, Freedom from Want: An Introduction to Human Security*, Toronto: University of Toronto Press, http://www.jstor.org/stable/10.3138/j.ctv2fjwz2p.

Harris, Clive and James, Winston (eds), 1993, *Inside Babylon: The Caribbean Diaspora in Britain*, London: Verso.

Hart, Ian, 1995, 'The Teaching of the Puritans about Ordinary Work', *Evangelical Quarterly: A Review of Bible and Theology*, 67 (3), pp. 195–210, DOI: https://doi.org/10.1163/27725472-06703002.

Harvey, David, 2005, *A Brief History of Neoliberalism*, Oxford: Oxford University Press.

Hay, Colin, 2016, 'Social Constructivism' in Bevir, Mark and Rhodes, R. A. W. (ed.), *Routledge Handbook of Interpretive Political Science*, Abingdon, Oxon: Routledge.

Hill-Collins, Patricia, 2008, *Black Feminist Thought: Knowledge, Consciousness, and the Politics of Empowerment*, New York: Routledge.

Hill-Collins, Patricia and Bilge, Sirma, 2020, *Intersectionality*, Cambridge: Polity Press.

Hirschberger, Gilad, 2018, 'Collective Trauma and the Social Construction of Meaning', *Frontiers in Psychology*, 9, 1441.

Hoelzl, Michael and Ward, Graham (eds), 2008, *The New Visibility of Religion: Studies in Religion and Cultural Hermeneutics*, London: Continuum.

Hollenbach, David, 2002, *The Common Good and Christian Ethics*, Cambridge: Cambridge University Press.

House of Commons Children, Schools and Families Committee, 2010, *Young people not in education, employment or training*, 24 March, London: House of Commons.

Ji-Sun Kim, Grace and Shaw, Susan M., 2018, *Intersectional Theology: An Introductory Guide*, Minneapolis, MN: Fortress Press.

John Paul II (Pope), 1987, *Sollicitudo Rei Socialis*, 30 December, Vatican City: The Holy See.

Joint Public Issues Team, 2013, *The Lies We Tell Ourselves: Ending Comfortable Myths about Poverty*, London: Methodist Publishing.

Jones, Owen, 2012, *Chavs: The Demonization of the Working Class*, London: Verso.

Jones, Patricia, 2019, 'Discovering the Common Good in Practice: The Catholicity of Catholic Charities, PhD thesis, Durham University, Durham, UK,' http://etheses.dur.ac.uk/13104.

Jørgensen, Marianne and Phillips, Louise, 2002, *Discourse Analysis as Theory and Method*, London: SAGE.

Kairos Theologians, 1986, *The Kairos Document: A Challenge to the Church, Theological Comment on the Political Crisis in South Africa*, revised edition, Grand Rapids, MI: William B. Eerdmans Publishing Company.

Kallsen, Kevin, 2014, 'Easter Sermon of the Archbishop of Canterbury', 20 April, http://anglican.ink/2014/04/20/easter-sermon-of-the-archbishop-of-canterbury-2, accessed 24.07.2024.

King, Matin Luther, Jr, 'The Quest for Peace and Justice', Nobel Lecture, 11 December 1964, https://www.nobelprize.org/prizes/peace/1964/king/lecture/, accessed 27.09.2022.

Kisby, Ben, 2010, 'The Big Society: Power to the People?', *The Political Quarterly*, 81, 4 (October–December).

Kretzmann, John P. and McKnight, John L., 1993, *Building Communities from the Inside Out: A Path Toward Finding and Mobilizing a Community's Assets*, Evanston, IL: Northwestern University.

Lederach, John Paul, 2005, *The Moral Imagination: The Art and Soul of Peacebuilding*, Oxford: Oxford University Press.

Leech, Kenneth, 1981, *The Social God*, London: Sheldon Press.

———, 1997, *The Sky is Red: Discerning the Signs of the Times*, London: Darton, Longman & Todd.

Leo XIII (Pope), 1891, *Rerum Novarum*, 15 May, Vatican City: The Holy See.

Levitas, Ruth, 2005, *The Inclusive Society: Social Exclusion and New Labour*, Basingstoke, Hampshire: Palgrave Macmillan.

Levitas, Ruth, Pantazis, Christina, Fahmy, Eldin, Gordon, David, Lloyd, Eva and Patsios, Demi, 2007, *The Multi-dimensional Analysis of Social Exclusion*, Bristol: Department of Sociology and School for Social Policy, University of Bristol.

Lévi-Strauss, Claude, 1955, 'The Structural Study of Myth', *Journal of American Folklore*, 68, 270, *Myth: A Symposium* (Oct.–Dec.), pp. 428–44.

Martin, Mary and Owen, Taylor (eds), 2014, *The Routledge Handbook of Human Security*, New York: Routledge.

Marx, Karl, 2024, *Theses on Feuerbach*, translated by Shaun Malley, London: Minerva Heritage Press.

May, Vivian, 2015, *Pursuing Intersectionality: Unsettling Dominant Imaginaries*, New York: Routledge.

McGarvey, Darren, 2017, *Poverty Safari: Understanding the Anger of Britain's Underclass*, London: Picador.

Methodist Church, 2023, *A Justice Seeking Church: A Guide to the 2023 Methodist Conference*, London: Methodist Publishing.

Morisy, Ann, 2004, *Journeying Out*, London: Continuum.

Muers, Ruth, 2021, 'Always with You: Questioning the Theological Construction of the Un/Deserving Poor', *International Journal of Public Theology*, 15(1), pp. 42–60, DOI: https://doi.org/10.1163/15697320-12341641.

Nixon, Rob, 2011, *Slow Violence and the Environmentalism of the Poor*, Cambridge, MA: Harvard University Press.

Nolan, Albert, 2007, 'Structures of Sin', *Angelicum*, 84, 3/4, pp. 625–37.

Norman, Edward R., 1987, *The Victorian Christian Socialists*, Cambridge: Cambridge University Press.

O'Donnell, Karen and Cross, Katie (eds), 2020, *Feminist Trauma Theologies: Body, Scripture, and Church in Critical Perspective*, London: SCM Press.

———, 2022, *Bearing Witness: Intersectional Approaches to Trauma Theology*, London: SCM Press.

Okri, Ben, 2018, 'Grenfell Tower 2017', https://benokri.co.uk/news/grenfell-tower-2017-poem-ben-okri/, accessed 30.06.2025.

Pass, Susan, 2004, *Parallel Paths to Constructivism: Jean Piaget and Lev Vygotsky*, Greenwich, CT: Information Age Publishing.

Patterson, Orlando, 1982, *Slavery and Social Death: A Comparative Study*, Cambridge, MA: Harvard University Press

Paul VI (Pope), 1967, *Populorum Progressio*, 26 March, Vatican City: The Holy See.

Paul, Kathleen, 1997, *Whitewashing Britain: Race and Citizenship in the Post-War Era*, New York: Cornell University Press.

Pears, Angie, 2009, *Doing Contextual Theology*, London: Routledge.

Pemberton, Charles, 2018, 'Between Ecclesiology and Ontology: A Response to Chris Allen on British Food Banks', *Political Theology*, 20, pp. 85–101.

———, 2020, *Bread of Life in Broken Britain: Food banks, Faith and Neoliberalism*, London: SCM Press.

Petrella, Ivan, 2006, *The Future of Liberation Theology: An Argument and Manifesto*, London: SCM Press.

Piketty, Thomas, 2014, *Capital in the Twenty-First Century*, translated by Arthur Goldhammer, Cambridge, MA: Harvard University Press.

Pinn, Anthony B., 1999, *Why Lord? Suffering and Evil in Black Theology*, London: Continuum.

Pixley, Jorge and Boff, Clodovis, 1989, *The Bible, the Church and the Poor*, Kent: Burns & Oates.

Plan B UK, 2012, 'Plan B - ill Manors [OFFICIAL VIDEO]', *YouTube*, 12 March, https://www.youtube.com/watch?v=s8GvLKTsTuI, accessed 30.06.2025.

Plender, Amy and Oldfield, Elizabeth, 2018, *After Grenfell: The Faith Groups' Response*, London: Theos.

Powers, Theodore and Rakopoulos, Theodoros, 2019, 'The anthropology of austerity: An introduction', *Journal of Global and Historical Anthropology*, 83, pp. 1–12.

Purcell, Liam and Purcell, Sarah (eds), 2016, *Church of the Poor? A Call To Action For The Churches In The UK*, Greater Manchester: Church Action on Poverty.

Putnam, Robert, 2000, *Bowling Alone: The Collapse and Revival of American Community*, New York: Simon & Schuster.

Radford, Wren, 2022a, *Lived Experiences and Social Transformations: Poetics, Politics and Power Relations in Practical Theology*, Leiden: Brill.

———, 2022b, '"A Stone You Need To Polish": Affect, Inequality and Responding to Trauma Testimonies' in O'Donnell and Cross (eds), *Bearing Witness: Intersectional Approaches to Trauma Theology*, London: SCM Press, pp. 311–35.

Radford-Ruether, Rosemary, 1983, *Sexism and God-Talk: Toward a Feminist Theology*, Boston, MA: Beacon Press.

Radstone, Susannah, 2007, 'Trauma Theory: Contexts, Politics, Ethics', *Paragraph*, 30, 1, *Trauma, Therapy and Representation* (March), pp. 9–29.

Rajikumar, Peniel, 2010, *Dalit Theology and Dalit Liberation – Problems, Paradigms and Possibilities*, London: Routledge.

Rambo, Shelly, 2010, *Spirit and Trauma: A Theology of Remaining*, London: John Knox Press.

———, 2019, 'How Christian theology and practice are being shaped by trauma studies', *Christian Century*, 1 November, https://www.christiancentury.org/article/critical-essay/how-christian-theology-and-practice-are-being-shaped-trauma-studies, accessed 22.07.2021.

Ratzinger, Joseph, 1984, 'Instruction on Certain Aspects of the "Theology of Liberation"', https://www.vatican.va/roman_curia/congregations/cfaith/documents/rc_con_cfaith_doc_19840806_theology-liberation_en.html.

Rauschenbusch, Walter, 1917, *A Theology for the Social Gospel*, New York: Macmillan.

Reddie, Anthony G., 2019, *Theologising Brexit: A Liberationist and Postcolonial Critique*, London: Routledge.

Ricoeur, Paul, 1970, *Freud and Philosophy: An Essay on Translation*, translated by Denis Savage, New Haven, CT: Yale University Press.

———, 1971, 'The Model of the Text: Meaningful Action Considered as Text', *Social Research*, 38 (Fall), pp. 529–62.

Robinson, Cedric, 1983, *Black Marxism: The Making of the Black Radical Tradition*, Chapel Hill, NC: University of North Carolina Press.

Rowlands, Anna, 2015, 'The Manchester Newman Lecture: The Politics of the Common Good: What does Catholic Social Teaching have to offer to electoral politics?', https://www.newman.org.uk/files/upload/Common%20Good%20Anna%20Rowlands.pdf, accessed 2.07.2025.

———, 2021, *Towards a Politics of Communion: Catholic Social Teaching in Dark Times*, London: Bloomsbury.

Runnymede Trust, 2018, *Austerity*, London: Runnymede Trust.

Russell, Cormac and McKnight, John, 2022, *The Connected Community: Discovering the Health, Wealth and Power of Neighbourhoods*, Oakland, CA: Berrett Koehler Publishers.

Sassen, Saskia, 1994, *Cities in a World Economy*, Newbury Park, CA: Pine Forge Press.

Saussure, Ferdinand de, 2006, *Writings in General Linguistics*, Oxford: Oxford University Press.

Scharen, Christian B. (ed.), 2012, *Explorations in Ecclesiology and Ethnography*, Cambridge: Eerdmans.

Schreiter, Robert, 1985, *Constructing Local Theologies*, Maryknoll, NY: Orbis Books.

Scott, Peter, and Cavanaugh, William T. (eds), 2004, *The Blackwell Companion to Political Theology*, Oxford: Blackwell.

Segundo, Juan-Luis, 2002 (1976), *The Liberation of Theology*, translated by John Drury, Eugene, OR: Wipf and Stock Publishers.

Sen, Amartya, 2000, 'Why human security?', *International Symposium on Human Security*, Tokyo (Vol. 28).

Sewell, Kenneth W. and Williams, Amy M., 2002, 'Broken Narratives: Trauma, Metaconstructive Gaps and the Audience of Psychotherapy', *Journal of Constructivist Psychology*, 15, 3, pp. 205–18, DOI: 10.1080/10720530290100442.

Shannahan, Chris, 2010, *Voices from the Borderland: Re-imagining Cross-cultural Urban Theology in the Twenty-first Century*, London: Equinox.

———, 2012, '"NEET" believers? An analysis of "belief" on an urban housing estate', *Culture and Religion: An Interdisciplinary Journal*, 13, 3, pp. 315–35, DOI: 10.1080/14755610.2012.706226.

———, 2014, *A Theology of Community Organizing*, London: Routledge.

———, 2018, 'The Violence of Poverty: Theology and Activism in an "Age of Austerity"', *Political Theology*, 20, 3, pp. 243–61, DOI: 10.1080/1462317X.2018.1543820.

———, 2019, 'Postmodernity and Urban Theology' in Beaumont, Justin (ed.), *The Routledge Handbook of Postsecularity*, London: Routledge.

———, 2022, 'The Grenfell 72: Austerity, Trauma and Liberation Theology', in O'Donnell and Cross (eds), *Bearing Witness: Intersectional Approaches to Trauma Theology*, London: SCM Press, pp. 269–93.

Shannahan, Chris and Denning, Stephanie, 2022, 'Politics, Poverty and the Church in an Age of Austerity', *Religions*, 14, pp. 59, https://doi.org/10.3390/rel14010059.

Shelter, 2019, *Building for our future: A vision for social housing*, London: Shelter.

Shenk, Wilbert R., 2005, 'Contextual Theology: The Last Frontier' in Lamin Sanneh and Joel A. Carpenter (eds), *The Changing Face of Christianity: Africa, the West, and the World*, New York, NY: Oxford University Press.

Shildrick, Tracy, 2018, 'Lessons from Grenfell: Poverty propaganda, stigma and class power', *The Sociological Review Monographs*, 66, 4.

Siddique, Haroon, 2013, 'Benefits changes will push children into poverty says archbishop of Canterbury', *The Guardian*, 11 March, https://www.theguardian.com/uk/2013/mar/10/benefits-children-poverty-archbishop-canterbury-welby, accessed 7.06.2024.

Sobrino, Jon, 1978, *Christology at the Crossroads*, London: SCM Press.

Social Exclusion Unit, 2001, *Preventing Social Exclusion – Report by the Social Exclusion Unit*, London: Cabinet Office.

Spivak, Gayatri, 1988, 'Can the Subaltern Speak?' in *Marxism and the Interpretation of Culture*, Cary Nelson and Lawrence Grossberg (eds), Basingstoke: Macmillan, pp. 271–313.

Stapley, E., O'Keeffe, S. and Midgley, N., 2022, 'Developing typologies in qualitative research: The use of ideal-type analysis', *International Journal of Qualitative Methods*, 21, DOI: 10.1177/16094069221100633.

Stewart, Denis, 1989, 'The Hermeneutics of Suspicion', *Literature and Theology*, 3 (3), pp. 296–307, http://www.jstor.org/stable/23924920.

Swinton, John, 1999, 'The politics of caring: pastoral theology in an age of conflict and change', *Health and Social Care Chaplaincy*, 2 (2), pp. 25–30.

Swinton, John and Mowat, Harriet, 2016, *Practical Theology and Qualitative Research* (second edition), London: SCM Press.

Szreter, Simon, 2002, 'The state of social capital: Bringing back power, politics, and history', *Theory and Society*, 31, pp. 573–621, https://doi.org/10.1023/A:1021300217590.

Tamez, Elsa, 1982, *Bible of the Oppressed*, Maryknoll, NY: Orbis Books.

Temple, William, 1942, *Christianity and Social Order*, London: Penguin.

Thomassen, Bjørn, 2014, *Liminality and the Modern: Living through the In-Between*, London/New York: Routledge.

Tillich, Paul, 1948, *The Shaking of the Foundations*, New York: Charles Scribner's Sons.

———, 1949, 'Beyond Religious Socialism', *Christian Century*, 15 June, pp. 732–3.

———, 1951, *Systematic Theology: Volume One*, Chicago, IL: University of Chicago Press.

———, 1968, *A History of Christian Thought, from its Judaic and Hellenistic Origins to Existentialism*, Carl E. Braaten (ed.), New York: Simon & Schuster.

Tronto, Joan, 2020, *Moral Boundaries: A Political Argument for an Ethic of Care*, London: Routledge.

Tyler, Imogen, 2020, *Stigma: The Machinery of Inequality*, London: Zed Books.

United Nations Development Programme, 1994, *Human Development Report 1994: New Dimensions of Human Security*, https://hdr.undp.org/content/human-development-report-1994, accessed 28.07.2025.

United States Council of Catholic Bishops, 1986, *Economic Justice for all: Pastoral Letter on Catholic Social Teaching and the U.S. Economy*, Washington DC, https://www.usccb.org/resources/economic_justice_for_all_1.pdf, accessed 27.10.2025.

Vincent, John, 1981, *Starting All Over Again: Hints of Jesus in the City*, Geneva: World Council of Churches.

———, 1982, *Into the City*, London: Epworth Press.

Ward, Pete (ed.), 2012, *Perspectives on Ecclesiology and Ethnography*, Cambridge: Eerdmans.

Ward, Peter and Tveitereid, Knut (eds), 2022, *The Wiley Blackwell Companion to Theology and Qualitative Research*, Oxford: Blackwell.

Watt, Nicholas, 2014, 'Bishops Blame David Cameron for Foodbank Crisis', *The Guardian*, 20 February, https://www.theguardian.com/politics/2014/feb/20/bishops-blame-cameron-food-bank-crisis, accessed 24.07.2024.

Weaver, Matthew, 2014, 'New Catholic Cardinal renews attack on "disgraceful" UK austerity cuts', *The Guardian*, 18 February, https://www.theguardian.com/society/2014/feb/18/cardinal-vincent-nichols-attacks-welfare-cuts-pope-francis, accessed 24.07.2024.

Weber, Max, 2011, *The Protestant Ethic and the Spirit of Capitalism*, translated by Stephen Kalberg, New York: Oxford University Press.

West, Cornel, 1985, 'The Dilemma of the Black Intellectual', *Cultural Critique*, 1, pp. 109–24, https://doi.org/10.2307/1354283.

———, 1999, *The Cornel West Reader*, New York: Basic Civitas Books.

White, Nadine, 2019, 'The SPAC nation story tells us what black people already knew about how the media and politicians value them', *Huffington Post*, https://www.huffingtonpost.co.uk/entry/spac-nation-opinion-media-politicians_uk_5dcd91f1e4b03a7e0296d035, accessed 25.07.2025.

Wilkinson, Paul, 2023, 'Two Child Universal Credit Limit Causes Poverty, Bishop of Durham Tells Peers', *The Church Times*, 27 March, https://www.churchtimes.co.uk/articles/2023/31-march/news/uk/two-child-universal-credit-limit-causes-poverty-bishop-of-durham-tells-peers, accessed 9.06.2024.

Williams, Andrew, 2014, 'Biblical lament and political protest', *Cambridge Papers*, pp. 1–4.

Williams, Elaine, Iyere, Ebinehita, Lindsay, Ben, Murray, Claude and Ramadhan, Zeyana, 2020, *Therapeutic Intervention for Peace Report: Culturally Competent Responses to Serious Youth Violence in London*, September, London: Mayor of London's Violence Reduction Unit.

Wilson, Brian, 1966, *Religion in a Secular Society: A Sociological Comment*, London: Watts & Co.

Wintour, P., 2013, 'Welfare Reforms: We will make work pay, says George Osborne', *The Guardian*, 2 April.

World Synod of Catholic Bishops, 1971, *Justice in the World*, available at https://officeforsocialjustice.org/wp-content/uploads/2025/01/Justicia-in-Mundo.pdf.

Wrenn, Mary V., 2021, 'Selling salvation, selling success: neoliberalism and the US Prosperity Gospel', *Cambridge Journal of Economics*, 45, 2 (March), pp. 295–311, https://doi.org/10.1093/cje/beaa048.

Yeo, Eileen, 1981, 'Christianity in Chartist Struggle 1838–1842', *Past & Present*, 91, 1 (May), pp. 109–39, https://doi.org/10.1093/past/91.1.109.

Yoder, Perry B., 1997, *Shalom: The Bible's Word for Salvation, Justice and Peace*, Eugene, OR: Wipf & Stock.

Zink, Jesse, 2017, 'Five Marks of Mission: History, Theology, Critique', *Journal of Anglican Studies*, 15, pp. 144–66.

Index of Names and Subjects